Personal Styles
and
Effective Performance

Personal Styles
and
Effective Performance

Make Your Style Work for You

David W. Merrill, Ph.D.
Roger H. Reid, M.A.

Chilton Book Company Radnor, Pennsylvania

Library of Congress Catalog Card No. 80-70389

ISBN 0-8019-6898-4
ISBN 0-8019-6899-2 *pbk.*

Designed by William E. Lickfield
Manufactured in the United States of America

18   0 9 8 7 6

To
our partner, associate, and friend
Gordon E. Brunson
who helped us succeed with style

Acknowledgments

We are indebted to all our staff at TRACOM for help in the completion of this book. We like to consider ourselves good teachers and researchers, but writing a book was a new challenge and the help, prodding, and creative contributions of our associates were invaluable. We would particularly like to single out Catherine Kilker, Jeff Larmer, Kathy Callahan, and Alys Novak for their writing and editing contributions. We also thank Virginia Cary, Luella Sanders, Barbara Thomas, and Dorothy Bannister for seemingly endless typing and retyping. And we must acknowledge the insights gained from our associates and the thousands of students who continually enrich our understanding of, and research on, social style.

Contents

Introduction

Theories on how to have successful human relationships abound, and almost everyone, especially in the business world, has a strategy for dealing with the "people factor." What usually happens, though, is that these theories work with one person and not with another. And when an effort fails to make a relationship work, the common reaction is: "My strategy worked before, so there must be something wrong with *him*."

We take another approach. Our position is that because people are uniquely different, each person merely responds individually to the behavior of others. By behavior we mean only those things you say and do, which others can observe and report about you. Our definition of behavior is limited to a person's social actions—nothing more—and we'll develop this theme throughout the book. Everyone has had the experience of saying or doing something that was perfectly acceptable to a friend or coworker and then being surprised when the same behavior irritated someone else. But aside from admitting that this happens, most of us are unable to draw meaningful conclusions from these experiences to help us perform more effectively with people in the future.

Our research into this aspect of human interactions has enabled us to assert that valid, meaningful conclusions *can* be drawn from one's own and others' behaviors, conclusions that will allow each of us to improve our relationships with those who share our careers and personal lives. Indeed, our message is disarmingly simple: All people exhibit patterns of behavior that can be identified and responded to, and if we can describe and adjust to these behaviors, we can achieve more satisfactory relationships. We can, in fact, increase our chances of success in any area of endeavor where the "people factor" is involved—without needing a deep understanding of people's inner selves.

This book is not, however, a new twist on popular notions of how to get along with others. Rather, it is an original theory based on years of empirical research and scientific observations of human behavior and its effects on business and personal relationships.

The name we give to the patterns of behaviors that others can observe is *social style*. In the following chapters, we will look at what constitutes social style, how it can be reliably measured, and how this knowledge can be used to increase the effectiveness of interpersonal relationships.

When we speak of interpersonal relationships (an interaction involving at least two people), we contend that no one can do much about what another person says or does, but each of us *can* do something about what *we* say and do. And because dealing with others is such a major aspect of our lives, if we can control what *we* say and do to make others more comfortable, we can realistically expect our relationships to be more positive, or effective, ones.

Now before going any further, let's clarify what we mean by the term *control,* because many people today react negatively to that word; they prefer to be spontaneous and free at all costs, to "tell it like it is." The irony that we face when we are spontaneous and free at all costs, however, is that we leave the control of an interpersonal situation to another individual. Then, if we aren't comfortable with what the other person says or does, we are likely to become so defensive that the relationship becomes nonproductive. We are neither spontaneous nor free, because we are simply reacting to someone else's words and actions.

But if we are in control—that is, if we consider the behavior of the other individual and that person's probable preferences—then we can use our insight, and perhaps a practiced repertoire of responses, to control ourselves and be less defensive—or at least to be defensive in a productive way. The result is freedom based on the knowledge of how to act appropriately in future situations.

Here's an example. Take the defensive unit of a football team. The greater the team's effort during practice to develop control over a wide variety of plays, the greater its ability to be spontaneous when the opposing team changes its offensive alignment. Such a defensive unit is freer because of its control than a unit that decides that only a few plays are necessary. Likewise, in a social relationship, if you take the time both to learn about the effects your actions have upon others, and to learn to control what you say and do when you are with them, you will be freer to enjoy the uniqueness of others—and not have to waste time and energy trying to resolve unsatisfactory relationships. You don't try to control others, manipulate them, or second guess them. There's no need to get inside their heads or souls. Just concentrate on controlling your own actions to achieve more productive relationships.

So, it's vital to understand your own behavior and how it affects others. Thus, we will spend the first part of the book defining the "you" in an interpersonal relationship. This focus naturally brings up the classic debate over whether the inner you or the outer you is the "real" you. Our perspective, which we believe is both valid and yet too often poorly understood, is that one's external, public actions are the only "you" most people get to know. To others, you are what you *say* and *do*—no more, no less. Most people do not know—cannot know—your motives or your inner thoughts. They can, though, hear and see what you say and do.

In the course of this book, we hope that you will gain some understanding of how others see you. We believe that such an insight will lead to less defensiveness in your interactions, more willingness to accept differences in personal styles, and more effective relationships in any situation.

The information that we will present describes what we have communicated to hundreds of human resource development workshops that incorporate the results of our research and observations. More than 100,000 people throughout the United States, predominantly in management or sales positions in business and industry, have attended these workshops, which are designed to improve interpersonal effectiveness. In addition, numerous firms, particularly in the life insurance industry, rely on our measurement of social style to make predictions about the success of their new employees.

As for the assumptions that represent our personal values, we believe that

People perform most effectively in a positive relationship.

A mutually productive relationship is an asset that one needs to work at to maintain.

The modification of one's approach in order to improve an interpersonal relationship does not constitute a lack of sincerity or a Machiavellian desire to manipulate. Quite the opposite, it demonstrates respect for another person's right to be unique.

One of the greatest insights in life is the mature recognition that others are at least as important in the greater scheme of things as oneself.

Developing a wide variety of skills and techniques for handling interpersonal relationships is a desirable objective.

The opportunity to misuse the skills and techniques we will talk about is real, but if they are misused, this will soon become evident to others, and these skills will lose their effectiveness in the hands of the misuser.

A certain amount of effort is required to develop new skills, and this effort is good in the sense that it represents a type of personal growth.

Those things that are out of one's control may be attributed to any source one desires, mystical or otherwise, but controlling what can be controlled—one's own actions—need not contradict one's beliefs.

This, then, is our value system. Of course, the option for you to disagree with what we say always remains open. We only hope that you will judge us after you have tried out some of the approaches we suggest.

We also believe that our method of understanding behavioral style and interpersonal relationships differs from other approaches in three very significant ways, and that it's important to understand these differences. First of all, whereas many self-help theories focus on the past—our parental relationships, our educational experiences—we will concern ourselves primarily with what is happening today, and how others see us currently behaving. We will only briefly discuss how or why we became the way we are now.

Second, a number of self-help approaches tend to concentrate on concepts such as the psyche, the id, the libido, the clinical idea of self—or, generally, on what goes on inside you. In contrast, we will emphasize the external you that others can see, describe, and agree upon.

Third, self-help theories often focus on specific techniques for modifying what people say and do, and their main emphasis is on changing human behavior. While some of these techniques might be appropriate, our purpose is more to help you to deal effectively with a number of types of social situations rather than recommend any one particular method—such as assertiveness training—as suitable for all occasions.

Thus, we take a practical view: Other people must deal with your actions every day, whether or not they understand why you behave the way you do. Because of this, your personal actions have an effect on your success. The way you act when you are with others—your social style—sends a message that influences the way that they, in turn, act with you. And thus, the better you understand these interactions, the greater are your chances of having positive relationships with people.

In the following chapters, social style—what it is, the messages it sends, and how it affects a relationship—will be discussed. We will explain that how you "see" yourself may be vastly different from how others perceive you. This can make dealing with people more difficult than would be the case if you had a better understanding of your style's effect on them. And, we will emphasize why *no one style is good or bad;* why social style is not the same as personality; and why any style can be successful, as long as the person uses it in a way that makes others comfortable.

Our book is obviously not a novel, yet neither is it a manual that will teach you a rigid set of rules. From time to time, though, we will describe various social situations in short narrative form to help you develop a mental image of the behavior and actions we call social style. These narrative pictures are exaggerations, taken out of context, which highlight the behavior, actions, and skills we'd like you to come to understand. A committed reader who has the opportunity to practice and get feedback from others about the actions we describe can increase his or her personal effectiveness. In addition, we will provide you with practice suggestions at the end of each chapter to verify what we say. In the final analysis, though, modifying one's approach to interpersonal relationships requires a fair degree of openness, personal risk, effort, and practice.

The first two chapters of the book will lay a foundation for understanding social style by discussing what we mean by behavior and its effect on our lives. In Chapter 3, we will put this information into a model that explains the patterns of behavior we have found common to most people. Chapters 4 and 5 will enhance this model, bringing it to life by showing how all styles can succeed. Then, Chapters 6 and 7 will discuss applications of social style at work, in the community, and at home. Finally, Chapter 8 sums it up. The Appendix will provide the reader with details about the development of our theory and the research upon which it was based.

Our hope is that this book will give you a new perspective on your interactions with others. Thus, we move into the first chapter by reinforcing this thought: Using social style effectively means being in control of your half of an interpersonal relationship, so that others are free to be themselves and so that you can enjoy the uniqueness of others. Some popular self-help books promote manipulative attitudes that essentially say "let the other fellow beware; I'm going to get mine." Our research and value system stands in sharp contrast to such approaches. Obviously everyone has the right to stand up for himself and, in truth, needs to be able to do so in a productive and effective way. However, if what a person says and does destroys relationships with basically self-serving actions, such behaviors become self-limiting. Our approach may require a little more study, but ultimately is self-freeing. Our approach means you will not succeed at the cost of others; you will not need to manipulate or control them. Instead, you will succeed in a way that is far easier and much more productive for you and the others in your life: You will succeed with style!

1

Behavior: Setting the Scene

When people ask, "Do I know myself?" the whole spectrum of psychology opens up before them. Many individuals try to answer this question by exploring their innermost feelings and thoughts, and while this is one approach to self-awareness, it is not ours. Instead, we are going to ask you to attempt to understand yourself by seeing yourself as others see you—to try to look at yourself objectively, much as a behavioral scientist would.

Your social style, the "you" that is on display every day, can be quite independent of what we may believe about ourselves or wish we were. But because others react to and draw conclusions about us mainly from our behavior, whether they know why we act as we do or not, our actions have a significant effect on our success in dealing with others.

But let's start at the beginning, with the fundamental concept of behavior. As we discuss some basic ideas about behavior, try to set aside the notions of psychology you might have that deal with the inner you. If you are still skeptical after our discussion, stay with us as we develop the next three chapters: At the end of your reading, we're confident our points will begin to make some practical sense to you.

DISCOVERING THE PUBLIC "YOU"

Our study of behavior revolves around one key principle: The conclusions that people draw about a person are based on what they observe that person saying and doing. Other aspects of an individual's personality, including abilities, dreams, ambitions, beliefs, likes, and dislikes, play no role whatsoever in discussion of behavior. In this book, the "you" that will be discussed is the you that says and does things, the public you. Your intentions are disregarded, because they belong to the private you.

This approach to gaining more understanding about ourselves by learning to see our behavior as others see it is rather challenging. It's difficult to stand outside ourselves, so to speak, as observers, and then to think about how our actions affect others. This challenge is made all the more difficult when we realize that others cannot feel what we are feeling nor think what we are thinking. They can only observe what we say and do. Yet learning to see ourselves as others see us can be a very rewarding way of understanding ourselves. More important, it can lead to improved relationships, without requiring dramatic changes in our attitudes or values. As we study how others react to our behavior, these insights about ourselves can become useful almost immediately.

Many people, when they initially hear of this concept, argue that the "inner me" who feels and thinks is much more important than the "outer me." A statement made a few years ago by a noted psychoanalyst, Dr. Willard Gaylin, will clarify our position:

   ❝ It was, I believe, the distinguished Nebraska financier Father Edward J. Flanagan who professed to having "never met a bad boy." Having, myself, met a remarkable number of bad boys, it might seem that either our experiences were drastically different or we were using the word bad differently. I suspect neither is true, but rather that the Father was appraising the "inner man," while I, in fact, do not acknowledge the existence of inner people.

   Since we psychoanalysts have unwittingly contributed to this confusion, let one, at least, attempt a small rectifying effort. Psychoanalytic data—which should be viewed as supplementary information—is, unfortunately, often viewed as an alternative (and superior) explanation. This has led to the prevalent tendency to think of the "inner" man as the real man and the outer man as an illusion or pretender.

   While psychoanalysis supplies us with an incredibly useful tool for explaining the motives and purposes underlying human behavior, most of this has little bearing on the moral nature of that behavior.

The inside of the man represents another view, not a truer one. A man may not always be what he appears to be, but what he appears to be is always a significant part of what he is.

Kurt Vonnegut has said, "You are what you pretend to be," which is simply another way of saying, you are what we (all of us) perceive you to be, not what you think you are.

Consider for a moment the case of the 90-year-old man on his deathbed, joyous and relieved over the success of his deception. For 90 years he has shielded his evil nature from public observation. For 90 years he has affected courtesy, kindness and generosity—suppressing all the malice he knew was within him while he calculatedly and artificially substituted grace and charity. All his life he had been fooling the world into believing he was a good man. This "evil" man will, I predict, be welcomed into the Kingdom of Heaven.

Similarly, I will not be told that the young man who earns his pocket money by mugging old ladies is "really" a good boy. Even my generous and expansive definition of goodness will not accommodate that particular form of self-advancement.

Saint Francis may, in his unconscious, indeed have been compensating for, and denying, destructive, unconscious Oedipal impulses identical to those which Attila projected and acted on. But the similarity of the unconscious constellations in the two men matters precious little, if it does not distinguish between them.

I do not care to learn that Hitler's heart was in the right place. A knowledge of the unconscious life of the man may be an adjunct to understanding his behavior. It is *not* a substitute for his behavior in describing him.

The inner man is a fantasy. If it helps you to identify with one, by all means do so; preserve it, cherish it, embrace it, but do not present it to others for evaluation or consideration, for excuse or exculpation, or, for that matter, for punishment or disapproval.

Like any fantasy, it serves your purposes alone. It has no standing in the real world which we share with each other. Those character traits, those attitudes, that behavior—that strange and alien stuff sticking out all over you—*that's the real you!*[1]

Saying that the inner man is a "fantasy" may overstate the case a bit. But Dr. Gaylin's statement is a provocative one, and

1. Willard Gaylin, M.D., "What You See Is the Real You," *New York Times,* 7 Oct. 1977.

it does help to explain our interpersonal perspective, which is one that defines "you" as being the you that says and does things, not the you that you intend to be.

BEHAVIOR VERSUS INTENTION

What we say and do, and how we say and do it, is our definition of behavior. The broad grouping of the things a person tends to say and do most often is called *behavioral preferences:* ways of talking and acting that we feel comfortable doing, that we come to like in ourselves and in others. But, these ways of behaving can sometimes become so habitual that they can get in the way of our intentions. For instance:

> You may *intend* to break the ice with a new client in a nonthreatening way (you decide to tell a joke), but that behavioral preference of yours (for joking) may cause your client to give you a cold stare, making you realize that you have gotten off on the wrong foot. "Obviously incapable of appreciating humor," you decide. "If I'd only known!"

> You may *intend* to critique your subordinate's work fairly and honestly (by going over the facts step by step, point by point, with methodical completeness), but that behavioral preference of yours (for being thorough and logical) may result in your being called picky. "Certainly not experienced or perceptive enough to recognize how I'm trying to help," you may conclude. "A total waste of my time!"

> You may *intend* to faithfully incorporate all of your superior's suggestions into the XYZ Report for the company vice-president (by illustrating his ideas with some dramatic little narratives), but that behavioral preference of yours (for describing things with a dash of color, just to underline the point) may cause others to say, "Stop trying to be clever. It distracts from our true purpose." "Unfair criticism!" you respond.

> You may *intend* to have everyone's best interests at heart at the office by running a tight ship: keeping things moving, on schedule, and everyone, including yourself, fully informed (you send out memos to the whole staff twice a day). But that behavioral preference of yours (for informing your staff of what needs to be done in a series of rapid commands) may cause staff members to

feel that their independence is being limited, which, in turn, makes them unresponsive to your demands. Then you fume, "My staff just isn't motivated!"

With a little effort, each of us can think of a number of instances in which these habitual ways of behaving can sometimes get in the way of our well-meaning intentions. In fact, it's fair to say that in more cases than not, it's what we say and do and how we say and do it that gets us in trouble with others, not our intentions. The kind of misunderstanding which occurs when one's behavior does not communicate one's intent can destroy what might have otherwise been a mutually beneficial, productive relationship. Let's look at an example of how this can happen.

Bob had just been promoted from field sales to the home office of a large Eastern insurance company as the director of product development. In the field, his way of going about things had been successful. He was fast-paced to the point of seeming driven, and he was decisive to the point of appearing closed-minded. He focused on one goal, greater sales, so much that his people viewed him as "a quota guy" who treated others as "so many bales of hay." Nevertheless, his people respected him. He had the ability to get them and their families to Hawaii or the Virgin Islands on annual reward trips. He helped, or drove, them to make money.

Sarah was a supervisor in the sales records department. She was a two-year business graduate with a degree in stenography but, as she liked to put it back then, "with no place to practice at present." The work was routine at best. But Sarah had shown an ability to keep morale up in her department, because she always had a willing ear for others' problems and she always found time for people and personal relations. People actually asked to be transferred to her department, and its efficiency had gone way up. Then Sarah got her big opportunity. Bob hired her as his administrative assistant.

Work went well the first few weeks. Both Bob and Sarah were trying extra hard, with that overenthusiasm that people assigned to new positions often show. Although there was some strain in their relationship—Bob couldn't understand Sarah's easygoing, sympathetic nature, and Sarah couldn't understand Bob's unfeeling, dominating manner—each knew the other's background and thought that the stress was just part of getting into a new routine. As time passed, though, it became apparent that something or someone was just not working out. Tensions built.

In October, three months after Bob and Sarah had been promoted, the company had its biannual national sales convention. Bob was responsible for planning it—a new challenge. Sarah, too, was challenged. Bob made her responsible for troubleshooting the entire convention and for heading up the spouses' program. Sarah got the job done, working slowly but well—her pace wasn't Bob's pace. For weeks, both Bob and Sarah put in long hours and shoved aside the irritation they were causing each other.

The convention ended—successfully—on a Thursday. Bob's staff was exhausted. That evening Sarah rested by taking a long bath and listening to some good music. She had understood that all the push, deadlines, and franticness prior to and during the convention were necessary evils. But she remarked to her husband, "Now things will get back to normal and I'm going to enjoy a little calm between storms."

Bob also was more tired than he'd expected. After having dinner with his family, he went into his study to relax. For Bob, relaxation usually meant sitting with a note pad and pencil in hand. And, true to form, he soon began making a list of follow-up things to do as a result of the convention's success. "I'll need Sarah's help first thing in the morning," he said to himself. "I'd better get to work a little early." Then, his last note before sleep: "Be sure to thank Sarah for all her help."

Friday morning Bob arrived at the office at 7 A.M. He'd had his morning cup of coffee, read the paper, and was just organizing his list of things to do when the other employees began arriving around 8:15. Sarah showed up about 8:30. At 8:35, as Sarah was chatting with her peers and organizing the morning mail, Bob got a call to meet with the vice-president of sales. Bob was ready, and he came charging out of his office.

Sarah was feeling very good about herself that day. She knew she had done a fine job and was looking forward to hearing praise from Bob. Instead, she met a man in mid-morning stride with an armful of papers, a purposeful set to his jaw, and a list of things to do.

"Good morning, Bob," Sarah said, expecting to receive a few compliments.

"Good morning, Sarah," Bob replied. "I've got a meeting with Vince in two minutes." Then he added, "You did a good job with the convention."

Sarah laughed modestly, "No, not really."

"Yes, you did. I even made a note to myself to remind me to tell you," Bob said, as he slapped down a memo and the crumpled piece of notepaper on Sarah's desk. He added, "We've got lots to do today. Here's a list of things you can begin working on, now that our vacation with the troops is over. And, I'll need ten copies of this memo when I get back." Then he was off.

Sarah sat there a moment, feeling lost in Bob's wake. She picked up the note and thought, "Boy, if that's all the thanks I get, he must not think much of me. What a louse." Angrily, she threw the note into her wastebasket and went to see the gang from her old work unit.

One hour later Bob came back to the office. He didn't see Sarah or the copies of the memo, so he got one of the girls in the typing pool to take care of the job. Once again, he felt himself becoming irritated with Sarah's apparent lack of a sense of urgency. But rather than taking his usual approach of pointing her mistakes out to her, Bob tried to push the irritation to the back of his mind. After all, Sarah had proven during the convention that she was a very capable assistant, and he admitted to himself that he hadn't taken time to thank her properly for the good job she'd done. As he made a mental note to take care of that matter, she returned. Bob jumped up with a letter he had been working on in his hand and went out to thank Sarah more adequately.

"Sarah, I just wanted to. . . ."

Thinking that he had another memo to be copied, Sarah exploded. "All you ever do is order me around with your memos and deadlines! I can't take it anymore!" She burst into tears and ran out of the office.

Bob, shocked, thought to himself: "Now what did I say?"

Neither of them got over the experience. Today Bob is still with the company, but Sarah gave up on corporate life to run an arts and crafts shop. A small matter? Perhaps. But it produced another new series of adjustments for Sarah and some nagging doubts for Bob about his own capabilities. What Bob had said and done, and how he had said and done it—his behavior, as a result of his behavioral preferences—had gotten in the way of his intention—to thank her for a job well done. Bob's message, "Hey, Sarah, I really want to thank you," got garbled on the way out. A potentially productive relationship between two talented people went sour. Bob's behavior preferences spoke louder than his words.

Of course, there are many factors that can make a relationship nonproductive, and certainly a lot of those things are beyond the scope of this book. But, undoubtedly, each one of us can recall situations similar to the one experienced by Bob and Sarah, when we failed to communicate to someone, and, as a result, lost a sale or didn't get approval of a proposal. In such instances we can ask ourselves: "Did I handle that relationship as well as I might have? Was it really a matter of not having the right information or the right intention, or was it just a matter of not presenting it in a way that made the other person comfortable?" Often the answers to those questions indicate that the relationship, which could have been an asset, was nonproductive, not because the information or intention was inadequate but because the presentation was a failure. Somehow, we did something wrong—created a bad first impression, or otherwise upset the other person so that he or she reacted negatively. If we only knew how we could have done it differently!

One of the primary reasons why these experiences are common to so many of us is that many people do not have a clear understanding of how their behavior affects others and what it does to an interpersonal relationship. This, combined with the inescapable fact that other people will always affect our lives and that they will always interpret what they think we mean by observing our actions, can too frequently lead to less than satisfactory relationships.

In the case of Bob and Sarah, Bob was unaware that his habit of behaving in a brusque, businesslike manner was a cause of tension for Sarah, since she interpreted this behavior to mean that he wouldn't take time to notice or appreciate her work. Sarah, on the other hand, did not perceive that she might be a source of irritation to Bob, since he found her easygoing, personal approach to her work inappropriate. But if Bob and Sarah could have understood that the judgments which they were making about each other were simply the result of differences in their behavioral preferences, rather than true criticisms of each other's ability, they would have had a much better chance of adapting to these differences. They could have devised a method for working together that would have supported each of their unique needs. Let's look at a case where this type of effort was made, and created a productive relationship.

Todd and Gayle are peers and both work for the testing and research staff of the personnel department at a Western paper firm. Todd is known as an intuitive person, always upbeat, always bouncing ten projects around at once in what appears to be a disorganized manner but with good results. Gayle, on the other hand, is quite the opposite of Todd. She's quiet and methodical, preferring to think each project through deliberately and logically. She isn't about to let Todd get away with too much. Both she and Todd, however, have come to accept their differences in style and have negotiated one of those rare working relationships between seeming opposites. They function well together, and Testing and Research has become one of the most respected units at the company.

This was not always the case, though. About a year ago, things had not been going well between Gayle and Todd, and their department was not highly productive or well respected. At that time Todd went to Ralph, director of Testing and Research, with a problem—his inability to get along with Gayle—and asked for advice. Ralph suggested that Todd attend a workshop sponsored by the company which was designed to improve interpersonal communication. Todd came back from the workshop enthused, as usual, but with a certain new moderation in his actions that pleased Ralph. Todd had learned a lot at the workshop about how he appeared to others, and what his actions said to them. Just a few days later the results of what Todd had learned became even more obvious.

It was a typical 9:00 A.M. Monday morning staff meeting, only this time there was a particularly urgent crisis. At 10 A.M. Ralph had to meet with the vice-presidents and produce a report explaining the firm's efforts to comply with existing Equal Employment

Opportunity (EEO) guidelines. It had to be done fast, and by somebody who was familiar with the subject. Since Todd was new to the company at the time, Ralph asked Gayle to compile the report.

Gayle knew that with only about an hour to prepare the rather extensive report, she was really going to have to concentrate. This meant having her secretary hold all calls, getting the documents with the necessary information laid out in a systematic series of piles, and developing an outline. Above all, she did not want to be interrupted. She did not like to work under so tight a deadline and, in fact, preferred to be deliberate, taking the time to do the job right the first time. Nevertheless, she set out to do her best under the circumstances.

As Ralph prepared for the meeting with the vice-presidents, he suddenly remembered a file of data which he thought would certainly enhance the report's credibility, and he asked Todd to take a look at the file and see if he could help Gayle out a bit.

As Todd read through the file, he suddenly came across a bonanza. Among the reports was one that seemed to be proof positive that the tests which the firm gave to prospective employees were firmly in compliance with EEO guidelines. His first reaction was to jump up with the file and run into Gayle's office to give her the good news—"our problems are solved." But he stopped himself, because he remembered one word from his workshop, one word that jumped out at him: *check*. Slow down and check out the appropriateness of your impulsive behavior. For instance, he had discovered that, although he felt great about responding quickly and enthusiastically with ideas and information, this was not necessarily the case for others. And, judging by what he had observed of Gayle's behavior, he felt that she was one of those others.

So, instead of barging into her office, he decided to have the statistics from the file typed in tabular form for inclusion in an appendix. He also decided to provide Gayle with a chance to review the data before preparing the final report. Gayle was more than pleasantly surprised when Todd handed her the additional material.

Ralph got the report for his meeting with the vice-presidents at 10 A.M. But the most rewarding result for T&R was that because of this success, Todd and Gayle began talking. Todd told Gayle about the workshop and what he'd learned. He also told Gayle he felt that his own behavioral tendencies had caused them to get off on the wrong foot. Gayle was impressed by Todd's apparent insights and showed an interest in learning more about the workshop. And that was when things began to turn around for T&R.

If you're beginning to wonder whether you are more of a Sarah than a Bob, or more of a Todd than a Gayle, read on. Later chapters will discuss in more detail what Todd learned at the workshop. But one point is clear: When you succeed with social style, you understand what effects your actions can have on others. You know how to make your behavior say to someone else what you truly intend to say. You do not let your typical behavioral preferences lead to a failure in communication.

Of course, achieving this understanding—and then doing something about it—will take a committed effort. But the value of the effort lies in developing and sustaining better relationships with the people around you—work groups, social acquaintances, and family members.

What's the first step? Probably our greatest challenge is learning to accept the fact that we all are creatures of habit—that everyone exhibits typical behavioral preferences. Next, it's necessary to learn what the basic patterns of behavioral preferences are, and which pattern our own preferences fall into. In Chapter 2, we'll begin by taking a closer look at some principles of behavior and at the techniques that you can learn in order to become an objective observer of social style.

PRACTICE SUGGESTIONS

1. All of us have run across situations in which, somehow, we created the wrong impression or received a negative reaction from someone. The next time you walk away from such an encounter thinking, "She just didn't understand what I had in mind," or, "I think they took that in the wrong way," ask yourself: Was a behavioral preference of mine (for example, for joking, or not expressing a definite opinion, or phrasing my words more like orders than requests, or trying to make friends rather than making a point) partially to blame for the poor results, rather than my intention, the value of the idea, or my competence?

2. Similarly, if you pass a judgment on someone else's idea or statement, and then find out later that the person really intended to communicate something else entirely, ask yourself: Was there something in the other person's behavior that caused my misjudgment? What was it? Did it go against my own behavioral preferences, irritating me and making me jump to conclusions?

3. Think of someone you know who makes you uncomfortable, someone you would prefer not to spend too much time with. What is it that this person says or does that causes you to react this way? How is his or her behavior different from yours? Do you limit your contacts with this individual, or at least keep them short? Do you suppose others often do the same thing with you? If you can recall such situations, you are recognizing the tension that occurs between people with different behavioral preferences.

2
Behavior: Looking at It Objectively

We all say and do things as a result of certain habit patterns, and people make predictions about us because they come to expect us to behave in a particular way. To illustrate this point, just think about some of the predictions we make about other people's behavior. For instance, when we give a dinner party, we have a tendency to seat our friends according to how we think they will get along with each other. Or, we tell our secretaries not to expect us back from a luncheon appointment with a client because "Joe will want to say hello to half the people at the club, and he'd be hurt if I rushed out without him." Or, we send George and Helen together on a sales call. George can sell them on the creativity of the idea, while Helen can support George with the facts. The examples go on and on.

But while we can easily ascribe patterns of behavior to others, we often resist putting the same labels on ourselves. We might argue, "Don't I behave differently with various individuals? Isn't my behavior too variable to make useful predictions from it?" The fact is that even though each of us is unique, we tend to act in fairly consistent, describable ways. All of us use habits we have grown used to—habits that have worked well for us, habits that make us comfortable—and these habits become the social style that others can observe.

Think about your own actions when you are uncomfortable in a social situation. Do you have a tendency to begin giving orders, or do you prefer to withdraw? On the job, do you try to joke with your peers to cheer them up, or do you smooth things over? Chances are, you tend to consistently behave more in one way than another, and even if you're not aware of this, your co-workers probably are.

THE ROOTS OF BEHAVIOR

Why do people develop these behavioral preferences? A brief look at the "roots" of behavior indicates that in the most elemental sense, people tend to do those things that make them comfortable and to avoid doing those things that make them uncomfortable or cause them tension. Once a pattern of actions receives positive reinforcement, we have a tendency to repeat it. These behaviors begin to develop early in life. For example, parents who want their children to be gentle tend to reinforce gentle actions rather than aggressive behaviors. Parents who believe their children should be fighters reinforce fighting behaviors. To reinforce these preferences, parents often seek out teachers, coaches, and other parental substitutes who support the same type of behavior.

Soon the accepted type of behavior becomes so automatic that a person may not even realize that it is a habit. People simply repeat the patterns that have made them comfortable in the past. Later they even tend to seek out social situations that will reinforce their habitual behavior and to avoid social situations that cause discomfort.

As an example, take Charlie, who is a big fellow, and who found out early in life that he could get by with being assertive. Moreover, his father reinforced this behavior, because he wanted Charlie to be a "real man." By the time Charlie became a teenager, he had long ago refined his behavior into a habitual style. For instance, one evening his father said, "Charlie, the lawn's beginning to look like a jungle. I want you to do something about it." Charlie, who hated cutting the grass, put the task off until the last minute and left it undone when his friends came by and wanted to play football. That evening when Charlie's father came home to find the lawn still not mowed, he called Charlie on the carpet. The next day, Charlie tried to persuade the other football players to help with the lawn, but to no avail. This time Charlie's father got really angry and made it very clear that someone would be in deep trouble if the grass wasn't cut by the following evening.

So, on the third day, Charlie tried the behavior that had always worked for him before. While his father was out, he grabbed his younger brother, Kevin, handed him the lawnmower and said, "Mow!" He cornered his sister Amy, gave her the clippers and said, "Trim!" Because Charlie was bigger than they were, they both unwillingly complied. Charlie's father, not knowing the circumstances, reinforced this behavior by giving Charlie a big smile, a pat on the shoulder and saying, "That's what I like to see, Charlie. The lawn looks great."

Because such behavior worked for Charlie, he began to choose activities and occupations that were extensions of this basic style and avoided social influences that disapproved of it or suggested other modes of behavior. For instance, when Charlie was encouraged to become a priest, he entered a school run by seminarians. One day he was taken aside by a teacher and told that his assertiveness was not appreciated; less forcefulness was regarded there as a more appropriate approach, and Charlie would have to change. But people don't change their behaviors; they change their circumstances instead. So Charlie wrote home and asked to be transferred to a military school. After military school he grew up and became a lawyer, a district attorney, and later a judge, always finding positions that allowed him to tell others what to do.

Thus, Charlie's choices reinforced his habits, and he limited his opportunities to develop a variety of ways for dealing with people in different situations. As the years went on, he grew even more reluctant to change. On the contrary, he tended to find fault with dissimilar people because they upset him. Today, Charlie probably doesn't realize that when he draws conclusions about others on the basis of his own preferences, he is really saying more about himself than about others. If Charlie sees a coworker behaving in an unassertive manner, he may conclude that this person is "gutless." What Charlie is really doing is assuming that his own behavior is good, and that therefore anyone who behaves differently from him must be bad.

Charlie's younger brother, who is much less assertive, grew up feeling uncomfortable with very assertive people and he, too, sought out career situations that supported his preferences. He became a marriage counselor with an easygoing, rather non-directive method.

This, then, briefly explains how behavioral preferences tend to develop and how they're reinforced over the years. It also explains why people tend to label as "bad" those who act differently from themselves, while people who behave similarly are seen as "good."

Additional reinforcement occurs when, as people observe each other's behavior patterns, they begin to seek out certain individuals when they need someone to exercise a particular behavior. For example, we look for the assertive person when we need someone to help us fight for a cause; we look for the cool-headed thinker when we need a problem solved; we look for the peacemaker if we encounter a dispute; and we look for the person who has a lively, warm demeanor when we need cheering up.

But while we can observe other people's habit patterns, most of us prefer to believe our own behavior can not be described this easily, that we usually have logical reasons for acting the way we do. For example, we might observe Mary, a woman who is not talkative at parties. If we ask her why, she might very well answer by saying: "Well, I try to be a good listener," or "I only say something when it's important."

In fact, though, if we could observe Mary in many different settings, we would probably find that more often than not she is quiet, and if we probed a little deeper, she might even tell us that she simply feels more comfortable when she takes an unassuming posture. Mary might admit, "When I have to speak up and assert myself, I begin to feel tense."

Let's look a little more closely at the tension Mary feels, because in a fundamental sense, tension provides the motivation for everything we say and do (or don't say and don't do).

TENSION: A STIMULUS TO ACTION

Tension, which can have either a positive or negative effect on us, is a stimulus that causes us to act rather than to remain inactive. Tension is simply a state of disequilibrium, an awareness that something disturbing is happening in our environment. More specifically, the tension we're concerned with in this book is the type that is felt between people. For example, we may experience tension in a situation as simple as having someone walk into a room where we happen to be sitting. We feel that something is different about our environment, and our nervous system goes on the alert. We may also feel elation, irritation, or indifference, but the fact remains that tension is present, and we'll try to reduce it, if only by looking out of the window and hoping that the person will leave.

Because we seek to reduce tension, or regain a sense of equilibrium, tension produces a response, and if the response leads to a reduction of tension, it's likely that we'll use the same response whenever we have similar feelings. For instance, when someone gets on a crowded elevator, we feel tension, and we respond in some way to make ourselves comfortable again. Some people automatically speak to the new passenger; others watch the floor numbers light up or stare straight ahead. But you'll notice that an individual's particular reaction to the tension in this situation rarely varies.

In short, we all display a set of behaviors based on a need to reduce personal tension. Since many of these behaviors work, we use them frequently. Other people observe these actions as belonging to habit patterns that are typical of us, and they can predict that we'll use them over and over. And, actually, it is difficult to vary a response to tension. This point can be demonstrated by using the elevator example again. If you usually stay silent and watch the floor numbers light when riding with someone else, next time, force yourself to greet the other person, instead. Not easy, is it?

We tend to think of tension as unpleasantness, but keep in mind that it can have both positive and negative effects. Tension is positive because it's the motivating force for virtually all living organisms. Tension provides ''go power'' for the human being. It gets us out of bed in the morning, keeps us on the job, and directs us in sustained activity through years of education and work. Defined in this way, tension is a natural and necessary part of everyday living. When tension is channeled toward personal goals and objectives, it leads to productivity, satisfaction, and success.

But behavior produced by tension can create negative results, too. As we learn to respond in certain ways to tension, we create "comfort zones" for ourselves—ranges or boundaries of behavior that make us feel comfortable. What we may not realize is that while we may be in *our* comfort zones when we behave in certain ways, we can be creating tension for someone else. Now in some cases, such as that of the military general who must order his troops into battle, raising others' tension by shouting commands might accomplish a necessary objective. But all too often the tension we cause another individual results in a nonproductive response: The person refuses to deal with us or argues bitterly against our suggestions. Similarly, we may react in the same way: If someone uses a kind of behavior that is outside our comfort zones, it causes tension for us, and we tend to become critical of the person.

The term for patterns of behavior used to protect ourselves in uncomfortable situations is *defensiveness*. Defensiveness is often nonproductive, because when we focus only on our tensions, we tend to explain the way we act by viewing what the other person is saying or doing as "bad." In other words, we do not strive for a mutual goal. Instead, we just reduce our own tensions in order to be comfortable. The other person becomes the antagonist, and we use some well-established habit pattern (a defense) to remove discomfort. Then, if both people experience negative tension, defensiveness—and a go-nowhere situation—develop.

Just as most of us are unaware of our behavior patterns, we are also unaware of our own defensive reactions, which are often unconscious and automatic. We can even become defensive when only anticipating discomfort, as well as when experiencing it. Utilizing the old adage that a good defense is frequently a strong offense, some of us use defensive behaviors that take the form of an attack. Other people prefer to cover up, or to avoid an unpleasant situation, rather than face it openly. These defenses become an essential part of our social style, and we'll discuss them in later chapters.

Now, let's go a step further and assume that someone is creating tension (either knowingly or unknowingly) for two people, Sam and Bill. Although both men consider it necessary to work with that person, they might have two different reactions:

> Sam may handle the discomfort by relying on his habitual defense, which is to try to satisfy the person by working hard on an assigned task. He is also trying to escape the problem, bury himself in the work. And quite likely he won't approach the task cheerfully, creatively, cooperatively, or productively. If this situation continues, performance suffers, and the person causing the tension might decide that Sam isn't motivated: "He has the wrong attitude about his job; he does as little as possible, just to get by."

> Bill, on the other hand, may attempt to deal with the relationship by resorting to his habitual defense: debating how the job should be done and taking time to discuss his feelings about his work. This can also be counterproductive, and the person causing tension might begin to feel that "Bill is a complainer."

Both Bill and Sam acted defensively in dealing with the tension that existed. But the comments "Sam has the wrong attitude" and "Bill is a complainer" are also defense mechanisms: they are reactions to the discomfort that Sam and Bill are causing. Our everyday defensive comments are so natural to us that we seldom recognize the tension they create for other people. But by responding defensively to someone else's defensiveness, we set up a vicious cycle that ultimately leads to unsatisfactory relationships for all concerned.

The reason that Bill's and Sam's reactions are so common relates to social reinforcement. In our society, we are taught that both achievement and acceptance are important. Our social values suggest that we will earn respect and material rewards for industriousness—*achievement*. They also emphasize the importance of being recognized as a nice person and a feeling human being—*acceptance*. People who exhibit either of these patterns or actions are rewarded by society.

The way most people handle confrontation can also be roughly divided into two responses. Some people habitually avoid confrontation (let's call this reaction *flight*) because to *fight* would cause further discomfort. This was Sam's case. Other people find it much easier to adjust their comfort some by tackling the situation head-on—debating points, the way Bill did, for example. All living creatures exhibit these "fight" or "flight" responses, and, since they were designed to keep us comfortable, they are neither good nor bad, but simply appropriate or inappropriate. Again, early in life we get reinforcement for our fight or flight responses to tension.

Although we don't employ either fight or flight approaches exclusively, just as almost everyone builds habit patterns that favor either achievement or acceptance, they also develop similar habits with respect to fight or flight. Thus, when tension is not directly tied to meeting basic needs, such as coping with hunger or pain, our behavior tends to habitually emphasize either fight or flight to gain social objectives. Note how one reaction to tension occurred because Sam was trying to *achieve*—complete the task—and hide from the discomfort (*flight*), while in the other case, Bill was trying to gain acceptance for his ideas by debating (*fighting*).

The problem with these defensive responses is that although they protect the individual temporarily, they don't resolve the interpersonal conflict that caused the tension in the first place. Because defensive responses tend to be self-centered and self-serving, they result in less than desirable results.

FINDING A TENSION EQUILIBRIUM

There is always some degree of tension between two people, which can either be productive or nonproductive. This tension is so natural it is seldom recognized or acknowledged until it becomes extreme. People are like thermostats; they're constantly seeking to reach a state of equilibrium or comfort. As soon as another person enters the picture, this produces a type of tension, and each one has to re-establish their balance and feelings of comfort. Whether the response is productive or nonproductive depends on how this equilibrium—or comfort zone—is established and managed. When people are attempting to work together, too little tension produces too few results. Too much tension also produces too few results and creates inappropriate or overly defensive behavior. Just the right amount provides the power to fulfill mutual goals.

Of course, we realize that defensive reactions are inevitable, and they can even be productive. The challenge for each of us, though, is to determine the proper amount and type of tension that will result in the greatest accomplishments.

If we are going to achieve this objective, we first need to develop skills to use in controlling the tension we create for others. This will require not only understanding what our behavior patterns are and when they begin to create nonproductive tension for others, but also expanding our comfort zones by accepting a wider range of behaviors from others before *we* become nonproductively defensive.

By reducing our own defensiveness through this approach, we not only avoid using other people but we can also prevent them from using us. As you have probably noticed, basically hostile individuals realize that they can capitalize on others' defensiveness and use it to their own personal advantage by keeping people afraid, threatened, or dependent. When we learn to be less defensive, we become stronger, more mature individuals who are not easily exploited by others.

But before we learn how to reduce defensiveness, we must become objective observers of our own and others' behavior. This book will focus first on observing other people, simply because it's almost impossible to stand outside ourselves and see our actions as others see them. But as you observe others, you will find that you will empathize with some people's behavior, while others' behavior will seem diametrically opposed to what you would say or do in the same situation. It's important to make these comparisons, because when we learn to relate the conclusions we draw about others to ourselves, we begin to understand how others probably describe our habitual behavior patterns.

OBSERVATION SKILLS

To ease the task of becoming objective observers of social style, let's narrow the concept of behavior. Our lives are made up of many separate facets and aspects of behavior. For example, there are those behaviors one engages in when alone. Some people whistle when they are by themselves, and most people probably don't smile much when they are alone. The concept of social style that we are developing for you does not concern itself with what people do when they are alone. Similarly, another facet of behavior—the way in which one deals with objects and private situations, not people—also does not involve social style. For instance, people behave in various ways when they come up against a piece of malfunctioning machinery. Some people are more likely to jiggle or kick the machine, while others sit back and study it to see if they can find the problem. Similiarly, some people may eat candy when alone but say "no, thank you" to a public offer of sweets.

The type of behavior that this book focuses on, in contrast, is interpersonal behavior—behavior that occurs when we are involved with one or more persons. As a rather extreme example, consider Richard, a man who takes high risk in his private world. He goes mountain climbing by himself every weekend and challenges the most difficult peaks. Yet among people, he's a person who dislikes conflict and argument. Thus his associates in the business world would probably be surprised if they found out that he was an aggressive mountain climber.

These differences in behavior are neither contradictory nor pathologic; they simply represent different areas of human adjustment. Richard's mountain climbing is not an aspect of social style, but his behavior when he's with other people is. Thus, as we begin learning how to observe our own and other people's behavior, we must remember that the behaviors we are interested in are those that occur during social interaction. Moreover, we're not seeking to define underlying causes or motives for this behavior, which would cloud our ability to see behavior objectively.

The following vignette is an exercise that will help you to practice sorting out objective and subjective observations of behavior. As you read it, concentrate on the behaviors of Frank, Jim, and Liz. In particular, pay attention to how Jim and Liz react to Frank—how their own behavioral preferences lead to defensive judgments of him and get in the way of an objective description. And, ask yourself whether you would respond to Frank more like Liz or more like Jim.

✔ Jim Berklund sat in his boss's office. Jim was recently hired as a management trainee at a large West Coast insurance firm and Bill Stanley was his boss. Jim was a bit nervous. The two men were meeting to discuss Jim's assignments and Jim didn't know what to expect from the day. He enjoyed spontaneity, had a personal preference for friendly, easygoing relationships, and he was suspicious of anything highly organized—including large corporations.

Soon Bill arrived and apologized for being late. He draped his coat over a vacant chair, dumped an assembly of files from his briefcase onto his desk, and gave Jim a friendly smile as he sorted papers.

"Well, Jim, how's your training going? As soon as we get a chance I'd like to spend some time with you, but right now we've got a meeting with Frank Johnson. He's senior vice-president for marketing."

Then Bill explained that he'd been up late the night before preparing a report for the meeting. He asked Jim to sit in and tape the discussion and then write up a summary.

On their way to the meeting, Jim smiled and nodded at the people they passed. As the two men entered the conference room, a number of people were already seated, and Bill introduced Jim to the corporate attorney, the director of marketing services, and the vice-president in charge of personnel. Jim seated himself next to one of the less important people present, a secretary, and began a pleasant conversation of small talk. As Bill passed around copies of his report, Senior Vice-President Frank Johnson was conspicuously absent.

Casual talk, followed by mock discussion of the report, seemed a comfortable way for everyone to pass the time until Frank showed up. "I'm enjoying this," Jim thought. Then, to Jim, the door seemed to open on a wave of energy as Frank entered the room. Without pausing for a hello, Frank launched into the meeting. "So, Bill, what's on the agenda?" Frank knew very well what the subject would be, but this was his way of saying, "This is my turf; you play by my rules."

Bill was familiar with Frank's way of asking this kind of question, with its very obvious answer. That's how Frank was, and Bill accepted it. "We're here to go over my preliminary report on the possibility of beginning our own management-development school.''

"Right. What have you got for me?" Frank's voice was resolute, and each statement was an assertion. He emphasized the word *what,* and spoke quickly, with a volume all could hear. This seemed unnecessary to Jim—and unpleasant.

Bill continued. "Frank, let's go over the high points first and then get into details. I'm recommending that we develop a feasibility proposal. We've done some preliminary research and it looks like there's enough value in such a school to at least put some numbers together.''

"All right, Bill''—Frank's voice became a bit lower, and more deliberate—"Tell me what you've dug up, but let's all understand that not all the facts are on the table. When they are, I'll see what's feasible.'' Again, he emphasized the *what.*

At that, Jim noticed that Bill began to shift slightly in his chair. Frank, too, seemed to sense Bill's uneasiness and started to lean toward him, facing him directly.

"Well, Frank''—Bill seemed to have forgotten the others in the room—"three conclusions from our research support the idea of a feasibility proposal.''

"Yes, yes. Okay, what are they?" Frank stood up and started to pace in front of the table.

"The first one is that most of our competitors are setting up these schools.''

"What are the details on this?''

"Of the big five, four already have plans for a centralized management-development school. I've talked with most of our regional vice-presidents, and . . .''

"Did you get ahold of Mac? What was his point of view?''

Bill hesitated, then haltingly admitted that he hadn't gotten through to MacKenna—a divisional manager whom Frank greatly respected.

All was silent. Frank leaned on the back of his chair. "Well, Bill, I mentioned last week that you better get hold of Mac about this. Doesn't look to me like you've got enough input yet.'' He slid his copy of the report back across the table toward Bill. Then reaching his hand to shut off the tape recorder in front of Jim, he spoke his first words to the new management trainee. "How's that for an introduction?''

Jim arrived home a little late that evening, and dinner was waiting. His wife, Liz, was slightly annoyed. Liz, who had risen quickly to the position of head accountant at a locally owned construction company, liked to stack one activity onto another in each weekday evening. Time, for Liz, was something to be organized—but she did not want to quarrel. Jim and Liz basically got along well, but saw some things differently.

Liz figured that if she could keep her tone of voice pleasant, her irritation at Jim's lateness would pass, so she said, warmly, "Hi, honey, how'd it go, today?" and gave him a kiss.

"Oh, all right," he said in a monotone, and returned the kiss affectionately.

"Just all right?" She sensed that he was equivocating, as he often did; it was one thing about Jim that bothered her.

"Yeah, just all right (Bill was still reacting to Frank's actions at the meeting). Tell you about it when I get changed." Upstairs, he hung his suit carefully, then threw his tie onto the closet floor with a flurry.

"Feel like telling me about it now?" Liz asked, as Jim mixed them a drink. Her irritation was under control, and she wanted to know about his day.

"Well, you know how it is. Lots to do." Jim wasn't really sure if he was ready to get into it.

Liz let him alone with his thoughts for a few minutes, then said, "Come on, I know something is bothering you. What is it?"

"Oh, nothing important. I had a meeting today with some of the big shots. This may be a tougher place to work than I thought."

"Why?"

Then Jim remembered that he had brought home the tape of the meeting, and he put it on the recorder, saying, "Here, listen. This will explain what I mean."

Liz listened attentively. When Jim had shut off the recorder, he said, "Can you imagine anyone being as callous as Frank? And look at his pictures in these company newsletters. He's always pointing at someone or ordering them around."

"Well, it sounded to me like Frank is a real leader," Liz responded. "He got right to the point and didn't waste any time. I'll bet you can depend on him to make decisions." After a few seconds she added, "And what's wrong with pointing? I think he looks like an intelligent, ambitious man. Besides, it says in this little article that he enjoys the symphony. How could someone who has a love of music be callous?"

Stunned, Jim asked, "But what about Bill's feelings? Frank never once even acknowledged all Bill's work. He just found out that Bill hadn't talked to this Mac guy, and that was it. You should have seen Bill. He was humiliated. I think Frank is a pretty arrogant guy. He probably pushes people around because he's not as smart as he wants people to think he is. To tell you the truth, I think the man's a conceited jerk!"

"Maybe he is demanding," Liz countered firmly, "but you have to be tough in his position. That's how my Dad would have handled it. Take charge. Get things done."

Jim sat there. He respected Liz, but this was hard for him to accept. How could she ever appreciate his concerns when she identified with a man who so totally repelled him? Jim went back to the bedroom, hung up his tie, and turned on the television to relax. He'd do that summary report in the morning, he decided. Liz, not wanting to waste the evening, went shopping. Neither of them brought up Frank Johnson again that night, but they both felt an unpleasant gap between them.

Sound familiar? Liz and Jim are not only describing Frank in terms of conclusions about his character, rather than stating objective observations, but they're also making different judgments of the man. On the basis of a variety of observations of verbal and nonverbal behavior, Jim has ascribed inner qualities such as "callousness" and "arrogance" to Frank. Liz, too, ascribed inner qualities to Frank, but she called him "intelligent," "ambitious," and a "leader." She reacted to him positively, saying, "That's how my Dad would have handled it. Take charge. Get things done." Jim, on the other hand, said, "I think the man's a conceited jerk!" And Liz also judged Frank according to the way she thinks he behaves when he's alone, rather than solely on the basis of his actions in the meeting. She said, "How could someone who has a love of music be callous?" Both their tendencies to judge another are natural human responses. We call it "reading into others"—trying to assign them motives or values which they may not have at all. Because of the mistakes that result, "reading into others" will almost always destroy the potential for a productive relationship.

Thus, Liz and Jim were reacting to Frank by assuming that he had certain inner traits or qualities, rather than by describing the specifics of his behavior. And because they each have behavioral preferences of their own, they reached different conclusions. Jim, who has an open, friendly manner (shown by his smiling a lot and trying to make small talk with the secretary at the meeting) and is concerned with people's feelings, labeled Frank's behavior as "bad" because it was so different from his own. Liz, on the other hand, who is more highly disciplined about time and takes a no-nonsense, serious approach to work, saw Frank's behavior as acceptable because it was somewhat similar to her own behavioral preferences. But neither of them really knows Frank's intentions or character. Their judgments became clouded because they were trying to box in and label Frank's behavior to make it fit in with their own views.

However, if Jim and Liz could have simply described Frank's behavior, they probably could have agreed about him—and saved themselves a tense evening. Objective observations about Frank might have been, for example, that he was fast-paced rather than slow, loud rather than quiet, aloof rather than warm, and rigid rather than compromising. These are behaviors that both Jim and Liz could have agreed upon. They are descriptions of behavior that avoid labelling it as either good or bad, even though Frank's actions had different effects on the couple and caused each to judge him differently.

As you read through this story, did you find yourself making rapid decisions about whether you liked or disliked Frank? If so, you, too, were not being as objective as you could have been. An objective observer is someone who can describe what went on in a situation so that others who were present and saw the same behavior can agree with the description.

If we are to observe behavior objectively and understand its impacts, we will have to take the subjectiveness out of our observations. To achieve this objectivity, there are two types of words and phrases that we should avoid. The first type are those words and phrases that describe the inner qualities of a person, such as the words *honest, intelligent, ambitious, motivated, interested, sincere, hypocritical.* The second type are those that describe our own reactions, feelings, and judgments about a person, words such as *likable, confusing, nice, odd.* The words we use to describe someone objectively are those that describe what a person is actually saying or doing in a social situation, words such as *loud, quiet, reserved, outgoing, aloof, fast-paced, slow, direct eye contact, indirect eye contact*—words and phrases that describe behaviors without attaching value judgments to them (see Fig. 2-1).

One way to increase this skill is simply to practice observing others. For example, if you are at a party, you might stand away from a group of people and observe the verbal and nonverbal

ONE Inner Qualities, Traits, or Characteristics	TWO Interpersonal Situations	THREE Reactions, Feelings, and Judgments
Honest	Loud • Quiet	I like him
Intelligent	Fast-paced • Slow-paced	She bugs me
Ambitious	Facially • Facially animated controlled	She interests me
Motivated	Inflected • Monotone speech speech	He seems nice
Interested	Rigid posture • Casual posture	He's strange
Sincere	Direct • Indirect eye contact eye contact	I hate him
Hypocritical	Dramatic speech • Factual speech	I trust her
	▲ These descriptions identify (1) an interpersonal situation in which two or more people interact; and (2) observable behavior which can be described by an observer and verified by observations made by others.	

Fig. 2-1. Common ways of describing people. Limit descriptions to type of words in column two to describe behavior objectively.

behavior going on. Identify the people who tend to dominate the conversation, the ones who speak in a loud, fast-paced manner. In contrast, which people tend to be more reserved, and voice their comments in the form of questions or support for someone else's statement? Which people show more animated behavior—smiles, finger-pointing, body movement? Which ones limit the amount of expression they show? By observing people this way, without paying attention to either the content of the conversation or to our like or dislike of the individuals, we can increase our ability to observe behavior objectively.

We've mentioned that it's important to observe both verbal and nonverbal behavioral clues. In fact, 70 to 80 percent of what people learn and believe about others is based on nonverbal communications—on what they see, rather than on the words they hear.[1] For instance, if someone says, "Boy, am I enthusiastic!" and yet at the same time shows no facial expression, very few people will believe the statement. They are much more likely to believe the nonverbal, unenthusiastic behavior that they see.

One caution: As we become people observers, we must constantly remind ourselves that our feelings and attitudes may be getting in the way of our objectivity. For example, if a person sits down beside you at the airport and avoids making eye contact or speaking to you, you might tend to think that this is some reflection on you. But if you move away and watch another stranger sit down next to the same person, it's quite likely that the response to the second person will be equally aloof. Thus, although we often can't help having a positive or negative reaction to someone's behavior, we should try to recognize these feelings for what they are—subjective, rather than objective, responses.

Another important facet of observing behavior is to try to determine how our behavior compares with the behavior of those we are watching. For example, as we observe opposites in behavior—the shy person versus the assertive one, the smiling, outgoing individual versus the serious, reserved one—we can ask ourselves, "whose behavior does mine resemble?" Our an-

1. A. Mehrabian, *Silent Messages,* Wadsworth, 1971.

swers will give us some clues about how others are perceiving our behavior, and may even begin to help us understand why this behavior draws positive reactions from some of our associates and negative ones from others. You can begin to see we are asking you to think about yourself in a different way. How do others see you acting, *not* who are you.

As you may have noticed, we are taking a scientific approach to learning about our effect on others. Like scientists, we are attempting to move from the unknown to the known in three careful steps:

1. By focusing on what we see and hear, we can objectively describe behavior.
2. By observing and describing enough behavior, we will be able to anticipate or predict a person's future behavior.
3. By learning to predict well, we can then exercise some control over how we respond to the behavior that we are describing and predicting.

Let's consider an analogy. A physicist observes a gas under a variety of conditions and can objectively describe what it does. With enough observations, it is possible for him to predict its reaction to different conditions. Ultimately the scientist can exercise some control over the behavior he uses when working with the gas. But note that the scientist cannot control the gas as much as the environment in which he places the gas. For instance, he could prevent the gas from getting so hot that it explodes, but he can't change the temperature at which it would explode.

Is there an analogy between this example and human behavior? Certainly. If we observe a person and learn that the person becomes visibly angry under certain pressures, it makes sense to avoid placing that person under those pressures. Thus, through observation we try to predict, and work to control, the environment, or climate, so that we can control the outcome of our interactions with another person. In most instances, we do not and cannot control the other person. To use this approach, we must exercise a great deal of self-control to achieve a desired effect in our relationships.

As you begin to observe your own and other people's behavior patterns in interpersonal relationships, you may feel that you have accumulated an array of unrelated observations, and you might become confused when trying to make sense out of the differences. Our analysis of social style provides a simple system for understanding these differences in behavior and how we can control our behavior to adapt to them. Chapter 3 will describe our social style model.

PRACTICE SUGGESTIONS

1. Perhaps, without even being aware of it, you have taken actions that capitalize on your knowledge that a person's behavior is predictable. For example, how did you seat your guests at your last dinner party? Did you try to seat a shy person next to a warm, outgoing one, predicting that the outgoing guest would make the shy one feel comfortable? Similarly, when assigning a committee to a project, did you try to combine someone who could explain the project to the boss in a dynamic, creative fashion with a person who, although more reserved, would provide the necessary facts and detail? Did tension arise between the two, or did one person try especially hard to make the other one comfortable in the situation? Keep behavioral preferences in mind the next time you are teaming people, and observe the productive and nonproductive tensions.

2. Sitting in an airport, or another public place, observe people's behavior without noticing the content of their words or making judgments about good and bad. Who, in a group of travelers, talks the most? Who talks the least? From this observation, can you predict who is more likely to talk most of the time in the next five minutes, and who is likely to listen better, without interrupting? Who talks in a loud, fast-paced fashion, and who uses more facial animation? Notice that if someone sits next to you and doesn't speak, this person probably won't speak to the individual sitting on his other side, either. You are observing the person's behavioral preference for being reserved—not a positive or negative reaction to you as an individual.

3. Recall a situation in which you were forced to deal with an individual who made you tense. Did the tension lead to productive results, so that you both reached a mutual goal? Or did so much tension result that you found yourself either arguing, or avoiding the individual?

Describe the other person's behavior, using objective words and phrases, and compare that description to how you believe you generally act. Were the two of you so different that you couldn't work at the same pace or move in the same direction? Or were you so much alike that as a team you got nowhere?

4. Try to write a list of phrases that will objectively describe how you think you behave in interpersonal situations. Use Figure 2-1 as a guide. Think of other people you know, and do the same for them. You'll probably find that describing others is easier than describing yourself, because we get wrapped up in thinking about our "inner selves" and lose focus on our interpersonal behavior.

5. Looking back at some of the characters we have described, think about them in terms of their behavioral preferences and your reactions to these behaviors. For example, remember Charlie, the assertive lawyer? Did you decide Charlie was obnoxious, or did you identify at all with his style? If you reacted negatively to Charlie, ask yourself if that is because Charlie's behavior is quite different from your own. Conversely, if your behavior is somewhat similar to Charlie's assertive style, you are more likely to see him positively, or at least be neutral.

And you can test your powers of observation with the Bob and Sarah story in Chapter 1. As we have said, people tend to show a preference to strive either for personal acceptance or achievement, and to react to conflict by either "fight" or "flight." Which posture do you think would be more likely for Sarah—which for Bob? If you identify Bob as an individual who seems to place high priority on achievement, and whose more assertive behavior would lead him to "fight" when feeling discomfort, you are right. Sarah, on the other hand, appears to place high priority on acceptance, and took "flight" when faced with an interpersonal conflict. What preferences do you have?

3

Your Style and Other Styles

When we begin to practice describing people's behaviors with objective, nonjudgmental words, we soon become aware that something is missing—a way to generalize about these behaviors. However, these observations can be put into a simple model of human behavior that will help us to generalize about others—but in a reliable way. The model we're referring to is our concept of social style.

Before separating the behaviors we've learned to observe into the categories of the social style model, though, it's important to remember that no one behaves in one way all the time. We all exhibit a range of behaviors, and this variability, combined with the other elements that constitute personality—such as our abilities, attitudes, ideas of what we are and of what we would like to be—make each one of us quite unique. But when we consider just social style—what other people can see us doing and saying—we realize that it's possible to generalize about the behavior of other people, and that they, in turn, can generalize about ours. We do behave in predictable ways *most of the time.*

As an example, think back to the story of Bob and Sarah, the pair who had a confrontation at the end of a successful national sales convention. Bob was ready to launch into follow-up details early the next morning, while Sarah wanted to take a breather and chat with her friends. We can generalize, and say that while there will be times when Bob will slow down and visit with his coworkers, he usually sticks to business. And although Sarah can be very efficient and businesslike, we can predict that she usually works more slowly and takes time out to develop her personal relationships.

Going further, ask yourself how you would behave under similar circumstances. You may respond, "Well, sometimes I want to plunge into work immediately, and sometimes I prefer to visit with my friends for a few minutes." But what do you do *most* often? Your answer describes the type of on-the-job behavior your acquaintances probably would remember as typical of you. In other words, even though we behave in a fairly wide variety of ways, we also tend to repeat certain behaviors—especially when we're with other people—because we've learned that these behaviors make us comfortable.

So, although each one of us is a unique individual, others rarely get to know our uniqueness. Instead, they generalize about us, and we generalize about them. And that's fine, as long as our generalizations are accurate so that we can predict the best way to communicate effectively with the other person.

That's where social style comes in. Our social style model, which is based on statistical research that has been validated through years of testing and refinement, puts objective descriptions of behavior into a simple, useful framework. It is not, though, the only social style theory in existence today, and, in fact, thoughts about social style have been with us for years. Let's take a quick look at the history of style concepts to get some background on the model that our research group developed.

EVOLUTION OF THE THEORY OF SOCIAL STYLE

Theories of social style are a product of the field of behavioral psychology. Behavioral scientists, such as the well-known B. F. Skinner, simply watch people and describe what they *do*, without making any attempt to analyze *why* a person behaves in a certain way. This is in contrast to psychoanalytical theorists, who try to analyze what a person *is*, and the motivation for his behavior. Sigmund Freud, with his descriptions of id, ego, and superego, was the founder of this school of psychology.

A number of style theories evolved out of the behavioral school of thought. These theories grew more sophisticated in the 1950s and 1960s, as psychologists and sociologists became interested in social interaction and human resource development.

For example, the well-known sociologist Erving Goffman characterized people as "actors" playing their special "parts," wearing "masks," being "on" and "off" stage. Psychiatrist Harry Stack Sullivan declared personality theories bankrupt. More important, he thought, was understanding characteristic human interactions—looking at people objectively in social situations. Even philosopher Jean Paul Sartre expressed the concept of social style when, in *Being and Nothingness*, he wrote, "But all of a sudden I hear footsteps in the hall. Someone is looking at me! What does this mean? It means that I am suddenly affected in my being . . . I now exist as myself . . . I see myself because somebody sees me."

In pursuing the theory of style in an attempt to determine the components of effective leadership, the United States Office of Naval Research conducted an extensive study in the 1950s. The study was done by researchers at Ohio State University, and the approach that they used was as unusual as the questions that were asked. First, the researchers made up a lengthy list of descriptive behaviors that leaders exhibit, or are thought to exhibit. Next, they asked people in various work situations to identify which behaviors they felt good leaders show. The result: a list of 150 behaviors that those questioned agreed effective leaders had in common. The final step was to organize this list of behaviors into meaningful categories or dimensions. This work was done with the aid of factor analysis—a statistical method of correlating the statements on the list with one another. With this technique, Ohio State researchers found four factors that seemed to account for effective leadership, which they called *consideration, structure, production emphasis,* and *sensitivity.*

Next, several questionnaires were developed to determine which factor characterized the best leader, but no reliable results were obtained. These disappointing efforts led University of Illinois researcher Fred Fiedler to look at the question from a new perspective. It doesn't make sense, he decided, to look at a person's leadership style in a vacuum and not consider the circumstances of leadership—or the environment. His conclusions were complex, but essentially he determined that we cannot talk about "good" or "bad" leadership styles. A leader who is effective in one situation may or may not be effective in a different situation, Fiedler said, and he found that both relationship-oriented leadership styles and task-oriented styles could be successful.

Other theorists have also drawn conclusions about style, but most of their descriptions have been made by generalizing from everyday observations made in clinical settings. Rather than statistically verifying results through repeated testing, a researcher simply observes a number of people, writes down his observations, and then generalizes about how a person's behavior is similar to, or dissimilar to, others'.

THE THREE DIMENSIONS OF HUMAN BEHAVIOR

When our research group began its study of social style in the early 1960s, it was aware of this previous work, but these earlier studies were not used in the new research. Instead, we based our conclusions on observations that could be verified without regard for any known system or theory. Thus, in contrast to research done in everyday clinical settings, our approach was to statistically correlate every aspect of the data, so that all results could be scientifically quantified. The computer was instrumental in conducting this type of research, because it enabled us to compare small units of description to each other. If these units statistically "clustered," or fell together in any way, it was probable that they measured a specific dimension of human behavior. Unlike the long descriptive phrases used by the Ohio State researchers, the unit of description that we used was the adjective.

The structured adjective checklist which we use in our research was developed in the early 1960s by Dr. James W. Taylor, a staff psychologist with a large United States corporation. Dr. Taylor began by asking a large number of respondents (1612 employees of the corporation) to check off the adjectives on a list which they saw as describing their own behavior. The original list consisted of 2331 adjectives selected from the dictionary. By repeated testing with this large population, Dr. Taylor narrowed his list of adjectives to a core group of 150 words which could be used to describe behavior precisely and which gave statistically reliable results.

After Dr. Taylor had developed the checklist, he went a step further by analyzing the responses to see if there was any correlation among the various adjectives chosen by each respondent. He found that if a respondent felt that a certain adjective described his behavior, then that same respondent would answer yes or no to certain other adjectives. In other words, there was a "clustering" of adjectives. This factor analysis process was done by computer. If there was a correlation of 0.35 or greater between two adjectives, these adjectives were considered to belong to one cluster, or scale. The scales were then analyzed to see if an overall word could be attached to them. Using this process, Taylor named five scales of human behavior: 1) self-confident; 2) considerate; 3) conforming; 4) thoughtful; and 5) rigid.

For our own research, we adopted (with his permission) Dr. Taylor's adjective list, but decided to use a different process in testing respondents. Instead of asking each person to report on himself, we decided to ask others to describe the person's behavior. The population which we used were 600 employees of life insurance companies. Each person being tested was asked to have three to five acquaintances fill out the checklist, choosing the adjectives which they felt were most appropriate to describe the individual. As Dr. Taylor had done earlier, we used a computer to cluster the adjectives (factor analysis). This time, however, the adjectives clustered in a different fashion than they had when a person reported on himself. The names given to the three clusters or scales that resulted from the computer analysis were: 1) assertiveness; 2) responsiveness; and 3) versatility. To our knowledge, this was the first time that anyone had attempted to factor analyze others' perceptions of an individual by using an adjective checklist. We discovered patterns of observable behavior that others use regularly to describe how people act. These patterns have a good deal in common with clinical observations, but our approach to measurement was significantly different than clinical studies. We used ordinary people describing the everyday actions of others and then looked for consensus data which would reliably picture how a person acts most of the time.

Briefly defined, *assertiveness* is the aspect of behavior that measures whether a person tends to tell or ask, and the degree to which others see us as trying to influence their decisions. *Responsiveness* is a dimension of behavior that indicates whether a person tends to emote or to control feelings, and the extent to which others see us as an individual who displays feelings or emotions openly in social situations. And *versatility* is the dimension of behavior that indicates the extent to which others see us as adaptable, resourceful, and competent; it is behavior that earns their social endorsement of us because it accommodates their preferences.

Because versatility has both positive and negative connotations, and because people's versatility can vary, this aspect of style will be discussed in the next chapter. In this chapter, we will concentrate on assertiveness and responsiveness, the two scales that form the Social Style Profile.

ASSERTIVENESS: WHO TELLS, WHO ASKS

As we think of people we have observed, it becomes obvious that some people are more likely to start an interaction quickly, to tell others what they think, and to make social moves which are definite. Others are less likely to start an interaction quickly and less likely to engage in active social behavior or to make definite statements.

Those described as mostly "telling" are individuals who state their opinions with assurance, confidence, or force. Adjectives which might be used to describe such a person are *demanding, aggressive,* and *forceful.* Those people who are seen as less assertive tend to "ask"; they seek information and raise questions more often than average and tend to avoid taking a stand with others. Adjectives such as *unassuming, contented,* and *quiet* might be used to describe these less assertive individuals. Those who are seen as having moderate assertiveness might be described as "sometimes willing to take a stand," or "sometimes forceful."

Levels of assertiveness are fairly easy to determine: we quickly recognize the highly assertive behavior of an individual who forcefully states his or her opinions. But high assertiveness, as we define the concept, is not just the amount of "air time" we take. Talking a lot or dominating a conversation may not make our ideas, beliefs, or opinions clear to others. In these cases our behavior may not be seen as assertive by others, even though we think we are being forceful. A person seen as assertive is described as someone who takes a stand *and makes a position clear to others.* It doesn't matter whether we hold strong convictions internally; if we don't publicly use actions that communicate our opinions effectively, we probably will not be described by others as assertive, no matter how much talking we do.

Another difficulty we might have as we try to decide whether we are more or less assertive than most people is that we might like to think that we are flexible enough to vary from shy to bold or from quiet to noisy. But, as we've stated before, what may seem variable to us is not perceived that way by others, and they are probably able to place us in general positions on the scale of greater or lesser assertiveness.

In the social style model that we are describing, the dimension of assertiveness is divided into four ranges. In our diagram of the assertiveness dimension in Figure 3-1, these ranges are labeled A, B, C, and D. Through research, we divided the norm population into four equal groups, or quartiles. Individuals who are seen as more assertive than 75 percent of the population are found in the A quartile. D indicates those seen as having the least assertiveness; B and C are in between the two extremes.

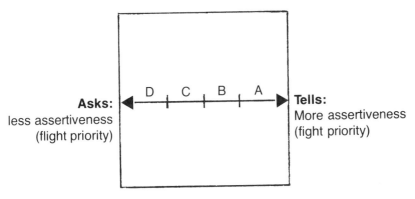

Fig. 3-1. Assertiveness dimension diagram. Each segment represents one-quarter of the normal population.

Less assertive individuals, those in the *C* or *D* quartiles, will be seen as more reserved, unaggressive, and easygoing. They rarely appear dominant, and tend to keep thoughts to themselves. Their behavior seems tentative, and others see them as individuals who do not communicate their ideas or beliefs without a specific need to do so. Less assertive individuals are often seen as cooperative, because they tend to listen to others and utilize opportunities to support the ideas and attitudes of others.

If we observe individuals who are often silent, express moderate opinions, seldom take charge, let others take the social initiative, and move slowly, we can place them on the "asking" end of the assertiveness dimension.

Where do you think your acquaintances or coworkers would place *you* on this scale?

At the other end of the scale are the more assertive individuals (*A* and *B*). They are often described as *active, forceful, aggressive,* and *ambitious.* A more assertive person tends to make his or her presence known, is perceived by others as liking to be in on the action, and tends to tell others what he or she thinks. Such a person will often initiate social contacts and communicate with others even when it may not be appropriate to do so.

If we observe someone who is outgoing, who seems to have a take-charge attitude, and a willingness to express strong opinions and make quick decisions, we can place this individual on the "telling" end of the assertiveness dimension.

To simplify this scale, remember: The more assertive person tends to tell, rather than ask; and when he or she is under tension, this person tends to "fight," or confront the situation, rather than to avoid it. The less assertive person tends to ask more than he or she tells, and when under tension, this person prefers "flight," or to avoid the situation, rather than to confront it.

As we begin to identify the amount of assertiveness displayed by an individual, we can rely on both verbal and nonverbal behavioral clues. By verbal behavioral clues, we mean how fast a person speaks, how much a person speaks, and how loudly he or she speaks. By nonverbal behavioral clues, we mean how the individual uses his or her hands and body, and whether he seeks or avoids eye contact (see Fig. 3-2).

When observing another person, consider all of the clues together. Don't try to evaluate them separately, or make an assumption about the person's assertiveness on the basis of only a few clues. You need to compound all of the behavioral information in order to see the dominant theme. Also, remember that a person under a great deal of stress will be trying to reduce tension, and may behave in a way that is not customary for him or her. A moderate amount of stress, though, will clarify the person's assertiveness theme. Compare yourself to those you are observing. Which behaviors do you think you display most often in social situations?

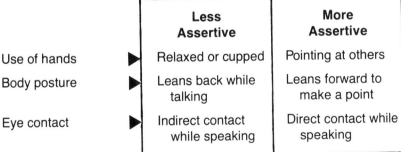

Verbal Behavioral Clues

	Less Assertive	More Assertive
Pace of speech ▶	Slower	Faster
Quantity of speech ▶	Fewer statements	More statements
Volume of speech ▶	Softer	Louder

Nonverbal Behavioral Clues

	Less Assertive	More Assertive
Use of hands ▶	Relaxed or cupped	Pointing at others
Body posture ▶	Leans back while talking	Leans forward to make a point
Eye contact ▶	Indirect contact while speaking	Direct contact while speaking

Fig. 3-2. Behavioral clues to assertiveness.

RESPONSIVENESS: WHO CONTROLS FEELINGS, WHO SHOWS THEM

The second dimension of behavior is called *responsiveness*. Responsiveness indicates how much feeling a person tends to display. The more responsively people behave, the more they appear to react to influences, appeals, or stimulation, and to openly express their feelings, emotions, and impressions. A more responsive person readily expresses anger, joy, or hurt feelings.

Once again, if any given part of the population is measured, the level of responsiveness will range from most responsive—or "emoting"—behavior to least responsive—or "controlling" behavior. As with the assertiveness scale, we used norms to divide the population into each of four equal ranges on the scale; these ranges are labeled *1, 2, 3,* and *4* (see Fig. 3-3). Those who are seen as less responsive than 75 percent of the population are placed in the quartile labeled *1*. Adjectives often used to describe these individuals are *cautious, intellectual,* and *serious*.

Controls Emotions

Less responsiveness (achievement priority)

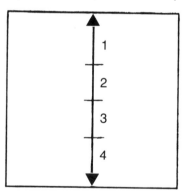

More responsiveness (acceptance priority)

Emotes

Fig. 3-3. Responsiveness dimension diagram. Each segment represents one-quarter of the normal population.

Those who display their emotions and feelings more readily than 75 percent of the population are placed in the quartile labeled *4*. These people are often described with adjectives such as *warm, emotional,* or *lighthearted.* Those between the two extremes (placed in quartiles *2* and *3*) might be described as *sometimes impulsive,* or *secretive sometimes.*

Less responsive individuals, those in the *1* and *2* quartiles, are seen as more independent of, or indifferent to, the feelings of others. They are seen as people who rely on reason and logic when making decisions, who are often formal, proper, or stiff in social relationships, and who tend to avoid personal involvement with others. A less responsive person appears precise, makes specific points, can be critical, with a no-nonsense attitude and a desire to get things done efficiently. Such a person tends to focus on ideas, things, and tasks, rather than on people, and seeks to gain approval through achievement.

If we observe an individual who dresses and speaks more formally than most, is a secretive, cautious communicator, who displays measured, factual opinions, and who has a strict, disciplined attitude, we can place this person on the less responsive, or "controlling," end of the responsiveness dimension. Individuals who seem difficult to get to know, who are demanding of themselves and others, and who are impersonal and businesslike in interpersonal situations also display less responsiveness.

At the other end of the scale (*3* and *4*) are more responsive individuals. These persons are often described as being self-indulgent, attention-seeking and involved with the feelings of others. They appear to be concerned with relationships, and act in informal, casual, and playful ways in social situations. Others may see the more responsive individual as having a tendency to talk in a general and imprecise way, showing a gamut of emotions ranging from frivolous laughter to dark depression—a person who appears to be unconcerned about getting things done efficiently.

If we observe a person who dresses and speaks informally, is an open, impulsive communicator, talks and acts dramatically, and who seems to have a permissive, easygoing attitude toward life, we can place this person on the more responsive, or emotive, end of the scale. Similarly, those who appear to dramatize their ideas, seem easy to get to know, and are open with themselves and others are displaying more responsiveness.

To simplify the responsiveness scale, remember: More responsive individuals tend to say and do things that show, rather than control, their feelings. These people will display responsiveness and work at maintaining relationships to earn *social acceptance*. Less responsive people, as we have said, tend to control emotions, and tend to focus on ideas, things, data, and tasks—rather than on people—to gain approval through *achievement*.

Figure 3-4 breaks down the responsiveness dimension into verbal and nonverbal behavioral clues. People who talk with feeling, using lots of emotions, expressions and enthusiasm, are more responsive individuals. Talking about people, telling stories and expressing opinions, rather than talking about ideas, things, tasks or facts and data, represent verbal clues of respon-

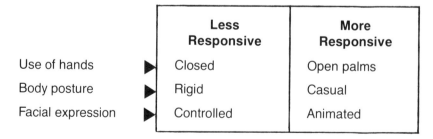

Verbal Behavioral Clues

	Less Responsive	More Responsive
Emotion in voice ▶	Monotone	Inflections
Subjects of speech ▶	Tasks	People
Descriptives ▶	Facts/Data	Opinions/Stories

Nonverbal Behavioral Clues

	Less Responsive	More Responsive
Use of hands ▶	Closed	Open palms
Body posture ▶	Rigid	Casual
Facial expression ▶	Controlled	Animated

Fig. 3-4. Behavioral clues to responsiveness.

siveness. Nonverbally, open posture versus crossed arms, relaxed, less formal posture and animated use of face, hands, or body, are more responsive signs of behavior. Once again, when you observe others, compound all these clues to see the dominant theme. And be willing to change your conclusion if you see new clues.

APPEARANCES ARE DECEIVING

These two dimensions of behavior—assertiveness and responsiveness—can be observed in everyone, and, whether consciously or unconsciously, we often decide how to deal with our acquaintances and coworkers on the basis of our perceptions of their responsiveness and assertiveness. But remember, when we do this, we are reacting only to other people's behavior—not to their intentions. The person who appears warm and friendly may not, in fact, like us any more than the one who appears serious and detached. Similarly, the dynamic, forceful-appearing individual may not have a better idea—or even believe in it as strongly—as the quiet, less assuming one. These labels do not define what a person is thinking or feeling; they only describe aspects of observable behavior.

As we begin improving our ability to observe these two basic dimensions of human behavior, it will seem that assertiveness is easier to identify. In fact, in our interpersonal relationships, we can almost immediately pinpoint a person's assertiveness. For example, we can all tell the difference between "shy" and "outspoken" people. Thus, with the clues which we have described, plus your previous understanding of assertiveness, you'll probably be able to recognize the extremes of this behavior dimension fairly easily, in others and in yourself. The responsiveness dimension, however, usually is more difficult to identify, even though our research shows that people respond to the emotional content in a relationship almost as frequently as to the assertiveness dimension.

ASSERTIVENESS + RESPONSIVENESS = SOCIAL STYLE

The Social Style Profile is the result of our measurement of how others describe a person. It is like a picture or map of what others can see you doing or saying, and shows where a person most frequently positions himself within the total universe of available actions on assertiveness and responsiveness.

Because we all display certain behaviors that can be placed on either the assertiveness or responsiveness scales, these two scales can be combined, permitting us to describe the various possible combinations of these qualities in people. During our research, we did this by placing them at right angles in the form of a cross (see Fig. 3-5). The horizontal axis shows the range from least to most assertive (as in Fig. 3-1). The vertical axis shows the range from least to most responsive (as in Fig. 3-3).

At this point, the social style quadrants emerge. Mathematically, an equal number of people in a randomly selected population will fall into each of the four quadrants or squares combining assertiveness and responsiveness. There is no predominance of any racial or sexual group in any one quadrant. We've labeled these quadrants as follows:

> Upper right-hand quadrant:
>   Less responsive + more assertive = *Driving* behavior
> Upper left-hand quadrant:
>   Less responsive + less assertive = *Analytical* behavior
> Lower left-hand quadrant:
>   More responsive + less assertive = *Amiable* behavior
> Lower right-hand quadrant:
>   More responsive + more assertive = *Expressive* behavior

In the model's upper right-hand quadrant, we can place individuals whose behavior is usually characterized by "telling," but who "control" their feelings. They are primarily assertive, serious people. These individuals make an effort to tell people what they think and require, and they appear severe because they don't display feelings or emotions readily. We call this social style *Driving*.

In the lower right-hand corner of the profile, we find the person who tends to "tell" and to "emote." This style is also assertive, like the Driving style, but these individuals are generally much more willing to make their feelings public. Rather than trying to control emotions, the person with this style will show both positive and negative feelings. This style is called *Expressive*.

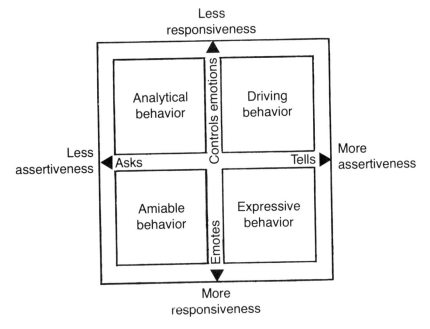

Fig. 3-5. The Social Style Profile.

As we move to the lower left-hand corner of the profile, we find a social style that "asks" and "emotes." Like the person with an Expressive style, this individual usually displays feelings openly, but is less assertive and more interested in being agreeable and cooperative. This is called the *Amiable* style.

Finally, as we look at the upper left-hand corner of the profile, we find a style that "asks" and "controls." This style is low in assertiveness, but high in control of emotions. Rather than being decisive or forceful, like the person with the Driving or the Expressive style, the individual displaying these behaviors will tend to ask questions, gather facts, and study data seriously. This style is called *Analytical*.

To imagine these styles, think of the following four television and movie personalities: Barbara Walters, television interviewer; Basil Rathbone, as Sherlock Holmes; Jean Stapleton, as Edith Bunker; and Robin Williams, as Mork. What social styles do these four people exhibit on the screen?

Barbara Walters, the no-nonsense, aggressive television interviewer, fits best in the Driving quadrant. Basil Rathbone, in his role as Sherlock Holmes, brings the most dastardly criminals to justice through his cool, disciplined detective work. His behavior is typical of the Analytical. Jean Stapleton portrays Edith Bunker as a woman who has a smile for everyone and who supports her husband Archie through thick and thin. Edith shows an Amiable style. And then there is Mork, played by Robin Williams. With his excitable, fast-paced behavior, Mork, from planet Ork, most certainly has an Expressive style. Now think of yourself. Where on the model do you think others see you?

To give you some idea of what your social style is, a self-scoring exercise is provided in Figure 3-6. In the spaces provided, list two people whom you see as more assertive, two who are less assertive, two who are more responsive, and two who are less reponsive. Use the behavioral clues in Figures 3-2 and 3-4 to help you. For each scale, ask yourself which of these people you act most like. By combining your answers, you can place yourself in one of the quadrants of the Social Style Profile. Admittedly, this exercise is not as accurate as the testing method which we use in our research, since it depends upon self-evaluation, but it will give you an indication of your own behavioral style and will help you to better identify with the style discussions in the rest of the book. In addition, one of the practice suggestions at the end of the chapter suggests a way to have others describe your behavior, and we've also listed some famous personalities, real and fictional, so that you can practice identifying the styles they exhibit on the screen.

Figures 3-7 through 3-10 show the nonverbal behaviors (facial expressions, postures, and gestures) of four individuals in an interview situation. Using the clues in Figures 3-2 and 3-4, what styles do you think these individuals exhibit? Try to reach your own conclusions before looking at the answers in the footnote which appears on page 55.

If you're thinking that this is a fairly shallow way to describe people, we agree. But remember that social style is not the same as personality; style refers only to surface behavior. And, as we

Assertiveness

Asks   Tells

1. _____   1. _____

2. _____   2. _____

Myself: _____

Responsiveness

Controls emotions   Emotes

1. _____   1. _____

2. _____   2. _____

Myself: _____

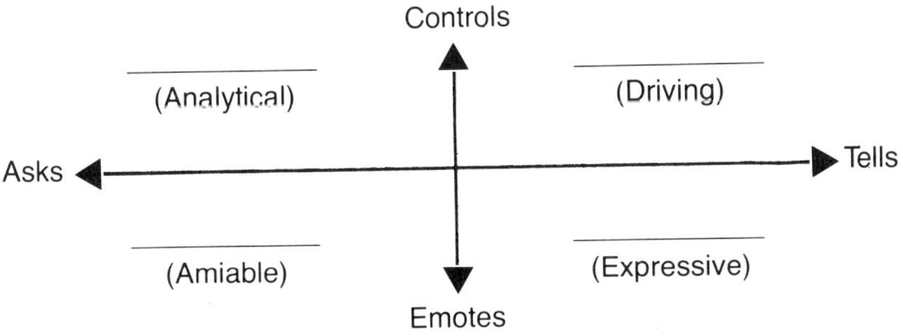

Controls

(Analytical)   (Driving)

Asks ◄——————————————————► Tells

(Amiable)   (Expressive)

Emotes

Fig. 3-6. Self-scoring exercise.

have said, social style is not an absolute; it is a matter of degree. Even though we tend to repeat some behaviors more than others, we all display a wide range of behaviors at various times. But people, especially those who don't know us well, will react to us on the basis of our observable, repetitive patterns of action—our social style—rather than on the basis of our capacity for variation.

1. Most people agree that Dorothy shows Driving behavior; Jim, Expressive; Bruce, Amiable; and Dave, Analytical.

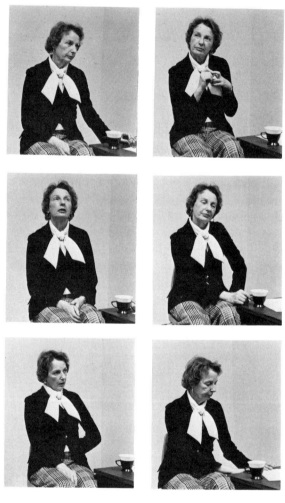

Fig. 3-7. Dorothy: Few smiles, little animation, controlled gestures, direct looks.

Fig. 3-8. Jim: Many hand gestures, facial
expressions, variability in style.

Fig. 3-9. Bruce: Warm, smiling, fewer hand gestures and less animation than Expressive.

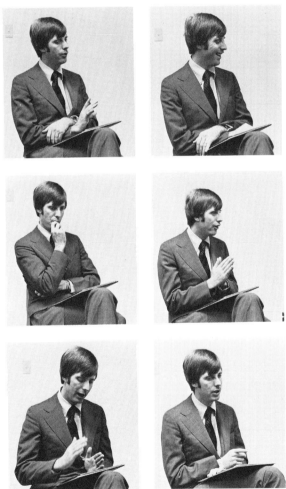

Fig. 3-10. Dave: Few hand gestures, little facial
expression, reserved smiles.

No "Best" Style

As mentioned earlier, we have chosen the adjective as the most accurate unit of description for defining style. Figure 3-11 lists some of the adjectives most commonly used to describe each of the four styles. Note that there are both positive and negative terms. This leads to the questions: Which quadrant has the good and successful people? and What is the best style? Research indicates that there is no "best" style. Each one has its good and bad points, and we tend to like or dislike individuals

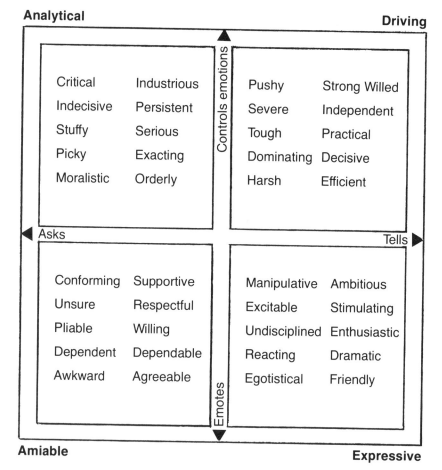

Fig. 3-11. Adjectives commonly used to describe the four styles.

displaying a particular style because of our own personal points of view, value judgments, or needs. Generally, if someone relates well to us, we describe that person's style with the favorable adjectives; if not, we will tend to use the unfavorable terms. But all styles can be successful, and there are no good or bad styles.

Still, because of our own behavioral preferences, some social styles may cause us more discomfort than others. Let's take a closer look at the four styles and learn what types of habitual actions we can expect from each of them. The focus is on three types of actions: typical actions used to relate to others; actions related to the use of time; and actions related to decision making. From these aspects of behavior, others get an impression of an individual's predominant social style.

As we are considering these aspects of behavior, try to decide which styles might cause you problems. Conversely, which styles do you think you would work with easily? For most of us, styles that most closely resemble our own create the least discomfort for us, and we feel positive about individuals with that behavior. Styles that differ most from our own probably create tension—violate our comfort zones—and we may tend to place a negative label on that behavior. Once again, we see how quickly we can let our objective observations of behavior become obscured by subjectively jumping to conclusions about people, especially when they make us uncomfortable by the things they say and do.

One other note: As you read about the four styles, remember that we all display some aspects of each of the styles, although we tend to act more one way than another. So, as you begin observing people, don't be surprised when you see variations in their style themes.

THE DRIVING STYLE: ACTION ORIENTED

Actions Used to Relate to Others

Individuals whose overall pattern of behavior gives the impression that they know what they want, where they are going, and how to get there quickly, have a predominately Driving style. In fact, "Let's get it done now, and get it done my way" is an appropriate slogan for persons with Driving behavior. Because driving actions seem more oriented toward getting results than toward pleasing people, individuals with this style often appear uncommunicative, cool, independent, and competitive in relationships with others. They tend to initiate action, and their actions are definite. However, their personal reasons for such action may not be clear to us, because they seldom see a need to share personal motives or feelings. Because of this, many people feel that they really don't get to know the Driving person on a close, personal basis. In a discussion about people, Driving individuals display an attitude that suggests that they have learned how to work with others only because they must, in order to achieve their objectives, not because they enjoy people. But they can also appear very pleasant, and even charming—on their terms.

Use of Time

Individuals with a Driving style tend to focus on the present. Their responses appear swift, efficient, and to the point. They tend to deal with the immediate situation rapidly and appear to have little concern for the past or the future. They work most easily with others who are able to move quickly. The further someone's behavior appears to get from that objective, the more restless the person with a Driving style becomes about the other person's attempts to communicate. Because of this tendency to be impatient, individuals with Driving styles get things done in a hurry, but the job sometimes has to be redone.

Approach to Decision Making

Persons with Driving behavior appear to want to make their own decisions; they seek power, and do not like being told what to do or what not to do. They are quick to express their conclusions about anything that concerns them, and when they encounter an obstacle between themselves and their perceived objectives, they will often seek to control the situation and get past the obstacle through the use of force. They generally base their decisions on facts and data, will take risks, and prefer to be presented with options from which they can choose.

THE EXPRESSIVE STYLE: INTUITION ORIENTED

Actions Used to Relate to Others

People with an Expressive style usually appear communicative, warm, approachable, and competitive. They involve other people with their feelings and thoughts. Their actions suggest that they want others as friends—but in the roles of followers and personal supporters of their dreams, rather than as competitors. Expressive persons consider power and politics important, since they seek to gain personal recognition and to recruit supporters to their causes. While relationships and people count to the Expressive man or woman, to their associates these relationships may frequently seem shallow and short-lived.

Use of Time

People with an Expressive style seem to spend much of their time and efforts moving toward some dream of the future. They generally act quickly, but are undisciplined in their use of time. Because of their focus on the future, they seem to have little concern for practical details in the present. They can easily change a course of action, and seem impatient to find the most exciting vision of the moment for themselves and others. As they move rapidly from subject to subject, they may forget to address specifics, such as who, why, what, and how. Changeableness is part of this style.

Approach to Decision Making

The Expressive individual will take risks in making decisions and will base the decision on personal opinion—his own or others. The opinions of people the Expressive individual considers important, prominent, or successful will mean more to this person's decision-making process than all of the facts and logic one might introduce. Expressive individuals appear to have more imaginative and creative ideas than do people with other styles; however, it is also easy for them to make mistakes, since they base their decisions on opinions, hunches, and intuitions, rather than on facts.

Expressive people like special, immediate, and extra incentives for their willingness to take risks and move rapidly. Personal social recognition or prestige often provides this incentive.

THE AMIABLE STYLE: RELATIONSHIP ORIENTED

Actions Used to Relate to Others

People who appear to place a high priority on friendships, close relationships, and cooperative behavior have an Amiable style. Because of this, Amiable individuals often lend joy, warmth, and freshness to social situations. Folklore, religious or family traditions, and even sentimentality can capture their attention. People seen as acting in an Amiable manner appear to interpret the world on a personal basis, and they get involved in feelings and relationships between people, frequently speculating on "who did what with whom, and why." They tend to look for personal motives in the actions of others.

As Amiable individuals attempt to achieve objectives with people, they use understanding and mutual respect, rather than force and authority. Paradoxically, though, people with an Amiable style appear to accept authority from another person, if the person is friendly and understanding. Power over others is not an important objective for them; however, being accepted by others does appear important to the Amiable man or woman.

Use of Time

Amiable people tend to move slowly and are undisciplined in their use of time, generally because they wish to take time to share personal objectives and feelings with other people. They focus on what is happening right now, and on how the actions of others may influence their lives. In some instances, talking and socializing can become so important that it is difficult for them to get back to the work at hand.

Approach to Decision Making

People with an Amiable social style appear slow or reluctant to change opinions that hold personal meaning for them. In fact,

Amiable individuals frequently stick with the comfortable and known, and tend to avoid activities that involve risk with the unknown—especially risks that involve personal relationships. They tend to use personal opinions in arriving at decisions, and they want others to provide guarantees that any decision made will minimize risk and assure the benefits promised. This need to feel safe in the decision-making process has the highest priority for an Amiable person. Consequently, one of the surest ways to alienate such a person is to provide assurances and guarantees and then not fulfill the commitment.

THE ANALYTICAL STYLE: THINKING ORIENTED

Actions Used to Relate to Others

People who are described as living life according to facts, principles, logic, and consistency have an Analytical style. Individuals with this general pattern of behavior are often viewed by others as lacking enthusiasm or as cold and detached. But although they are seen as cool and independent, they also appear cooperative in their actions, as long as they can have some freedom to organize their own efforts.

Individuals with Analytical behavior tend to be cautious about extending friendship or showing personal warmth, and initially will be more concerned with how things can get done without the need for personal involvement. People and friendships may be very important to this person; however, it might not seem so in initial contacts. Facts and logic will appear to have greater importance.

People with an Analytical style have a "show me" attitude. They tend to be suspicious of power or leverage until they can see a predictable pattern in the way power is used. Once they determine how power is systematically used to achieve stated goals and objectives, they begin to identify with its use and may even incorporate such power into their own efforts.

Use of Time

Although persons with an Analytical style seem to move slowly, they use time in a deliberate, disciplined manner. These people are interested in facts, and they prefer to consider information in a calm, common-sense way, and avoid flashiness. Because they want to look at the facts in a systematic, accurate manner, they focus on the past to give them direction for the future, and they prefer to work on a predictable schedule.

Approach to Decision Making

Analytical individuals appear to make decisions on the basis of facts, and they tend to avoid risks. They look for evidence to support the validity of their decisions. The evidence should be solid, tangible, practical, and realistic—not just someone's personal opinion. They also require assurance that any decision made today will remain reasonably valid in the future. Because of this desire to be ''right,'' Analytical people move with caution and deliberation when making a decision. While they may appear to be overly concerned with details and organization, once made, the decision will be lasting.

STYLE THEMES

You should now have a good understanding of the most common patterns of action found in each of the four basic social styles. To summarize, the major thrust of each style can be described as:

Driving: action oriented
Expressive: intuition oriented
Amiable: relationship oriented
Analytical: thinking oriented

As you have read, these four styles can be used to characterize the observable behavior of most human beings. And while at times people will combine the actions of several, or all, of the social styles, a person's basic social style represents his or her system for coping easily and comfortably with the varied relationships encountered in the course of a day.

Figure 3-12 summarizes the key features of each style's theme. Remember, we all have behavioral themes running through most of our actions, and others will recognize those themes (even if we don't), and deal with us in terms of our styles. The style themes of the characters being described next are pur-

Analytical   **Driver**

Analytical	Driver
Slow reaction	Swift reaction
Maximum effort to organize	Maximum effort to control
Minimum concern for relationships	Minimum concern for caution in relationships
Historical time frame	Present time frame
Cautious action	Direct action
Tends to reject involvement	Tends to reject inaction
Unhurried reaction	Rapid reaction
Maximum effort to relate	Maximum effort to involve
Minimum concern for effecting change	Minimum concern for routine
Present time frame	Future time frame
Supportive action	Impulsive action
Tends to reject conflict	Tends to reject isolation

Amiable   **Expressive**

Fig. 3-12. Behavior typical of the four styles.

posely exaggerated, and are designed to help you begin to recognize style characteristics. After reading each example, you might practice identifying style by relating the described behavior to people you know.

The Amiable

✔ John and Sue needed to buy some life insurance. One salesman had already called at their home, and they were expecting another one that evening.

"I hope this guy isn't like the last one," John said to Sue. He was dressing, and as he spoke his voice rose at intervals. "He was too hard-sell. He thought he had all the answers and tried to press me for a decision. I don't like to buy anything from someone like that, let alone life insurance."

Sue pointed out that John could have been a bit firmer during the sales call and that sometimes others took advantage of his cooperative nature. John agreed: "Well, I suppose I could have been. This evening I will be." But Sue recognized that John was rarely assertive, and she realized that he wouldn't be tonight, either. "What did you think of him?" John asked, and Sue replied, "I thought he was o.k.—just a little confused.

"You didn't *tell* him you *wouldn't* buy," she explained. "He gave his whole talk, and you just kept saying yeah, uh huh, and nodding your head."

"I guess I didn't want to offend him," John said. "He's a nice guy down at the club, but I never realized he could be so pushy. This option and that; this benefit and that." Then he added, "This new guy sounds real nice though. Tonight, let's serve the coffee and cake first. That should loosen things up."

Sue agreed to the coffee idea, but also suggested that during this interview they concentrate on getting a few more facts.

"Sure. We will. But you know, I can always get my brother to look at the policy later. It's the service, the follow-through, the personal concern that really makes the difference. Some of these salesmen forget that. It's people who buy and sell policies—not policies that buy and sell people!"

"That's true," Sue conceded, "but if we're going to have your brother look it all over before we decide, I think we had better try to get as much information as possible."

"Oh, don't worry, we'll figure it out."

Just then the doorbell rang. John rushed to answer it, while Sue stayed behind and picked up a pad and pencil before following him down the stairs.

The Analytical

It was her second interview with the company, and Miller said to her, "Jan, all the testing showed you're a perfect sales candidate."

"Thank you, Mr. Miller." Her formality surprised him. He expected her to show a bit more something—he didn't know exactly what. Perhaps she'd at least drop the "Mr. Miller."

Jan was conservatively attired, and she always seemed to be taking notes, if not on paper, then in her head. He could see this by the way she paused thoughtfully between sentences.

Miller was surprised that the sales aptitude testing had come out so well, considering her reticence and apparent shyness. "Well, Jan, the next step is to set up an evaluation interview."

Again the pause; then, "That makes sense." She was processing, he saw: one, two, three. "Mr. Miller, would it be possible for me to talk with some of the other women who've been here for at least a year?"

"Sure, why not? So you still have some questions?" He laughed a little, as if encouraging her to do likewise.

She smiled slightly to acknowledge his attempt to lighten things up, then continued, not skipping a beat. "Yes. I'm quite concerned about how the training program has been adjusted to meet the needs of women."

"Oh, I'm sure you'll find it very helpful."

"Well, if I can be sure of that." She seemed skeptical. "I have several opportunities to consider, and I want to be certain. The time I invest now could save me much more in the long run." Then, feeling encouraged to go more deeply, "You see, as you know from my resume, I've had one poor experience. It really bothered me." She sensed his surprise at the personal turn their conversation had taken and was herself a little self-conscious at this unexpected show of emotion. Not accustomed to putting her feelings on display, she pulled up short and remained quiet.

Miller could see she'd reined herself in. "It's important for you to have all the data possible." It wasn't a question, or a confrontation. He wanted her to feel comfortable again.

"Yes. Exactly." The balance was restored.

"Fine. Why don't you talk with my secretary and set up an appointment for an evaluation interview. And, Jan, have her line up some of our women agents to talk with you about their experiences."

She paused, thinking, and then, with it all in order, thanked him, stood to shake his hand, and said good-bye.

"A very logical, organized person," Miller thought to himself. "I hope she'll go with us."

The Expressive

After the encounter with Tom, Mike felt as if he had suddenly been ejected from a plane with a parachute.

Tom had nabbed him in the parking lot. "Hey, Mike, where are you going?"

Mike replied, and asked Tom the same question, but Tom, on his way to some mysterious appointment, would only say, "Oh, I've got some unfinished business. Across town. You don't know him. Well, it's kind of business, kind of not. Don't ask." Then, before Mike knew it, they had reached Tom's car.

"Get in, Mike. I'll take you, even if it's only a block. You look on top of it. Great day, huh?" Though Mike made it clear he was only going a short way, Tom insisted. "What's the matter? You won't ride in an import?"

Tom had a way of getting you to say yes before you really knew what it was he was asking. You said yes to his enthusiasm; then quite casually you might find out what was up. One suspected Tom rode the crest of his wave quite blindly. But, oh, was it done with verve!

"Want a lemon drop?" Tom asked as he drove, pulling a half-empty sack from the cavity in the console between the seats. "Go on, take it. Save it for later. Where'd you say you're going? Whoops, I gotta turn here."

As they spun around the corner, Tom gave Mike only seconds to answer one question before he was off to a new, totally different subject. "Hey, I saw the playoff game last night. You? What do you think of the new guy at work?"

Then, with Tom's mission suddenly pressing, they pulled up to a stoplight. "Hop out here," Tom said, "quick, before the light turns!"

Tom's foot was pumping the brake, and the car, with its idle set a big high, jumped with each release of brake pressure.

"See ya, Mike." And Tom roared off.

Mike was left standing on the sidewalk, having barely translated Tom's good-bye from ear to brain. As he walked down the street, it took a few minutes before he felt his world slowing down once again.

The Driver

The door was solid-cored and oaken, and below the name "Smith & Bellows, Attorneys at Law," it had a highly buffed, silvery handle. Jason reached for the handle at the precise moment that Samuel Bellows, Esq., pushed outward from inside.

Bellows was looking over his shoulder as he pushed the door open, giving some final instructions to his secretary.

"Be sure to get those letters out in the 1:30 mail, and I'll expect a draft of my closing statement for the Jacobs trial by the end of the day."

"But, Mr. Bellows, there's no 1:30 pickup today, and . . ."

"Oh, yes, and I'll be in a little late tomorrow," Bellows said, seemingly not hearing the secretary. He turned toward the door and came face to face with Jason.

The timing was a surprise to each, and each was faced with the question of who must move aside. Bellows dealt with this dilemma silently. Although he said nothing, he remained standing squarely in the opening of the door, and his physical presence could not be ignored. Jason sensed that the attorney's silence did not mean that Bellows would defer, so he offered a pleasant smile, a "pardon me," and then moved aside.

It was only a small confrontation, but it was one of those little daily occurrences that quite subtly say a lot about a person. Bellows, reacting to Jason's action, responded with a thank you. His gratitude was expressed without a hint of a smile, but the flat tone of his voice carried emphasis. Then, Bellows rushed quickly through the door and disappeared down the hall, as Jason wondered if he'd ever get to know the man.

SOCIETY'S CHILDREN

Why do people develop these social styles? As was discussed in Chapter 2, our habitual ways of acting, or behavioral preferences, developed with years of reinforcement from important people in our environment, people such as our parents, teachers, and friends. When we received positive reinforcement for certain patterns of action, we repeated them. This process begins very early in life, and it is estimated that we develop our social styles by the time we are five or six years old. We experiment with these styles during our teens, often imitating peers we envy, but usually finding ourselves most comfortable with our earlier habits, and returning to them as young adults. Of course, individual patterns of development may vary by several years.

We have also discussed the values our society places on both achievement and social acceptance, and the way we develop behaviors to satisfy these social demands. As humans we are all social beings, and we all learn ways to gain acceptance and to achieve. However, the different styles vary in the actions they take to reach these goals and the emphasis put on each. For example, people with more responsive styles—the Amiables and Expressives—are especially open and obvious in the actions they take to gain social acceptance. They seek to build and maintain personal relationships—gain acceptance—as they pursue achievements. They may, in fact, use their skills in developing good personal relationships as tools to seek achievement. It is a matter of priority; gaining acceptance makes achievement easier, or so it appears to more responsive styles.

The Amiable man or woman gains social acceptance first through efforts to be "secure" within social surroundings. Once a person has this acceptance, he or she goes on to seek achievement. The Amiable's efforts toward achievement are characterized by a deliberate, congenial, people-oriented approach and a generous use of time and supportive behavior.

An Expressive person seeks social acceptance first by capturing other people's attention, and then goes on to achieve a goal. This effort is reflected by a style which displays an impulsive, excitable nature, more people orientation than task orientation, and a stimulating, competitive push for attention.

People with less responsive styles—the Drivers and the Analyticals—are more obvious in their actions to gain achievement. People with these styles take the approach of accomplishing a task first, which they hope will lead to acceptance by others. Their priority is to get the job done and that seems to be their key to later acceptance. But they do not tend to *openly* seek social acceptance. One way to gain acceptance through achievement is by being in charge. This approach is reflected in behavior that is self-directed, independent, and fast; a task orientation as opposed to a people orientation; and competitive actions. Whose style are we describing? The Driver's, of course.

The Analytical person also seeks to gain acceptance through achievement, but his achievement is to be "right," in the form of having a thorough plan or picture of whatever situation he is attempting to deal with. This effort is reflected by actions that are deliberate, calculating, and cool; by a task orientation; and by a generally cautious, slow approach.

Thus, as we observe behavior, we can see that persons with each style act in ways that reflect their priorities—either to achieve first or to be accepted first—as a means of reaching the secondary goal. (Fig. 3-13 summarizes these style priorities.)

BACKUP STYLES

What happens when these efforts are frustrated by someone else's behavior? As we might expect, tension builds. Earlier, we said that some tension can be positive, because it creates the impetus, or go-power, for us to act. But at a certain point, others can create so much tension for us that we can no longer focus on our goals or care about the relationship. Instead, we are concerned only about reducing our own tension.

The way that we deal with this tension is a reflection, in part, of our social styles. People who have Driving or Expressive styles, for example, being more assertive, prefer a primary defense of confronting the situation head-on—fighting—rather than avoiding the situation. Obviously, of course, if a "fighting" response doesn't work, the person may be forced to try a "flight" response. People with Analytical or Amiable styles show an initial preference for "flight" defenses—they try to smooth over the conflict or avoid the fight. If this attempt doesn't work, people with these styles may then resort to a "fight" response.

More particularly, when we resort to nonproductive ways of relieving tension we use an exaggerated form of our social styles. We retreat even further into our own behavioral preferences to make ourselves comfortable, even at the expense of our relationship with the other person. Because of this phenomenon, it's possible to predict the manner in which people with each of the four social styles will act in an attempt to reduce tension. We call these typical responses *backup behavior.*

For example, when people who normally behave in a Driving fashion are put under continuing pressure, they will probably exaggerate their behavior by becoming overassertive and overcontrolling, to such an extent that they become *autocratic.* The effort they make to take over no longer proceeds within the bounds of a mature interaction. Rather, it now represents a selfish move to have things just the way the Driver wants them.

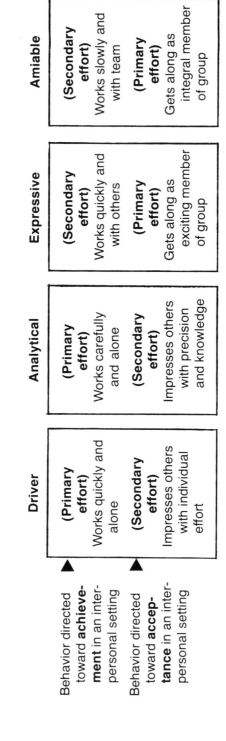

Fig. 3-13. Style priorities.

Other people do not matter, and it's almost as if they are unnecessary to the attempt to achieve objectives.

Similarly, Expressive behavior under continuing pressure becomes overly assertive and emotional, to the extent that it becomes a personal *attack*. If we observe individuals with Expressive styles who are under pressure and who are no longer trying to keep the relationship productive, we'll recognize their emotional, assertive, attacking behavior. They attack with personal condemnations and putdowns in a total effort to discredit the other person. The Driving and Expressive backup behaviors can occur as a flash reaction, which can startle others and catch them unprepared to respond.

Persons with Amiable styles who resort to nonproductive methods of reducing their tension will become less assertive and more emotional, until they appear to *acquiesce* in everything. Acquiescent behavior attempts to retain a relationship at all costs, and to do so with minimal interpersonal tension; however, it can still make an interaction nonproductive. It looks like agreement, but in reality it is neither agreement nor any form of commitment.

Analytical behavior, when nonproductive under pressure, becomes less assertive and more controlled, as the individual seeks to *avoid* the situation. He tells none of his feelings about the situation at all, and does not offer any more ideas. Once again, the immediate result of this behavior is a release from interpersonal tension, but frequently it also means an escape from the relationship and a retreat into self-serving solitude. Analytical and Amiable backup behaviors may not immediately seem to others to be the nonproductive reactions that, in fact, they are.

As you think about your own nonproductive reactions under stress, you may observe that if your preferred backup behavior doesn't relieve the tension, you'll try something else. This is true of each of the four styles. For example, when people with Driving styles are put under pressure and tension builds, they may try to reduce the tension by reacting autocratically. However, if this backup behavior does not lessen the tension, we may see "avoiding" backup behavior. If this fails, such behavior may even be followed by a "personal attack," which, if unsuccessful, may finally force the individual to "acquiesce."

When the normal behavior is extremely assertive, very little time will be spent in less assertive avoidance or acquiescence. Similarly, those with less assertive styles will not experiment long with very assertive attacking or autocratic behavior. After the initial frustration and backup behavior occur, people will seldom try different behaviors unless the situation remains unchanged for a fairly long period of time.

As we observe these nonproductive efforts to relieve tension, it's not hard to imagine the potentially toxic situations that can arise when styles clash. Let's look at this aspect of style a little more, because the better we understand the factors that increase our own and other people's tensions, the better prepared we will be to take the next step: to become more versatile, or adaptable, in order to reduce tensions and to keep relationships productive—the subject of Chapter 4.

STYLE CLASHES

When we talk about people and their differences in assertiveness and responsiveness, we note that each of the dimensions of social style has some positive and some negative characteristics. If we use the positive adjectives, speaking, for example, of an "industrious" Analytical, a "practical" Driver, an "enthusiastic" Expressive, or a "supportive" Amiable, we see that any style can complement another, that sharply different qualities do fit together well. In fact the whole thrust of using style effectively is to encourage people to understand and appreciate the positive side of style differences.

But at the same time, if we look at negative style characteristics, it becomes apparent that problems can occur when different styles interact, especially when the individuals involved make no effort to adapt to each other's behavioral preferences. The result: What was a potentially productive relationship can become a toxic one. This is particularly likely to happen when styles differ on both the assertiveness and responsiveness dimensions, as do the Driving and Amiable styles, and the Analytical and Expressive.

For example, picture Doris, a Driver, and Allen, an Amiable, working on a report together. Doris is extremely assertive, efficient, and strong-willed, so much so that she could be called pushy, dominating, and unresponsive. Allen is easygoing, unassertive, and has a friendly manner, so much so that he might be considered conforming, dependent, and unsure. Doris may wonder about Allen's ability to write the report convincingly enough or whether his oral presentation will be hard-hitting enough. In working with Allen, Doris could build up so much tension that she would revert to her backup style and become "autocratic," insisting that she handle the entire presentation herself, quite possibly to the detriment of the report.

Allen, the Amiable, may think that Doris is so overpowering that she will annoy the management group by demanding too much. Or, he worries that she won't listen to the opposite point of view and will move too quickly for the group, while Allen would prefer to find out more about opposing feelings. But because of his unassertive nature, he may "acquiese"—go along with Doris's decision and withdraw from the unpleasant relationship, just to keep peace and reduce his own level of tension—and thus he decreases his effectiveness in the relationship.

Often, the central problem in such a toxic relationship involves a conflict between the personal priority to achieve and the personal priority to be accepted. Because Doris gives a high priority to achievement, she places greater emphasis on the task, while since Allen gives high priority to acceptance, he requires personal attention when he interacts with other people. Since Doris directs her energies toward getting the job done she is less likely to give Allen the attention he seeks. This creates tension for Allen. The Driving person, on the other hand, develops a feeling of tension about achievement, because she fails to see how the Amiable person's slower, more easygoing behavior—so different from her own—could help them to reach the project goal.

As another example, the other two directly opposing styles—the Analytical and the Expressive—can also create problems because they have opposing behavioral preferences.

Suppose Alice, an Analytical, and Eddie, an Expressive, have been given the responsibility for an annual budget report. Alice, serious and unresponsive, begins to collect the necessary data, works slowly, and impersonally reviews each fact carefully. Eddie, the Expressive, shows a great deal of enthusiasm about the task and collects data quickly, without stopping to check for accuracy. He talks as he works, sharing personal feelings and experiences, and suggests quick, exciting ways to wrap up the assignment.

Can you see the potential problem here? Alice will probably begin to feel frustrated by Eddie. She may feel irritated at his constant talking, which disrupts her careful thinking. And, discovering that his portion of the report is not precise, she may refuse to be a part of the project. She may withdraw and completely "avoid," rather than take responsibility for the results.

Eddie, on the other hand, may feel angry at Alice's stiffness and lack of responsiveness. He may get impatient with her slow pace and become upset because she seems critical of his work. These tensions could cause him to "attack" her in typical Expressive backup behavior. Both Alice and Eddie have become nonproductively tense, and their teamwork suffers as a result.

We've been illustrating the style clashes between people who are different from each other on both the assertiveness and responsiveness dimensions of the Social Style Profile. But, it should be noted that toxic relationships can also develop when there is only one difference in terms of style dimensions. For instance, similarities between two people on the responsiveness scale can help to make their interactions more comfortable, but differences on just the assertiveness scale alone may be cause for concern.

Thinking back to Alice the Analytical, and Doris the Driver, here are people whose two styles have similarities: both are fact oriented, and both are less responsive. However, they differ on assertiveness and that difference can create tensions. They can easily understand each other's task orientation. But they could run into problems concerning pace. The difficulty could occur, for example, when Alice and Doris set up a company-wide pay-for-performance system. Both employees work quietly and efficiently, gathering data, writing job descriptions, and comparing payroll statistics, and toward the same priority: job-related achievement.

But let's add a time deadline. Alice, the Analytical, works cautiously and slowly, while Doris, the Driver, displays a fast pace. Doris may feel that Alice is dragging her feet and worry that the task won't be finished in time for the board meeting. Alice could feel that Doris is pushing and react negatively to that. If they resort to backup styles, Doris may become autocratic and try to control Alice or take over the whole task. Alice, seeking to avoid the unpleasant relationship, may withdraw from the task. The result? A toxic relationship and probably inferior results, or an unfinished task.

Any style can conflict with another style, but our point is that if you can recognize and accept style differences, you can do much to minimize tensions which are unnecessary and clearly unproductive.

CONFLICTS OF HABITS

We should point out again here that we are talking mostly about tensions created between people because they act differently. Behavioral differences are causing the problem, not differences in beliefs or values. Two people, for example, may agree on the importance of profit or the importance of marriage, but the way they say and do things to move toward making a profit or making a marriage work can get in the way of the relationship. Each of us tends to feel that our own way of acting is the right way (and indeed it is, for us). But how someone else acts is also the right way *for them*. Unfortunately, most of us refuse to adjust to these differences.

What's the answer? The key is to develop a sensitivity to, and tolerance for, the behavioral preferences of other individuals— whatever their styles. If we can observe the effect our behavior has on others—predict the differences and possible conflicts between ourselves and them—we can control our own actions so that we don't create additional tensions. Then, instead of wasting time defending ourselves and our own actions, we can open ourselves up to creating the most effective relationship possible. Chapter 4 will expand upon this skill.

OBSERVING STYLE

Our sensitivity to others' behavioral preferences begins with learning to observe their styles. To identify other people's styles, keep in mind the following:

1. Avoid trying to define a style too quickly. Since we all tend to jump to conclusions, we should try to observe a person in as many situations as possible. If we force style identification too quickly, we might create a self-fulfilling prophecy. Use a suspended reaction to confirm the validity of observations. Avoid taking sides in an interaction; hang back, get out of the picture as much as possible. Don't grasp onto one bit of observed behavior and ignore others that don't fit. Rather, let the behaviors add up, and be willing to add more later, if necessary.

2. Get out of the way. Our personal feelings toward the people we are observing can only hinder the accuracy of our objective observations. We should attempt to forget how we are feeling and reacting and concentrate instead on how the other person is acting. Give people a "second chance" to display more behavior.

3. Learn to observe more accurately and describe what a person does without making early "good," "bad," or "why" judgments. Our natural response to others is an early "like" or "dislike" judgment. More often than not, this is a style reaction, and gets in the way of objective observation. The test of the skill of accurate observation is to describe a person's actions in such a way that others can readily agree. For example, the observation that "Charlie sat quietly during the meeting and had an expressionless face" can be quickly verified or denied by others who attended the meeting. But the statement "Charlie wasn't interested" is an interpretation, not an objective description, and it can lead to serious errors in predicting Charlie's future behavior. Concentrate on observing behavior until you can predict someone else's typical action pattern; don't worry about motivations.

4. Separate style clues from assigned authority or roles. We often jump to conclusions based upon assigned roles; for example, we might say, "He's a football player, a competitor, so he must be assertive." This statement is not necessarily true. Assertiveness is *how* someone says or does things with a relationship, not how well someone competes in a contact sport. Many football players are socially unassertive when off the field.

5. *Moderate stress clarifies style.* As already mentioned, we often fall back on those patterns of action that have worked well for us in the past—our styles—in social situations that cause us moderate tension. It's fairly easy to use different, less comfortable behavior patterns when the situation doesn't put us under stress. But watch a person "snap back" to old habits when the situation is not so comfortable.

6. *Set the stage for the person being observed.* If someone is busy reacting to you and your social style, you will find it very difficult to observe that person's style. Thus you must give the other person a chance to show his or her style by effectively "setting the stage." To do this, approach the individual in an open, nonthreatening way; demonstrate an interest in the person. After the normal greetings, begin the conversation with nondramatic questions, rather than with statements. Take an information-gathering posture, but don't ask questions that are too personal or specific. Instead, you might say, "I understand you are involved in _____. Can you tell me something about it?" or, "Can you tell me a little bit about your current situation?" or ask some other general question appropriate to the meeting.

In this way, you will be showing interest in the person and giving the individual a chance to display his or her habitual style. This technique works best if you standardize your actions at the beginning of the process. The key to the technique is to provide as few clues as possible about how you expect, or want, the person to act. This creates an ambiguous situation and mild stress, which causes people to rely on their own styles. The less other people know, or think they know, about what you expect, the more they will rely on their most comfortable behavioral habits, that is, their social styles. And, the more they use those habits, the clearer their styles will become to you. However, even at this point, do not leap to any quick conclusions. Take time to be as open as possible to all of their verbal and nonverbal actions. Then, once you feel confident of your observations, you can form a tentative style judgment.

To test this judgment, look for clues that suggest a different style. If you only look for confirming behavior, you may filter out all other types of behavior that could suggest another social style. By looking for clues that differ from your initial judgment, you face one of two possibilities. You may not find any differing clues, and thus you can confirm your tentative judgments. Or, you may find many clues that suggest that your first assumption needs revision.

Once you have settled on a style theme, you are ready to put your observations to the final test. React to the person according to what you believe to be his or her style preferences (see Chap. 5 for information on how to do this). Does the person respond favorably to your approach? If the person reacts negatively, you will need to reexamine your style considerations and adjust your actions appropriately.

SOCIAL STYLE—IT'S DIFFERENT

Now that we have described our concept of social style, we can explain how it differs from other current psychological theories that you may be familiar with. We identified the dimensions of style—assertiveness, responsiveness, and versatility—through empirical measurement methods. As we have mentioned, other researchers have discovered similar scales; in fact, there is strong agreement about the general dimensions of social style. This remains true, even though methods vary greatly for collecting information about how people interact. There are, though, several distinctions between our idea of social style and that of others who teach style concepts.

The first distinction is one of *source and type of measurement.* Social style as outlined in this book is based upon socially reported measurement. And it is based on others' impressions of a person, not someone's self-impressions. This is in contrast to most behavioral measurement techniques, which ask people to report about themselves. These self-report sources of data are useful only for providing feedback about how one sees oneself.

However, when people report about themselves, their perceptions are often significantly different from those of others who see them acting. That's why we emphasize that the style identification exercise earlier in this chapter cannot be considered totally accurate.

In addition, the social style model we have described is based on information that came from a consensus of at least three people, so that an "average" was obtained. And the 150-adjective checklist that we mentioned earlier has a broader range of application than measurements that rely on describing behavior in a specific situation, as in the statement, "At work, this person tends to be cooperative."

The second major distinction is that this concept of social style is limited to objective, observable behavior. That is, social style, as we define it, is concerned only with the "is"—not the why, the cause, or the motivation of behavior. The focus is on what our behavior is likely to do to someone else, how that may work to our advantage or disadvantage, and what we can do to negotiate an interpersonal relationship so that both parties achieve mutually satisfactory goals.

The final major distinction is that our concept of social style is *nonjudgmental;* there is no good or bad, right or wrong style or formula for success. Never is it suggested that you imitate someone else's style for succeeding. In fact, our social style research suggests that there is little we can do to change our behavior. We can make our actions work more effectively for us by *adding* something to our customary habit patterns, but we don't need to *eliminate* or *change* existing behavior. Some other approaches prescribe the best of a desired style—or the right way to act to be a success.

This nonjudgmental approach allows us to concentrate on understanding our own behavior, instead of trying to figure out other people's motivations or the deeper aspects of ourselves. Social style training helps us to improve perception, delay making value judgments about good and bad, or mature and immature behavior, and learn to accept and work with each person's differences. Attaining this kind of understanding pays off in improved communication skills, because the emphasis is on learning to reduce defensiveness in relationships by doing something about how we appear to others. This approach, teaching us to be less defensive in our own actions, allows us to work *with* others instead of trying to manipulate them by capitalizing on their defensiveness.

Another way to explain the difference between this concept and other approaches is to look at the differences in training emphasis. Obviously, different training programs have different objectives and achieve them in varying degrees. And, depending on a person's objectives or expectations, may serve them well. Social style training can be best understood by reviewing Fig. 3-14. Note that at the left end of the continuum are approaches that suggest we gain control over our inner selves. What we feel and think is analyzed in an attempt to achieve a certain inner understanding. These approaches may be characterized by the broad term "sensitivity training." Though such approaches often succeed at helping a person achieve self-awareness, this focus can be at the sacrifice of others' needs, resulting in the attitude, "If you don't understand me, that's your problem." At the other end of the continuum are approaches that suggest we should exercise control over others. These approaches may be characterized as "prescriptive training." Here we find most of the formulas that show how to manipulate others or the environment to meet our own objectives and needs. These approaches usually suggest that there is just one way to win or

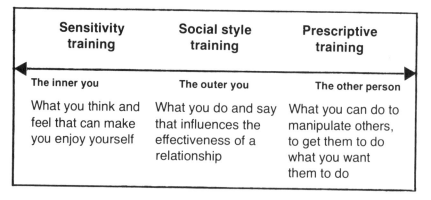

Fig. 3-14. The training continuum.

succeed, and don't encourage using broader understanding or adaptive techniques with others.

Somewhere in the middle is our concept of social style training. This training recognizes that, although we can manipulate others to fit our needs, or work from the inside out to gain understanding, either approach tends to be self-serving, like "how do I get my act together," or "how do I win," without addressing the interactive requirement for succeeding with others. In contrast, social style training says that by simply controlling our defensive tendencies, we can create productive relationships.

PRACTICE SUGGESTIONS

1. When we objectively observe behavior, we begin to pick up clues to another person's style. For example, the next time you're in a restaurant where people seat themselves, watch the behavior that occurs when a group enters the establishment. Who takes charge and suggests a table? When that person is seated, does he or she take part in the conversation, or remain quiet? If you can overhear the voices, does this person tend to speak loudly and talk fast? These are common traits of more assertive individuals. Which member of the group shows a lot of facial animation—smiles, laughs, grimaces—uses hand gestures, and is dressed casually? These are common characteristics of a more responsive individual.

2. The next time you meet a stranger at a party, pay attention to what is happening to you during the first five or ten minutes of conversation. Are you observing this individual the way you might observe an actor on television, or are you just reacting unconsciously to the way the person affects you? Make a conscious effort to note three verbal and three nonverbal behavior patterns that this person exhibits. Later on in the evening, try to talk to this person again, and see if you can confirm these six behavioral clues.

3. Have people told you that you are a talkative, outgoing person? If so, experiment with *a,* below. If others describe you as quiet and reserved, experiment with *b.* If you really don't know how others describe you, go on to *c.*

a. If you are a rather talkative person, at your next social gathering, deliberately remain quiet for the first fifteen minutes or more. As you'll probably notice, people may become uneasy when your behavior is not consistent with your usual pattern, because you have thwarted their tendency to generalize about you. You may hear comments like, "Don't you feel well?" or, "You're so quiet tonight! What's wrong?"

b. If you are normally a reserved, quiet person, at your next social gathering be prepared at the outset to tell a couple of stories or jokes one after another, or to state some opinions. Watch the reaction. Ask anyone if they would like to hear another story, and be prepared if they would. As you'll probably find out, people will be surprised by your change in behavior, and may remark, "What's gotten into you tonight?" or, "I've never seen you this lively before!"

c. If you do not know how others might describe you, try both *a* and *b* with the same group of people, but on separate occasions. When you try *a,* and no one asks you if there is anything wrong, you'll know that others see you as a less assertive person. When you try the jokes or opinions suggested in *b* and people react as though there's nothing unusual, you'll know that people see your behavior as generally more assertive.

4. Using the adjectives in Figure 3-11 and the typical behavior of the four styles described in Figure 3-12, prepare four 3 × 5 cards, listing the characteristics of one style on each card. Then give the cards to people who know you (other than family and very close friends) and ask them to rank the cards in order from most like you to least like you. Do this with five to seven people, and see which style is chosen most by the group to describe you. If you find it difficult to identify a group of five to seven people who are not close confidants or family members, that may indicate that you are a less assertive individual who tends not to venture beyond relatively close, safe relationships. This is particularly true of people with an Analytical style. More assertive individuals tend to have a wide sphere of casual friends. People with an Expressive style, in particular, seem to have the widest sphere of social friends. Driving individuals may tend to prejudge

this assignment and say that it isn't necessary, thinking they already know what their style is. If you react this way, you may take the same approach to other assignments, and this may cause tension for those you work with.

5. What styles do the individuals and characters listed below display? Pick out the three whom you are most familiar with, and try to determine their styles. The answers are at the end of the quiz.

a. Ralph Waite, as John Walton, in "The Waltons"
b. Irving R. Levine, television newsman
c. Lucy, "Peanuts" comic strip character
d. Karen Grassle, as Caroline Ingalls, in "Little House on the Prairie"
e. Amanda Wingfield, the mother in *The Glass Menagerie*
f. Carol Burnett, entertainer
g. Former President Dwight D. Eisenhower
h. William Christopher, as Father Mulcahy, in "MASH"
i. Johnny Carson, on the "Tonight Show"
j. Carroll O'Connor, as Archie Bunker
k. Nigel Bruce, as Dr. Watson, in "Adventures of Sherlock Holmes"
l. Eliza Doolittle, character in *Pygmalion/My Fair Lady*
m. Bob Newhart, as Bob Hartley, in the "Bob Newhart Show"
n. Dan Rather, television newscaster
o. Robert Walden, as Rossi, in the "Lou Grant Show"
p. John Denver, singer
q. Vic Tayback, as Mel, in "Alice"
r. Former President Gerald Ford
s. Falstaff, character in Shakespeare
t. Meryl Streep, as the wife, in *Kramer vs. Kramer*
u. Jane Eyre, novel heroine
v. Charles Bronson, television and movie actor
w. Bette Davis, in *All About Eve* and *Jezebel*

a. Amiable; b. Analytical; c. Driver; d. Amiable; e. Driver; f. Expressive; g. Analytical; h. Amiable; i. Expressive; j. Expressive; k. Amiable; l. Expressive; m. Analytical; n. Driver; o. Driver; p. Amiable; q. Driver; r. Amiable; s. Expressive; t. Analytical; u. Amiable; v. Driver; w. Driver.

4

Versatility: The Extra Dimension

In 1914, psychologist William James wrote, "The great thing, then, in all education, is to make our nervous system our ally instead of our enemy."[1] How easily the same thing could be said of social style!

Those who have made their social style an ally have indeed achieved a "great thing." They have learned to control their behavioral preferences when those habits create nonproductive tension for another person, and they know how to make their words and actions communicate their intentions. In short, they are able to create and maintain valuable interpersonal relationships.

We call the ability to handle our behavioral preferences in this skilled way *versatility,* the third dimension of human behavior. Just as the other two dimensions of behavior, assertiveness and responsiveness, are independent of each other, versatility is also a separate facet of human behavior. Statistical research demonstrates that people who are seen by others as highly versatile in interpersonal situations can be found along all ranges of the assertiveness and responsiveness scales, as can those people who are seen as less versatile. What separates the versatile from the nonversatile is the amount of endorsement that they receive from others regardless of style.

Endorsement means that people approve of our behavior. People give us their endorsement because they remain comfortable and nondefensive when they deal with us. Nevertheless, the interaction retains enough tension so that the people involved reach their goal, whether it is finishing a complex corporate

1. From *Habit* (New York, Henry Holt, 1914).

88

budget report or having a pleasant party conversation. People who are more versatile are described by others as using their styles in a resourceful and impressive manner. Those who have more difficulty making their relationships "work" are described as limited or defensive with their styles and are perceived as having lower versatility. High versatility means that people are comfortable or impressed with our behavior; *it does not necessarily mean* that they like us as individuals.

In other words, versatility as we measure it represents how others view a person's ability to adapt to others and deal with relationships effectively. It reflects the effort that a person makes to have a relationship succeed, the skill shown in this effort, and, finally, the endorsement that he or she earns as a result of it. For versatility, in our sense of the term, all of these elements must be present. For example, some people may try to be versatile, but fail. Some have skills, but don't try. And, of course, unless their efforts result in a mutually productive relationship, they won't earn endorsement from it.

Versatility is not simply the ability to get along with others. Rather, it is dealing with others in such a way that they come away from encounters with us feeling better about themselves, thanks to what we said and did. In other words, a truly versatile relationship increases the effectiveness and productivity of both parties.

A DYNAMIC DIMENSION

Fortunately, for those of us who lack versatility, it can be learned. The skill consists of the ability to listen well, handle confrontation, and resolve conflict. Versatility is quite a dynamic quality, and, unlike assertiveness and responsiveness, which are aspects of our behavior that will remain more or less constant during our lives, versatility can change. Depending on the effort and skill we put into a relationship, we can receive smaller or greater amounts of endorsement from others. Our endorsement can vary over a period of time or even among different groups of people who know us. For example, it is possible that Jill may be an excellent bridge player, and the life of the party, too, thus earning her a high endorsement from her bridge club. But at the office, her joking behavior and less than persistent sales effort may earn her a lower endorsement from her boss. Both her bridge partners and her boss would probably describe her responsiveness and assertiveness levels similarly, but her bridge group sees her behavior as appropriate for the club, while her boss sees her behavior as inappropriate for the sales situation. Thus, their endorsement ratings—their judgment of her versatility—probably will vary. Versatility is behavior that can cause others to put positive or negative labels on our actions. Our versatility rating answers the questions, How well do you use your style with others? Are your actions in a relationship very self-centered? Or, do you manage your actions in a way that prevents tension from getting out of hand?

Versatility is a skill that is practiced in a dynamic manner. It means constantly monitoring your behavior and shifting your actions so that they don't interfere with a relationship. If your actions don't appear to be self-centered, and if you do monitor the tensions you may be causing for other people, you will be seen as versatile, and it is likely that the person describing you will use the positive adjectives listed in the social style quadrants in Figure 4-1. If you are seen as self-centered and your behavior seems concerned only with your own tensions, others may react negatively to you and use the negative adjectives listed in Figure 4-1 when describing you.

Let's go back to a couple of the vignettes in Chapter 1 and look at the characters again, thinking about the endorsement rating they would probably receive from their coworkers and the adjectives that would be used to describe their behavior.

Take, for example, Bob and Sarah, the two people who put in long hard hours organizing their company's national sales convention. Bob deeply offended Sarah by failing to thank her adequately for her good work. How would we rate Bob's versatility in this situation? To answer that, let's consider the elements that contribute to a high versatility rating and decide whether Bob had them or not. First, how much *effort* did Bob put into making the relationship succeed? Not enough, obviously. Although Bob's intention was good—he did want to thank Sarah—he

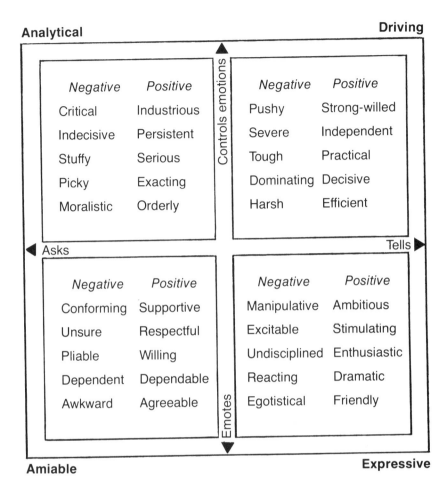

Analytical   **Driving**

Controls emotions

Negative	Positive		Negative	Positive
Critical	Industrious		Pushy	Strong-willed
Indecisive	Persistent		Severe	Independent
Stuffy	Serious		Tough	Practical
Picky	Exacting		Dominating	Decisive
Moralistic	Orderly		Harsh	Efficient

◄ Asks   Tells ►

Negative	Positive		Negative	Positive
Conforming	Supportive		Manipulative	Ambitious
Unsure	Respectful		Excitable	Stimulating
Pliable	Willing		Undisciplined	Enthusiastic
Dependent	Dependable		Reacting	Dramatic
Awkward	Agreeable		Egotistical	Friendly

Emotes

Amiable   **Expressive**

Fig. 4-1. Positive and negative adjectives used to describe the four styles.

didn't put out much effort in making sure that she understood his thanks.

Second, how much *skill* did Bob show in his effort to make the relationship succeed? Again, he showed little skill. First of all, he didn't seem to realize that, although he was comfortable with his fast-paced, rather aloof style, Sarah was not. Her preference was for a slower-paced, more personalized approach. If Bob had had the skills to recognize this, and also the skill to do something about it, he probably wouldn't have tossed a crumpled-up note on her desk and assumed that she would understand it as a sincere expression of his appreciation.

And third, what *endorsement* did Bob earn from the encounter? Very little. In fact, we learn that Sarah soon left the company to go into another business. A potentially dynamic team of two hard-working, intelligent people fell apart, partly because of Bob's lack of versatility in dealing with Sarah.

Looking at the adjectives in Figure 4-1 again, Bob's style could probably be described as Driving, but which group of adjectives do you think Sarah would have used for Bob? Chances are she would choose the negative ones, such as *pushy, dominating,* and *harsh,* rather than the more positive ones, such as *thorough, decisive,* and *efficient.*

But before judging Bob too harshly, remember that versatility, like assertiveness and responsiveness, is only an aspect of behavior—what we say and do—*not* a part of our inner self, that part of our personality that intends to do right and feels sincerely grateful. Bob truly did not want to offend Sarah, and he *did* believe that her work during the convention was outstanding. But he was unable to communicate this to Sarah because his versatility—his ability to use his style to his and Sarah's advantage—was limited. You can probably recognize that Sarah's versatility also needed improvement; she shouldn't have taken refuge so easily in a "flight" response, but should have told Bob her feelings and talked it out.

However, as we have said, versatility is an aspect of behavior that can change. In fact, this happened to Todd, one of our other characters in Chapter 1. As you'll recall, Todd restrained his natural impulse to interrupt Gayle when he found some material that he knew would be useful for her report, and figured out an appropriate time and way to give it to her. In this episode, Todd did not try to permanently change his fundamental pattern of behavior, which could be described as Expressive, but he did make an effort to control his behavior when he knew that it would create nonproductive tension for Gayle. Let's look at Todd in light of the factors that add up to a high versatility rating.

First, how much effort did Todd put into making the relationship succeed? It's obvious that Todd made an effort when he decided to control his own behavioral preference to run into Gayle's office with the exciting news. Instead, he did something that appealed to her preferences: he prepared an accurate appendix that could easily be added to her own report.

Second, how skillful was Todd in making the relationship succeed? As we read, Todd had acquired the skills to understand how and why his behavior could cause tension for another person. He also had the skill to observe Gayle and decide what he could do to moderate his own actions in order to accommodate her style (probably Analytical).

Finally, what endorsement did Todd receive from Gayle? He received a high endorsement from her, not only because he produced the information that she needed to make the report complete, but just as important, because he presented it in a way that did not raise her tension level. And, because of this incident, Todd and Gayle began talking, trying to understand each other's differences a little more and to appreciate each other's strengths. They became an effective team. Because of Todd's versatility, they began a productive, successful relationship.

Because of the success of their relationship, it's likely that if we asked Gayle to describe Todd, using the words in Figure 4-1, she would place him in the Expressive quadrant, but would choose the positive adjectives: *enthusiastic, friendly,* and *stimulating,* rather than the negative adjectives she might have chosen if Todd had used his style in a less versatile manner: *excitable, undisciplined,* and *reacting.*

If we are versatile, we do something to ourselves which, in turn, causes others to feel comfortable with our actions. The versatile person, in this case Todd, recognizes that he can control only his half of a relationship and that it's easier to modify his behavior than to attempt to change other people. The versatile person asks: "What can I do to *me* to make it easier for the other person to relate to me?" In this sense, versatility involves awareness, sensitivity, and appropriate social responses. It requires acting in a manner that shows concern for the impact our behavior has upon people around us.

TENSION AND VERSATILITY

In the two episodes we just looked at, tension arose between the characters, and each of them took defensive actions. Bob created tension for Sarah by his brusque, aloof manner, and unfortunately, he did not manage the tension he was causing. Instead, the tension grew to such a point that Sarah eventually left the company.

Todd and Gayle also had behavioral preferences that caused tension between them. But Todd managed the tension by taking creative action: The memo which he prepared for the report satisfied his need to contribute to the group and also met Gayle's preference for logic and order. In other words, because of Todd's higher versatility, he managed tension in a productive, rather than nonproductive, way.

We have discussed earlier the fact that tension arouses us to action and that when tension occurs, we respond to it by making a defensive move. An individual who shows little versatility reacts to tension defensively, serving his or her personal comfort needs alone. This form of reaction contains ingredients that create even more tension for the other person.

For example, Bob may have placed a high priority on getting the job done, which reduced his tension and made him more comfortable. But in the process, he behaved in a less than sensitive way toward Sarah and thus made her more and more uncomfortable until she finally blew up. Bob was so concerned to meet his own needs that he neglected to consider Sarah's.

We can also carry concern for another's tensions to the other extreme. This can often happen with Amiable and Analytical styles: they do everything possible to avoid conflict, and frequently yield to the other's needs. When this occurs, others may have more positive feelings about their sensitivity, but they may also feel a different kind of tension, because they see someone who will not take a stand or hold firmly to an opinion, approach, or goal. Thus, even though they may avoid an obvious conflict, the behavior is still nonproductively defensive. Remember, we must experience enough tension in a relationship to move toward a goal.

Ultimately, the key word in versatility is *appropriate*. The more appropriate our behavior in a given situation, the more likely that we and those we deal with will achieve our goals in a socially effective, mutually satisfying way. When we monitor tensions effectively, we recognize when people are being detrimentally affected by too much or too little tension. And, if we then have the ability to deal constructively with people under those circumstances, we will have achieved a successful interpersonal relationship.

The ability to handle tensions productively is a skill that individuals with any of the four styles can have. Even though all of us have personal investments in our styles because they make us comfortable in interpersonal situations, the versatile individual is willing to take the emotional risk of objectively observing the effect of his or her style on others and then doing something about it. Versatile individuals are willing to become concerned with the tensions of others and to learn how to effectively use their particular styles in order to create mutually satisfying, successful relationships with a variety of people and in a variety of situations.

As an added bonus, when we take this risk and see a relationship work, we will become more comfortable and willing to make the effort to be versatile again in the future. The results are similar to what happened to the football team when it added more plays to its defensive team: it became more spontaneous. When we learn a wide variety of social skills which permit us to be productively defensive in a wide variety of ways, we'll anticipate the "game"—the social encounter—with less tension, because we'll be confident that we can handle most situations to our own and the other person's satisfaction. In fact, our level of comfort in a variety of social situations is a good way for us to estimate our own versatility.

How to Recognize Versatility

It is relatively easy for us to recognize versatility in someone else. Gayle and Sarah, in fact, might have had trouble identifying Bob's and Todd's styles, but they could probably have pinpointed the men's versatility skills quite easily. In our own lives, we may have difficulty determining whether or not someone exhibits Driving, Expressive, Amiable, or Analytical behaviors, but we'll almost immediately know whether or not we're comfortable with them. And if we are comfortable with someone—if that person helps us to achieve our goals without making us defensive or nonproductively tense—we sense that we are dealing with a versatile person.

In contrast, think of someone who made you extremely uncomfortable in the first few minutes of an interaction, merely by the way he acted or by what he said. More than likely, you reacted defensively to this less than versatile person because his actions or words seemed inappropriate, or self-centered, to you.

Notice that we say words *or* actions. A person doesn't necessarily have to make a crude or awkward comment for us to consider him nonversatile. The individual who refuses to give us *any* signal, by avoiding making a statement or taking any action at all, can also cause us discomfort.

AM I VERSATILE?

While it's easy to know whether another person makes us comfortable, it's a bit more difficult to decide whether we ourselves are versatile. Many people tend to think that if they engage in many different kinds of activities—play golf, paint pictures, sell real estate, tune a car—they are versatile. But this definition of versatility—engaging in many varied activities—is not the concept we are interested in here. Rather it is social versatility—the ability to interact with many different types of people and to monitor tensions to create productive relationships. Some suggestions to help you decide where you rate in this dimension of behavior follow.

1. Evaluate the level of your social endorsement. It is difficult to evaluate the level of comfort we create for others. We can, though, ask ourselves several questions that relate to our social endorsement. For example, we can ask ourselves: Do people choose me to work with and relate to me in a variety of circumstances? Would I win, not just a popularity poll, but an endorsement poll in a variety of circumstances? Do I seem to do better in technical interactions, rather than social ones, or vice versa? Are there limitations to the range of situations and people who would choose to work with me? Does my endorsement relate to some specific skill or capability, or does it carry over from formal to informal circumstances, and from one group to another?

2. Determine whether you are versatile in many groups. With regard to the last question, you'll recall that a person's versatility rating can vary from one group to another; the bridge club may endorse us, but the boss may not. But, if we are truly versatile, we will succeed with many groups. For example:

If you say that someone is versatile because you feel comfortable in your relationship with that individual, you may call the person versatile—with you. But unless you can observe this person in a variety of circumstances with other people, you cannot generalize about his or her versatility.

So, it's important to recognize that if we think our versatility ratings would be high among a very selective, homogeneous group of people who have a specialized type of contact with us, those ratings are fairly limited. Members of a tennis club or a volunteer organization who comment on our versatility provide a weak basis for generalizing about how we might perform in relationships as a manager, salesman, teacher, or parent.

3. Distinguish between versatility and position power. We should also not make the mistake of assuming that a title or position assures versatility in the eyes of others. A person with authority in a position may be able to order other people to do things, but it is only the person with broad competence and effective social skills who can lead others without creating conflicts and arousing defensiveness. Success in terms of achieving position power is no guarantee that those who interact with you see you as resourceful, adaptive, and impressive.

4. Evaluate messages from others. As we examine our own versatility, there's one other caution to keep in mind: People will tend to tell us what we want to hear (or what they think we want to hear). So it is very unlikely that others will report low versatility to us if we ask them, point-blank, what they think. They may

Instructions: Read each statement and place an X in the box that best describes your reaction to that statement. Mark either "Very True," "Somewhat True," "Somewhat False," or "Very False."

	Very True	Some-what True	Some-what False	Very False	Score
1. Before I dress for the day, I stop to consider those I might meet for the first time, and then dress in a way that will have an appropriate impact on them.	___	___	___	___	___
2. I recognize the importance of first impressions and, for this reason, give special effort and attention to my physical grooming and dress.	___	___	___	___	___
3. My manner of dress is one of my ways of expressing my individuality, and it's not my problem if someone is put off by the impression I create.	___	___	___	___	___
4. I am a skillful speaker and find it easy to communicate my ideas to people I meet, both in groups and in one-to-one situations.	___	___	___	___	___
5. I must admit that there are times I will say things just to impress people with my vocabulary and my knowledge of a subject.	___	___	___	___	___
6. I sometimes have difficulty expressing my ideas in a clear, concise, and organized manner.	___	___	___	___	___
7. People ask my opinions on a variety of subjects, and appear to respect my judgment even if they disagree with me.	___	___	___	___	___
8. At a social gathering or party, I tend to seek out one or two people with interests similar to mine, and spend most of my time with these people.	___	___	___	___	___

Fig. 4-2. Versatility self-scoring questionnaire.

	Very True	Some- what True	Some- what False	Very False	Score
9. I find I have some difficulty socializing with people who have educational backgrounds or experience different from mine.	——	——	——	——	——
10. I am usually very frank and candid with others and can usually disagree with them without causing hurt feelings.	——	——	——	——	——
11. I seldom let it be known if my feelings are hurt by something someone says to me about the way I feel.	——	——	——	——	——
12. I am equally good at taking directions from others and giving directions to others when the situation calls for me to do so.	——	——	——	——	——

Scoring Instructions: Indicate your score for each statement, using the following answer values.* Add your scores for the twelve statements. Interpret your total score as follows:

0–24	Less versatility than most people
25–30	Mid-range versatility; typical
31–36	Most versatile

	Very True	Some- what True	Some- what False	Very False
1.	3	2	1	0
2.	3	2	1	0
3.	0	1	2	3
4.	3	2	1	0
5.	0	1	2	3
6.	0	1	2	3
7.	3	2	1	0
8.	0	1	2	3
9.	0	1	2	3
10.	3	2	1	0
11.	0	1	2	3
12.	3	2	1	0

*Most people completing this questionnaire tend to underestimate their versatility since the statements are written to challenge the way you would normally think about how you handle your relationships.

admit: "You can be difficult at times." "You are opinionated." "You are uncompromising." But usually they will qualify these observations with some positive statement, like: "But you get the job done." "People know where you stand." "You make your plans and stick to them."

5. *Use this self-scoring tool.* Figure 4-2 is a self-perception questionnaire that will give you a rough approximation of your versatility. Bear in mind as you fill it out, however, that it has a serious drawback because it records your impressions of yourself, not others' impressions of you. Most people tend to underestimate their versatility on this test. We believe, as we've said before, that a truly accurate measurement of versatility can only be achieved through use of the computer-graded 150-adjective checklist mentioned in Chapter 3.

RANGES OF VERSATILITY

Figure 4-3 shows the versatility scale which we use in scoring the 150-adjective checklist. The scale indicates whether people perceive an individual as focusing more on making himself or herself comfortable and tension-free or on demonstrating some degree of concern for the tension this person creates for others. The opposite ends of the scale are labeled "Concern with others' tensions" and "Concern with my tension." If you rated yourself low on the self-perception questionnaire, you can place yourself on the left side of the scale; if high, place yourself on the right side of the scale.

For example, on this scale, Bob, who hurried past Sarah on his way to a meeting with the vice-president, showed more concern with his own tension than with Sarah's tension, so Sarah would

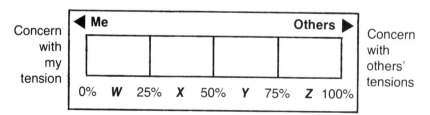

Fig. 4-3. The versatility scale.

probably place Bob on the left-hand side of the scale. Todd, in contrast, realized the tensions he would create for Gayle if he dashed into her office. Because he showed concern for Gayle's tension and did something about it, Gayle would probably place Todd on the right-hand side of the versatility scale.

Of course, just as in the assertiveness and responsiveness dimensions, there are ranges of versatility. Thus, the scale is divided into four segments, with each segment representing one-fourth of a sample population. The quartiles are labeled W, X, Y, and Z.

W Rating

At the lower extreme is the W level of versatility. By definition, 25 percent of the general population will receive a W versatility rating.

A W rating suggests that people with this versatility level might have a more difficult time monitoring the tensions their styles could create for various people. Persons who consistently operate with low social versatility usually seek situations that capitalize on their technical skills, abilities, and knowledge, rather than using their social resourcefulness as a means for building mutually productive relationships.

X Rating

Persons with an X level of versatility display more versatility than approximately 25 percent of the population. An X level of versatility represents a form of balance. In other words, people displaying this level of versatility do a low average job of managing relationships in a concerned and appropriate manner. Usually, though, they tend to do better with specific groups of people, and are less able to move smoothly from one group to another.

Y Rating

People with a Y level of versatility fall within the range of the upper 50 percent of the population. These people do an above average job of managing relationships in a concerned and appropriate manner. Typically, they move smoothly from one social situation to another and meet the needs of a variety of people. They meet strangers well and handle new or unusual social situations in an aware, concerned, and appropriate fashion. But they are not so very versatile that they appear extremely individualistic or overwhelming in their efforts to demonstrate concern for others.

Z Rating

Z represents the highest range of perceived versatility. People in this group are seen as more versatile than approximately 75 percent of the population. These people appear impressive and unique in their interactions. At times they can become so individualistic that they have difficulty subordinating these needs when dealing with others. Individuals with this level of versatility may require unusual independence and an opportunity to "do their own thing."

These, then, are the four ranges of versatility. Figure 4-4 shows typical adjectives used to describe people at various levels of the versatility scale. Figure 4-5 lists examples of versatile and nonversatile behavior.

We may seem to be implying that low versatility is "bad" and that high versatility is "good." So let's look at the two extremes, W and Z, a little more closely to clear up some misconceptions that can easily occur when people learn about versatility.

Limited Adaptability (W)	Balanced Adaptability (X, Y)	Extreme Adaptability (Z)
Apprehensive	Resourceful	Provocative
Conforming	Adaptive	Individualistic
Blunt	Tactful	Polished
Argumentative	Reasonable	Compromising
Overcritical	Perceptive	Unbiased

Fig. 4-4. Adjectives commonly used to describe levels of versatility.

Concern with My Tensions		Concern with Mine and Others' Tensions
Stipulates a relationship: "I'll tell you how it should be."	►◄	Negotiates a relationship: "Let's discuss it."
Rigid opinions and actions: "I'm right."	►◄	Flexible opinions and actions: "I see your point; we'll do it your way."
Inflexible attitudes: "There's only one answer."	►◄	Adaptive attitudes: "There's more than one way to approach this problem."
Single-mindedness: "I stick to my guns."	►◄	Resourcefulness: "Let's try several ways."
Narrow, traditional interests: "It has always been so."	►◄	Broad, unusual interests: "I'm always looking for new ideas."
Seeks certainty and clear rules: "Be specific."	►◄	Accepts uncertainty and enjoys freedom from strict rules: "Give me my head."
Tends to be a specialist and relies on his specialty: "I do my thing very well."	►◄	Tends to be a generalist or a resourceful specialist: "I'm a 'Jack of all trades'."
Indifferent about impact and impressions: "Take me or leave me."	►◄	Tries to manage impact and impressions: "How can I best relate?
Takes a clear stand: "This I believe."	►◄	Takes a flexible position: "It depends."
Blunt, straightforward: "You're wrong."	►◄	Tactful: "I want to understand."
Uses position power to influence: "Do it, because I'm in charge."	►◄	Uses personal power to influence: "We can work this out."
Predictable, consistent, believable: "You always know where I stand."	►◄	Unpredictable, may appear inconsistent and, therefore, unbelievable: "I seldom do anything the same way twice."
Seeks and maintains personal advantages: "I win. You look out for yourself."	►◄	Tries to meet the needs of others: "How can I help?"

Fig. 4-5. Examples of versatile and nonversatile behavior.

W: Pros and Cons

There is a strong tendency to label someone who has W versatility as "bad," which is a mistake. Individuals exhibiting low versatility are not bad people; they are simply not skillful at developing comfortable, productive relationships. Their values, efforts, and intentions may all be sterling, but the relationships they have with others do not lead to improved productivity for all involved.

For instance, a man we know tells us he has always had a poor, nonproductive relationship with his mother. He realizes that her values, intention, and effort to help him cannot be questioned. But because of her rigid, uncompromising statements and advice about how he should live his life, he became very defensive when he was with her. He was determined to run his own life, and finally the situation with his mother became so tense that he moved to another state, in order to avoid constant contact with her. In other words, her lack of versatility, he feels—not her intention—contributed to the poor relationship between them.

On the other hand, there are times when it is advantageous to subordinate concern for how others respond to us to other objectives. For example, consider General Patton, faced with the objective of winning a battle. His officers and troops certainly described him as *pushy, severe, tough, dominating,* and *harsh*—all adjectives that indicate low versatility. But General Patton won quite a few battles. In this case, General Patton's behavior was appropriate to the situation, and his lack of versatility was actually a virtue.

In the business world, we know of many examples of people with low versatility who appear to be successful in their areas of endeavor. For instance, some individuals working alone on a job can stick to specific objectives or tasks with a vengeance, resulting in very high levels of personal productivity. But if they do not make enough effort to control the impact of their styles on others, their relationships may suffer.

Similarly, in management we all can name several corporate heads who display very low versatility. They have enough position power, however, to order things done and to require others to conform to their requests. Thus they can get a job done, but usually at the expense of the relationships involved. If they pay their staff high enough salaries, and the product is good enough, these men and women may prosper. But a closer look at such an organization often reveals poor morale, high turnover, and efforts to unionize. So in one sense the organization is successful, but just think how much more productive the corporation might be if the boss took care to improve his relationships with his staff.

Z: Pros and Cons

At the other extreme of the versatility scale is the high Z rating. The advantage of a high versatility rating is clear. People are perceiving an individual as resourceful, adaptable, and able to deal with many different interpersonal situations effectively. This behavior leads to high endorsement, but the rating can be a mixed blessing. For example, some of these very versatile people can raise the tension of others because they appear changeable and unpredictable. This changeable, smooth, or even slick social manner can cause others to question or mistrust these individuals' actions. The actions are impressive and can lead to personal successes, but others may view them as self-serving and doubt their motives.

Some of those who score beyond the 90th percentile may continuously be on the move, seeking new challenges to prove outstanding personal resourcefulness. This extreme mobility or flexibility in actions can create tension for others, because they can't seem to pin the individual down. In addition, there are some highly versatile people who create a chameleon effect, diminishing their ability to work well with a group of people over any extended period of time. People are impressed initially by the adaptive resourcefulness of the individual, but at a later date they may feel that they were somehow used.

Versatility is a "what have you done to me lately" measurement, so it is possible for a person to be seen initially as very versatile, but later lose that endorsement if the individual's actions create nonproductive tensions for others.

People with Z versatility can do a lot to prevent their adaptable ways from creating tensions for others by making goals and objectives clear and by sticking with them. As long as the effect of very versatile action is to help others to reach their goals without exploiting them, people can learn to deal with the tension that changeable or flexible behavior might create.

DEFENSES AGAINST TENSION

In essence, we see that both extremes in versatility indicate a type of defensiveness. For example, when persons with W versatility exhibit behavior that is direct, narrow, or rigid, and when they seem to be almost unaware of the effect their behavior has on others, they may be reacting defensively to the awkwardness that they feel in social situations. When unsure of a situation, such people may restrict what they say and do until they become more comfortable. But when they finally speak up, it is generally from one point of view—theirs. Their styles are usually very clear to everyone but themselves. It appears that individuals with W versatility have weak self-reflective skills.

The type of defensiveness displayed by persons with a Z versatility revolves around their impressive, multidimensional behavior. When they are unsure of a social situation, they, too, may hang back a bit. But unlike persons with W versatility, they carefully size up the situation to determine the most appropriate behavior. They may even show many aspects of many styles in order to impress others, and thus their social style may be unclear. Others may notice that such individuals seem to have a smooth, slick, or pat answer for everything. They may say something that sounds good without saying anything really specific.

Individuals in the middle range of versatility often have more success because they seem more solid to others; people feel they can understand them, and thus they feel comfortable with them. That is why we call the middle range, X and Y, the Golden Mean.

However, even though both W and Z levels can cause nonproductive tension for others, individuals with Z versatility are probably more successful with people relationships than are W-level individuals. This is because people with Z ratings are highly visible, impressive individuals and are often admired for having these traits. But because both W and Z levels can be seen as types of self-serving behaviors, the middle range of versatility is usually preferable.

CHANGING VERSATILITY

As we've emphasized, versatility is a dynamic dimension; it can be changed with practice and effort. But there must be motivation to try to change, even if that involves some failure and pain as new skills are learned.

Why make the effort? Quite simply, if we assume that we'll be involved in situations where success hinges on working with other people, then building productive relationships with others will be essential to reaching the greatest level of success.

Sometimes, of course, we might not want to make the effort to be versatile because the outcome of the relationship is not valuable to us. In fact, unless versatile behavior becomes almost automatic, it's unrealistic to assume that anyone will want to expend the energy required to make the best of every interpersonal situation that's encountered, whether it be with a salesclerk at a department store or a stranger on a bus. Some encounters we'll simply write off. That's fine, as long as we're aware of what we're doing.

But if a relationship is important, we must be willing to state to ourselves: "I will take on some personal tension in order to make this relationship work. I will let the other person do things his way, because I am farseeing enough to understand that this present tension is worth the price if it results in a successful outcome."

But what do we *do* to increase versatility? First, we must be sure that we want to make the effort to try new skills. Second, we do *not* try to change our social style. We do not try to be more or less assertive or more or less responsive. Instead, we add appropriate behaviors to our repertoire of social skills so that we simply use our own style more effectively. For example, when it's appropriate to listen to another's opinion, we'll do so; when it's appropriate to state our opinions, we'll do that. We monitor the interpersonal situation and determine what action will help most to keep the relationship productive. We don't *always* listen and never give an opinion; neither do we *always* give an opinion and never listen.

Third, and more specifically, there are four factors that particularly affect our versatility ratings. We can acquire some techniques for using these factors appropriately to increase our versatility. These factors are: appearance, presentation skills, breadth of competence, and skill in using feedback. No matter what your style is, you can increase your versatility by concentrating on these four factors. Some pointers for making the best use of each of them are discussed in the following paragraphs.

APPEARANCE

The individual who has a pleasant physical appearance and is appropriately groomed will make a better impression than someone who is not as physically appealing. Almost everyone makes value judgments about others that are based in part upon appearance, even though that first impression may not be valid. But after people have developed a first impression, they are reluctant to change their opinions, even if later exposure suggests that this first impression might be incorrect.

Very often, dramatically unusual personal appearance in terms of hair style or clothes can create tensions in others and lead them to form quick conclusions about us. For instance, unkempt, dirty hair may suggest social indifference. The person wearing it appears to take the attitude: "If you don't like my hair, that's your problem—not mine. It's comfortable for me." And observers of this person may avoid such an individual because of the unappealing impression he or she creates.

Of course, we're not discouraging individuality in dress and appearance. We are suggesting that your versatility can be improved by considering the impact of your appearance on others.

For example, are your dress and appearance appropriate for each situation you encounter? Do you vary your dress to meet the needs of others, or do you dress for yourself? In many cases, it is possible to do both.

Development Direction Hints: When dressing for any occasion, but especially a business one, consider what style of dress and appearance will make others feel the most comfortable about you. For example, if you're making a sales call to a group of well-established older executives, don't play up your youth and relative inexperience by dressing in an extremely casual, faddish way. Dress the part of a knowledgeable professional, so that their first impression will be the one most beneficial to you. On the other hand it could be equally inappropriate to overdress to sell farm equipment to a rancher.

Oral Presentation Skills

Good oral presentation skills involve the capacity to communicate in a way that satisfies others. This includes behavior such as using correct grammar, good diction, appropriate vocabulary, and clear enunciation, and organizing ideas to meet the needs of the audience.

Effective oral presentation is different from knowing the job, although that is a basic requirement in business. For instance, a sales representative may possess outstanding knowledge of the product or service offered for sale, but he also needs the ability to speak clearly on the telephone and in face-to-face encounters.

Development Direction Hints: Using slang, technical words, or, for that matter, profanity, might create tension for the listener. So if you are talking to someone about a subject you'd like them to find interesting and motivating, monitor the impact your presentation has upon that person. If you produce too much tension, the individual may resist or avoid what you have to say; if you don't produce any tension at all, the person may not pay attention to you.

Saying too little or too much about what you wish to communicate can also influence tension levels. Others may say, for example, "Sam never says enough to let you know whether he agrees or disagrees with you." Or "Sue talks so much I shut her out, even when she has a good point to make. She just overdoes it."

To help improve oral presentation skills, try to prepare ahead of time; think through what you have to say and whom you will be saying it to. Enrolling in a speaking course can also improve your presentation ability.

DEVELOPMENT OF COMPETENCE

One of the most meaningful and solid ways for an individual to earn lasting, real respect and endorsement from others comes from developing competence that others can use to accomplish their goals. If you develop competence—understanding and awareness of things that others are interested in or feel are important—and use this competence to help them achieve their needs, you will be seen as more versatile.

As an example, some people talk regularly about sports but have limited interest in art or music; some can easily discuss Picasso and Beethoven, but have never heard of the Phillies. Others get interested in, and talk about, their work, but have few outside interests or activities. Developing the skill to converse with almost anyone, and finding some common ground for sharing interests or ideas, takes time and effort on your part, but it's worth it. We don't recommend that you become an expert in many things, or for that matter, become competent in many areas. Instead, exhibiting breadth of competence is simply a matter of being alert to a variety of activities and being able to listen and learn from others about their interests.

If you're not familiar with art, for instance, how willing are you to extend yourself and ask an art enthusiast to help you understand that world of interest? Admitting your lack of understanding about the subject and seeking ideas that broaden your knowledge can build common ground for future discussions in this area. Building adequate—not exceptional—understanding about wide areas of interest and activity helps develop versatility.

Why does this ability increase versatility? Just think of someone you know who talks only about those things which interest him or her. Such a narrow range of interest can make us avoid that person in favor of someone else. In other words, when we can't establish common ground, we raise tensions in others, and that tension can cause them either to take over the conversation or to limit the discussion with us. The ability to hold up our end of a conversation on a variety of topics is a part of versatility.

Another important point is to understand that the way we communicate our competence in a given area to others is more important to our versatility ratings than the competence itself. This is why, incidentally, we do not find any correlation between our versatility ratings and intelligence or actual technical competence on the job. For example, two equally good doctors with competence in their specialized fields may vary in success with their clients. The one with the good "bedside manner" may attract more patients because of an ability to express competence in a way that makes patients comfortable. The other physician, although just as competent, may alienate patients because the inability to express this competence makes patients tense and uncertain.

Of course, we must realize that no one should set out to be all things to all people. But anyone can develop broad competence if he or she takes the time and effort to do so.

Development Direction Hints: As a suggested approach, work toward developing one area of competence at a time. After mastering the selected area, take on another challenge. Reading about a variety of subjects is helpful—not just sports, sales or management but all three areas, as well as others.

The skill of simply knowing how to ask good questions, even when you know little about a topic, can also improve your versatility. Get the other person to talk about his or her work, hobbies, vacation, or reactions to current events. Because you are sharing another's interests, that person will see you as having greater breadth of competence.

USE OF FEEDBACK

The most dynamic aspect of versatility is the use of feedback. Proper use of feedback makes possible a two-way communication process in which we send and receive both verbal and nonverbal messages with a minimum of tension and a maximum of understanding. When we achieve this balance, we are displaying the ability to collaborate and negotiate with others to reach our own objectives, while helping them with theirs. We say that the feedback skill is dynamic because we use it actively in shaping a personal relationship. We can use specific skills to improve this aspect of versatility.

When we have good communication skills, we send our signals

in a clear, accurate, and definite manner, so that others can understand us. At the same time we monitor our behavior and become sensitive to the tension our signals may create in others.

In other words, after sending a message to someone, we check to see whether it was received and understood, as well as to find out how the receiver feels about the message sent. We stay open to the communication signals others are trying to send to us, and we let them know whether this communication is causing us undue tension.

Our skill in handling two-way communication in a candid and open manner, with a minimum of defensiveness, is essential to versatility. To be seen as versatile, we must share our feelings and thoughts about the messages we receive from others, and we must check our own messages.

For instance, if we just tell others what we think and feel without asking them to report back to us on our messages, we miss the boat on feedback skills. On the other hand, if we tend to ask others what they think and feel but seldom tell them how we react to their messages, we fail at sending feedback. A balanced approach to listening and speaking is essential for good communication. Avoiding tensions entirely or creating tensions unnecessarily will block this process. Some tension is both desirable and inevitable, and dealing with this tension when we communicate is a key to developing good feedback skills.

As an example, if someone takes an opposing stand on an issue that we feel is important and we can't discuss both sides without becoming upset, if we refuse to talk about it, or if we challenge the other person's right to his or her position, we are displaying weak feedback skills.

Recent research into this aspect of versatility indicates that the balancing process in achieving good communication is composed of two factors: interpersonal understanding and interpersonal strength. Let's look at these factors more closely.

UNDERSTANDING AND STRENGTH

By interpersonal understanding, we mean our ability to: 1) let others know us; and 2) let others know that we are trying to understand them. Interpersonal strength is our ability and willingness to meet our own objectives in situations of conflict or confrontation without allowing others to remain defensive. When one demonstrates both understanding and strength in interpersonal situations, one is communicating with versatility. There are specific skills a person can learn to use which will improve interpersonal understanding and interpersonal strength. It is not our purpose here to detail these skills, but for the interested reader we have listed two excellent books at the end of this text which cover these skills in great depth, *People Skills* by Bob Bolton and *You and Me* by Gerard Egan. Essentially, the skills are in the areas of reflective listening, confrontation, and conflict resolution.

Before discussing these feedback elements further, it is important to realize that the words *strength* and *understanding* can be misleading if thought of in terms of social style. There is no relationship between the typical behaviors of particular styles and interpersonal understanding and strength. For example, people displaying Expressive and Amiable behaviors appear to show more interest in personal relationships, feelings, and emotions. This does not mean that they are naturally better able to understand the tensions they are producing in others, or to understand their own behavior. They may respond to someone else in a personal way, but so quickly that they seem unable to sort out important messages. When this happens, they are seen as flighty and overly responsive—not understanding. Likewise, more assertive individuals do not necessarily demonstrate strength, as the term is used here. Just because they tend to state an opinion quickly—tell, more than ask—does not mean that they know how to handle conflict or confrontations so that nonproductive defensiveness is kept out of the encounter. Demonstrating understanding and strength simply means that we can communicate clearly, without letting our own and others' biases, beliefs, or opinions get in the way of the message.

To explain a little further, consider the typical message sending and receiving process. Most of us "code" our messages in some way as we send them, by including—usually nonverbally, or even subconsciously—our attitudes, beliefs, and prejudices. We say something to a person, but the message has a deeper meaning—to us, anyway. By the same token, the one who receives the message typically also has his own beliefs and prejudices. Thus, when he receives the message, he reads his own interpretation into it. No wonder so many of our encounters end up with each party thinking something different has happened!

But when we use proper feedback skills, we try to circumvent this coding process. When we deliver a clear message, and when we make sure that we receive the message the other person is trying to send to us, we demonstrate interpersonal understanding and strength.

As a simple analogy, good use of feedback skills can be thought of as resembling tennis practice. When we practice our tennis skills, we try to volley the ball back and forth across the net. The object is not to "ace" our partner—not make him our opponent—but to keep the ball in play so that we can each work on our skills. Likewise, in good use of feedback for communication, we give and receive messages in a way that keeps the ball going on a straight course. We don't send it over the sidelines with inappropriate comments, or completely over the fence by letting our biases lead to misinterpretation of the message. We also keep our end of the game up. We don't walk away from the court and leave our partner standing there alone—refuse to send messages back. Nor do we refuse to receive and try to understand the other person's messages.

At its best, good use of feedback is a two-way process, but if our partner does not have interpersonal feedback skills, we can still keep up our end of the game. We can lob easy shots to our partner—even run off the court to return his shots. Thus, even though it takes more effort on our part, we both keep the ball in play—keep the communication going in a productive way.

Obviously, this effort can create tension, because we won't always be able to behave in the way that's most comfortable for us. And, of course, if in the process of changing our own approach to a situation we create so much internal tension for ourselves that we cannot be effective, then that is an inappropriate change. An appropriate change is to do what is necessary to help the other person function more effectively, while still attaining our own goals. And, as we've said before, if we understand that our partner simply has limited feedback skills, then we'll probably develop more tolerance for him—and feel less tension personally.

THE FOUR STEPS

In essence, then, improving your versatility is a four-step process.

First: Know yourself. Know the impression you make on others; how your behavioral preferences can cause tension for others; how your appearance, oral presentation skills, breadth of competence, and feedback skills affect your ability to communicate effectively with others.

Two: Control yourself. Make an effort to take advantage of your strengths and minimize your weaknesses. For example, if your strength is the ability to present an idea well, don't hold back. Use that skill. If your weakness is to interpret others' messages in terms of your own beliefs and prejudices, recognize this and try to prevent yourself from doing it.

By controlling yourself, we also mean: Learn to be tolerant of others' behavior without becoming tense. In a relationship, allow some time for the other person to respond to you in a nondefensive way. Don't posture and position yourself so quickly that the other person *has* to react defensively to you.

If you give people time—even just a few minutes—to become comfortable with you, you'll learn more about their preferred mode of behavior than if they must immediately react to you. When other people try to react in ways they think you want them to, you may not see their usual behavior. Instead, you'll get crossed signals.

Three: Know others. By observing others' behaviors, we can learn about their tension levels, how they respond to our messages, and what we can do to make them more comfortable and effective.

Four: Do something for others. Once we know what makes another person comfortable, try to accommodate his preferences. For example, if we are most comfortable when dressed in a sloppy, very casual way but the person we want to work with is more at ease with conservative attire, we can take some measures to accommodate this preference. When we say, "do something for others," we don't suggest you give up your objectives, beliefs, ideas or values. We are simply saying, do something to manage relationship tension.

Taking even one of these steps is bound to improve our versatility. For instance, if we know ourselves, we are likely to do a better job of dealing with the tension we cause other people; we adjust our behavior almost unconsciously. If we then make a conscious effort to control ourselves, we'll see even better results. Again, if we have insights about other people, we will make an almost automatic adjustment to them. And, if we make a deliberate effort to adjust to these individuals, then our versatility will become greater still.

As we begin to practice these skills, it's important to recognize that there is no such thing as instant versatility. We must be persistent in our efforts to gain experience and develop competence. A willingness to stick with versatility goals is necessary, even if frustration and occasional discouragement are an inevitable part of the growing process. Developing a tolerance for frustration is part of the price one must pay to gain additional social competence.

But the frustration and tension we initially feel as we work at versatility skills will subside. As we've stated several times, the more we learn about ourselves and others, the more tolerant and accepting we will become of behavior that is different from our own. We won't feel the need to automatically assume that anyone who behaves differently from us is bad, and this alone will greatly reduce our tension levels when we deal with others.

In addition, we don't have to be "on"—constantly showing versatility—all the time. Rather, we use our versatility early in a relationship to establish a comfortable environment for the other individual, then we relax and carry on our normal activities. We keep in tune, though, with what the other person is feeling and, if necessary, adjust our behavior to reestablish comfort in the relationship.

As you recall, Chapter 3 helped us understand the different behavioral preferences that most of us exhibit—the four social styles—and how these styles can both complement and create tension for people with other styles. Chapter 5 will relate style to versatility by providing some suggestions for working effectively with each of the four styles.

PRACTICE SUGGESTIONS

1. One of the best ways to understand versatility is to observe its effect on us. As an example, the next time you are in a group and someone is "called on the carpet" for something, watch to see which of these reactions you have: Do you immediately become tense as you anticipate the individual's response to the challenge? Or do you remain fairly relaxed, because you know that the individual will be able to handle the confrontation well? If the latter is the case, you are observing an individual displaying versatile behavior—and it doesn't matter what that person's style happens to be.

2. A versatile individual receives endorsement from a wide variety of people in a wide variety of circumstances. Versatility is not just the ability to perform the technical side of the job. To illustrate this, make a list of people you know who do their jobs well. Now, rank them in terms of how well they get along with their fellow workers. Third, rank them in terms of their ability to represent their fellow workers at an organization meeting. Ask: 1) would they be chosen to represent the work group; 2) would they use social skills to handle the new responsibility well; 3) would they be able to overcome a poorly planned meeting to achieve their objectives? As you go through this process, you are demonstrating your awareness of people's versatility. The individual you rank as the one most likely to be chosen to represent others and achieve the objectives of the group is the individual you see as the most versatile person in your work group.

3. Nonversatile responses to tension can take many forms. By observing them in others, we gain insights into our own responses to tension. For example, some people won't accept any fact or data that conflict with their own preconceived notions. Think about people who declare, defensively, "I just know that can't be right." Another nonversatile reaction is to reject a suggestion in a judgmental way: "It's no good." "It's not worth talking about." A third common reaction is to distort what was said in order to make the statement compatible with what one wants to do or think. "No, she didn't mean she was bored with the project. She meant she doesn't care about her job, which I've known all along."

4. As we have emphasized, learning versatility skills can take a lot of energy and effort. We may consciously choose not to be versatile in some situations, such as when the paper boy comes to the door to collect his money and we're trying to catch up on some important work. You might speak sharply to him or hand him the money without speaking. That's okay, if you accept the consequences. The paper might be on your roof tomorrow!

But also try choosing a relationship that you feel is important to keep productive and use some of the recommendations given in this chapter. You'll probably notice your tension level rising, at least at first, but you'll probably also notice that the other individual is feeling less tension than usual. As you become more understanding of that person's behavior, you will probably also find yourself becoming less tense and more tolerant of his or her behavioral differences. That's a sign of versatility!

5

Putting Versatility into Social Style

In the previous chapter, we recommended four steps to follow to improve versatility: know yourself, control yourself, know others, and do something for others. Now, let's apply these steps more specifically to the four social styles, to highlight some practical tips for dealing versatilely with different types of behavior.

KNOW YOURSELF

Every style has positive and negative aspects, which we touched upon in Chapter 3. The following discussion will recap some of these points, because once we understand the strengths and weaknesses of our own social styles, we will have taken the first step toward improving our versatility: know yourself. With this knowledge, we can easily move to the second step: control yourself.

As you read about the advantages and disadvantages of the four styles, don't just concentrate on your own. Look at the sections about the other styles as well, because this information will help you to take the third step: know others.

As you read, you'll note that the negative aspects of a style are often the result of overworking our behavioral preferences to the point where they create nonproductive tension for others. For instance, the individual who displays Expressive behavior tends to show others his or her feelings. This can be an important asset in building solid relationships. But when the person insists on disclosing feelings to someone who is uncomfortable hearing personal revelations, the Expressive person is not using this style appropriately. He or she is not behaving versatilely in this situation, and what could be an asset, under different circumstances, is now a liability to the success of the relationship.

Later in this chapter, we'll provide hints on what individuals can do with their own styles to minimize the negative aspects of their behavior—to control themselves. Then we'll discuss some ideas for modifying behavior to work better with other styles. That will complete the fourth step in building versatility: doing something for others.

STRENGTHS AND WEAKNESSES OF THE AMIABLE STYLE

People with Amiable behavior tend to be very supportive; they are usually polite and do not interrupt or push their own interests ahead of others'. They are good listeners and are sensitive to others' feelings. Because of this, they can be very helpful in monitoring morale problems, even before such problems become significant.

Given their typical approach, people with Amiable styles tend to make sure that relationships are firmly established and that a positive attitude exists, before they move into a task. They are typically strong, loyal team players. And while they can be very energetic, they also lend an air of relaxation to the groups they work in, fostering a leisurely work pace.

Another behavior characteristic of the Amiable is the fact that they work very hard not to let people down and are willing to go an extra mile to respond to the needs of others. They'll not only help others with a task, but also will give them personal attention—a willing ear or a shoulder to cry on.

On the less positive side, Amiables tend to be slow to act, sometimes to the detriment of finishing a task before a deadline. They may stop to consider feelings unnecessarily. And their reluctance to move forward independently may irritate people who want faster, more definitive action. Thus, Amiables can sometimes create tension for others because of their personal insistence on doing things in a slow-paced, warm and friendly, responsible but unaggressive way.

People with other styles react in fairly typical ways to the Amiable. For example, an Expressive person may see the Amiable man or woman as pleasant, but too easygoing and slow-moving. This can make the Expressive impatient with the Amiable.

People with a Driving style see much the same thing, but, in addition, they may become so impatient with Amiables that they begin to feel that they cannot expect timely action and tough, initiating behavior from them. Consequently, Drivers may either place strict demands on Amiables, or simply take over the job from them completely.

Individuals displaying Analytical behavior can also have trouble in their relationships with Amiables, because Analyticals require attention to facts and details, and they don't get much of this from Amiables. Thus, Analyticals often find themselves taken by surprise over the concern for everyone's feelings ultimately expressed by Amiables. Analyticals not only wonder why the Amiable person allows relationships and feelings about others to influence objectivity, but also why the Amiable expects others to deal with these subjective feelings.

To portray the typical way an Amiable person would do a job for us, let's put an Amiable man, Joe, in the hypothetical situation of planning a luncheon meeting. In this situation, we might expect the following behavior:

Joe will probably put in a lot of hard work on the assignment, perhaps with no haste, but with a tendency to be meticulous about doing a good job. He will probably seek the direction, and consider the preferences, of others, trying to please everyone, and may work overtime to give sufficient attention to detail. What Joe might minimize, however, is the value of negotiating the best deal with regard to price, facilities, and so on, unless failure to bargain would displease his boss.

As he looks for a place to hold the meeting, Joe would be likely to limit the number of vendors he investigates. He will probably make a personal call on a few of them and will want to become involved in actually selecting dishes, seating arrangements, and so forth, so that the arrangements will not disappoint those attending.

STRENGTHS AND WEAKNESSES OF THE EXPRESSIVE STYLE

Persons displaying predominantly Expressive behavior have a number of positive traits that can make them a pleasure to work with. They tend to move very quickly, and to do it with fun and *joie de vivre.* They inject humor and excitement into situations, and can be very stimulating and persuasive. Expressive people need few precise instructions, because they can make decisions without such structure. At the same time, they can think in terms of what will please others; they can figure out techniques that are people oriented; and they can recognize social situations that need to be enlivened with a few sparks of drama or humor.

Of course, Expressives can cause problems for people if they joke, laugh, and brush off situations that are not taken lightly by others. When Expressives try to stimulate and excite for the sake of getting approval in a business situation, without having the facts at hand to justify their actions, they can cause tensions for others. In addition, their sensitivity about their relationships with others, while an advantage in some cases, can become a problem if they become so thin-skinned that they must be handled with kid gloves. And their need to be constantly doing exciting things may result in what other people see as careless and impulsive behavior.

For example, a person with an Amiable style might become envious of dramatic, stimulating Expressives, or, worse still, might think their friendliness is false, because, although Expressive people develop relationships rapidly, they don't pause long enough to develop them in depth.

People with a Driving style may find Expressive behavior particularly difficult to accept, because, while Expressives are competitive like the Driver, they are more interested in approval than in achievement. Their tendencies to have fun and have people respond warmly to them—behaviors that are part of the Expressive style—may not have the structure, direction, and the stated objectives that the person with a Driving style typically wants.

Individuals with Analytical behavior are least like the Expressive, and therefore they may have more trouble accepting Expressive people as comfortable to work with, or may find it hard to deal with them at all. An Analytical man or woman's discomfort with an Expressive can be expressed by statements such as: "Can't you be serious?" or, "You really don't have enough facts to say that."

If we assigned Peg, a person with Expressive behavior, to organize the luncheon meeting, her approach would probably be to seek to build a grand experience. Peg might pay a great deal of attention to colorful dishes, foods, and decorations. She would tend to find a dining place that people would enjoy, rather than considering the exact cost or the purpose of the luncheon. On the other hand, if Peg was not enthused about the assignment, she would quite likely put together a hasty "that's good enough" affair.

Like the Amiable person, Peg probably wouldn't be too concerned with price, and she would use personal contact to establish relationships with the vendors. But she might make more calls and take the approach of selling them on the fact that they ought to provide "extras," rather than analyzing who would provide the best deal. Peg would count heavily on developing a relationship with the vendor to get what she asks for, even if she pushed the vendor to provide more than he cares to supply.

STRENGTHS AND WEAKNESSES OF THE DRIVING STYLE

People seen as having primarily Driving behavior are fast-paced, fairly businesslike, and goal-oriented individuals. They are willing to take the responsibility for moving ahead and making decisions. They will make the open statement and take the definitive stand. Drivers have the ability to deal with tough interactions without becoming upset by criticism or personal rejection. They get the facts and move on, without appearing to worry about whether or not they are liked. Thus, if we work with Drivers, we can utilize their ability to present a position in a confident and forceful way—whether or not all the evidence for their stands actually exists.

Of course, Drivers can also be seen as somewhat rough and tough—very impatient and less likely to seek, hear, or respond to information from others. Drivers frequently accept data from coworkers in an off-hand way, without giving credit to the source, incorporating the information in their ongoing activity as though the facts were their own.

Both Expressives and Amiables see Drivers as lacking human qualities and being businesslike to the exclusion of the good relationships that people with Expressive or Amiable styles feel are important. Thus, unless the Driver's leadership abilities are needed, Expressive or Amiable persons tend to minimize contact with the Driver.

The Analytical person's trouble with Drivers occurs because Drivers don't need as much data and logic as the Analytical does. Because of this, the Analytical sees Drivers as people who are willing to exercise quick options and confidently make decisions on the basis of data that seem insufficient. If the Analytical had no more data than these individuals, he or she would be unwilling to state a position, and because of this, the Analytical sometimes assumes that Drivers are truly sure of themselves. The Analytical can then be disillusioned to find out that a Driver's opinion may not be based on information as complete as the Analytical had supposed.

If Kay, a woman with Driving behavior, organized the luncheon, we could expect her to move quickly with little advice from others and gather just enough information to feel comfortable choosing among several options. Then Kay would probably concentrate her efforts on getting the luncheon arrangements done and ready on time—sometimes so far ahead of schedule that she could redo the plans two or three times before the actual luncheon date.

When choosing a place for the luncheon, Kay would tend to make two or three calls on vendors, state the objective, make an effort to strike a hard bargain, and then push for completion of arrangements. For the actual execution of her plans, she would choose one of two extremes, either retaining complete control over the details herself, or fully delegating responsibility to the vendor, thinking, "I'll hold him fully responsible for getting it done."

STRENGTHS AND WEAKNESSES OF THE ANALYTICAL STYLE

When we work with individuals showing Analytical behavior, we can appreciate their fact-oriented, data-gathering approach to problems and their tendency to move cautiously and not create problems with precipitous action. Their objectivity, willingness to listen, and cool, collected responses to troublesome situations are aspects of their behavior that others can use when working with them. Of course, this is not to say that Analytical people won't be upset when they make a mistake, or that they won't ever be assertive about something they are quite sure about.

On the flip side of the coin, the tentative behavior of Analyticals can cause problems for others who seek suggestions or conclusions from them. Analyticals do not respond to emotional appeals, nor can they be stimulated to move quickly. Instead, they prefer holding to their own data-gathering pace. Others may think Analyticals express ideas in a negative fashion, when, in fact, they are only unwilling to be positive until they have examined all sides of a question.

When working with Analyticals, individuals with Driving behavior can become impatient with their lack of decisiveness and unwillingness to take risks. Drivers may feel compelled to hurry Analyticals along, seeing their preferences for gathering more data as unnecessary. Expressives also question Analyticals' dependence on facts. In addition, Expressives tend to be put off by Analyticals' critical, "stuffy" behavior, their impersonal approach to relationships, and their lack of enthusiasm for dramatic ideas.

Persons with Amiable behavior may admire Analyticals' cooperative, organized approach to tasks, but will often be critical of their lack of warmth and close relationships. Analyticals' reliance on facts and figures, to the seeming exclusion of humans, can also cause tension for Amiables.

If an individual with Analytical behavior, Greg, was given the luncheon assignment, he would probably first seek information about why the luncheon was being held and then examine a number of facilities, menus, and prices. His objective would be to get the job done right once, without having to redo any aspect of it. Thus, the arrangements might be spartan, because only activities that could be done with certainty would be fully explored.

When dealing with vendors, Greg would probably make a tentative approach to two or three to determine what each could offer, giving away nothing until a commitment was necessary. After he had made his choice, however, Greg would give the vendor all the information needed about timing and objectives. Once this was done, he might not make many decisions for the vendor, leaving details up to the person he had chosen to handle the luncheon.

As we can see, people with all four styles can successfully handle the luncheon meeting. Each individual may approach the assignment differently because of different style preferences, but each can obtain satisfactory results.

CONTROL YOURSELF

Thus each style has strengths that others can use to advantage in achieving mutual goals. At the same time, the weaknesses of each style can limit our effectiveness. What can we do to minimize the adverse effects of our style's weak points? By focusing on the weak points and asking ourselves what behaviors our style seems to lack, we can decide what "growth actions" will help overcome the weaknesses. We can add behaviors to our repertoire of responses which will allow us to "control ourselves" appropriately when dealing with others.

GROWTH ACTION FOR THE AMIABLE: INITIATE

Amiable behavior is characterized by a congenial, people-oriented, supportive nature, and by a generous use of time. If these characteristics are carried to an extreme, thus maintaining safe comfortable relationships at the expense of other business objectives, what would be a logical growth action for the Amiable? With their great need for relationship security, Amiables are probably reluctant to take the initiative in directing a project that involves others. Thus, the Amiable's growth action would be to initiate action.

By initiating action, we mean that Amiables should try to reduce the tension in a relationship by providing direction when it's needed and sticking to objectives and goals—even if there's a risk involved of creating some relationship tension.

When Amiable persons become too involved with people on an emotional level, they may be seen as subjective, soft-hearted "nice guys," and consequently have difficulty influencing others. Learning to develop a more businesslike, serious-minded manner can be helpful. For example, Amiable individuals might learn to limit the extent to which they take fellow workers into their confidence about personal matters. Developing a close personal relationship with all those they want to influence is unnecessary, and can even work against them.

In addition, Amiables should learn to make demands on others, because very often people need to be challenged to achieve results beyond their own personal expectations. Since people often consider Amiables easy to get around, because they respond readily to feelings, Amiables should learn to control their feelings in interpersonal situations and keep job communications in line with business.

Amiables can also work to provide stability and calm in the face of disturbing situations, and to present factual, rather than emotional, points of view. Because Amiables are sometimes seen as "submissive," they should express opinions—and even be the first one to share an idea, rather than waiting to see what others might have to say.

These opinions might conflict with someone else's, but Amiables should realize that often the best ideas grow out of resolving different points of view. Simply supporting existing ideas may make others like Amiables, but it won't help them in their roles of parents, managers, or leaders. So, Amiables should learn to speak up and disagree while listening to others' ideas. Think of disagreement as a sign of interest in someone's ideas or opinions, not as expressing dislike of the individual. Conflict is an integral part of change, and if Amiables want to influence others, they must realize that they cannot avoid disagreements. Learning to manage conflict, rather than avoid it, is necessary to reconcile differences and establish good communication.

Obviously, these are not behaviors that Amiables are most comfortable with, but if they use them appropriately, they will be seen as more versatile than Amiables who refuse to use anything other than their customary habit patterns.

GROWTH ACTION FOR THE EXPRESSIVE: CHECK

The man or woman with an Expressive style is characterized by an impulsive, excitable nature, by an orientation toward people rather than tasks, by quick decision making, and by a stimulating, competitive need for attention. When striving for attention, Expressives are usually not very good at "checking" their behavior—slowing down long enough to consider the facts and feelings of others, rather than relying on their own points of view. Thus, the growth action for the Expressive is to "check."

By checking, we mean that Expressive individuals should practice some of the following actions, even though they are not as comfortable for them as their customary behavior patterns. For example, rather than having to be the center of attention, Expressives should try to show a willingness to accept other individuals' actions without reacting negatively. They should try to focus attention on the needs and requirements of those they wish to influence, rather than centering the conversation on themselves. Expressives can practice skills such as allowing time to ask questions, considering other points of view, acknowledging and incorporating useful points made by others, and developing cooperative, rather than competitive relationships.

Expressives should be able to admit that they are not always right. They can admit that they don't know all the answers and not lose face, thereby showing confidence in their ability to obtain the facts needed to solve the problem. Expressives should understand that they often project attitudes of impatience and restlessness. Thus it would help them to pause, study, or delay their responses. People can feel downgraded when they encounter individuals who always have answers for everything on the tips of their tongues.

In addition, Expressives should avoid overwhelming others with their ideas or apparent capabilities. Confidence and decisiveness are quite different from cockiness or aggressiveness. The very assertive Expressive needs to learn to place emphasis on problem solving and good communication, not on social self-gratification.

Expressives can tone down their emotional reactions to events by presenting factual information and assisting in defining goals or objectives that will resolve, not increase, personal conflicts. They can limit the extent to which they take others into their confidence about personal matters. Think of it this way: One of the basic reasons for separating officers from enlisted men in the military is that it is easier to lead others if officers do not get too close to their troops. Rather than responding only to the feelings of others, Expressives should work toward keeping their job communications on a business, rather than personal, level.

Expressives who remain calm and stable during a disturbing situation, and who talk more slowly, quietly, and less, will be seen as more versatile than Expressives who consistently react to situations in an excitable, emotional way.

GROWTH ACTION FOR THE DRIVER: LISTEN

A Driving style is characterized by self-directed, independent, fast, action-oriented feedback; a task orientation, rather than a people orientation; and competitive behavior. Because of their need to be in charge of situations, nonversatile Drivers often do not take time to listen to other peoples' opinions and feelings. Thus, since people rarely enjoy being pushed into decisions or actions without having their side of the story heard, the growth action for the Driver is to "listen."

By suggesting "listening," we ask Drivers to practice the following less than comfortable behaviors: to express a willingness to accept another person's actions without reacting negatively; to allow time to ask other people questions; and to fully consider and acknowledge different points of view. Drivers who can admit that they are not always right will gain more endorsement from others than those who give answers and make decisions without the necessary facts. Thus Drivers should avoid the temptation to come forward with the answer to a question immediately. Such an approach can overwhelm others with Drivers' ideas, apparent capabilities, or need to have the last word.

Persons with Driving behavior should also work to develop cooperation in their relationships by talking about other people's ideas. For example, accepting the merits of another point of view helps good communication. Individuals who can incorporate aspects of the other sides of issues into their positions with their original commitment and conviction demonstrate more strength than persons who never listen to others with an acknowledging attitude. And, if Drivers do incorporate another's idea into their positions, they should openly recognize the source of the idea.

We also recommend that Drivers work on showing more concern for others' tensions by giving emotional support to the feelings or attitudes of people, and try to convey a healthy excitement and sense of involvement in relationships. Drivers should not be reluctant to express some sentiment, admit to feelings, or talk personally with people about their ideas. They should learn to visit with others by making social small talk and realize that expressions of personal excitement or disappointment can help communicate their ideas more meaningfully.

If we think back to the Bob and Sarah episode, we can see that if Bob had allowed more time for his relationship with Sarah and had displayed his feelings of thanks in a more open, emotional way, Sarah's tensions would not have built up quite so much. She might still have seen Bob's actions as essentially Driving, but she would have considered him resourceful and impressive— what we would call versatile—because he tried to meet her preference for a warmer relationship.

Growth Action for the Analytical: Declare

Analytical behavior is characterized by deliberation, calculation, cool nature, task orientation, and by a generally cautious nature. In their unwillingness to take risks and their preference for sticking to the facts, Analyticals have difficulty "declaring": taking a stand or making a decision. Thus, growth action for Analyticals is to "declare."

To practice this growth action, Analyticals should try to provide direction and decisions when they are needed; to stimulate timely action; and to take part in decision-making discussions. Analyticals should work on becoming more candid and frank in expressing their opinions—perhaps being the first person to provide an idea or opinion, rather than waiting for all the facts to be brought out. Such assertions needn't be rigid declarations of fact, but simply statements of how one sees a point. Don't always wait to be asked, and don't wait until the discussion requires an opinion to be given.

When this kind of dialogue begins, Analyticals should expect some conflict with other points of view. If these disagreements can be handled well, the differences can be reconciled, and the best solution can be found. In other words, Analyticals should learn to be willing to negotiate with others, even if they feel they have the facts to support their own conclusions. It takes time to influence others, so Analyticals should try to settle for some gains and work for additional agreements later.

In addition, when making their positions known, Analyticals should simplify their points so that others will understand them. Technically detailed disagreements with others can hurt feelings or make others angry because they cannot understand the points being made. Good communicators assert themselves well when they express opinions in everyday terms, so that others can grasp them easily.

Analyticals should also try to lessen the negative aspects of their cool, factual styles by showing emotional support for the feelings and attitudes of others; by openly displaying emotional qualities and feelings in nondefensive ways; and by being willing to show some excitement and involvement in relationships. Expressing feelings and concern for traditional humanistic ideas is neither foolish nor indiscreet. It's good to be businesslike and rational, but such an approach should not exclude personal warmth. Holding feelings in at all costs does not contribute to better communication. The restrained Analytical needs to avoid appearing too serious and stiff, and should work to establish rapport with others.

One way to make this adjustment is to talk personally with people about their ideas, rather than dwelling only on technical and abstract subjects. Social conversation, mixed with technical or job-oriented conversation, can often improve one's ability to influence the decisions of others. In addition, if Analyticals express how they feel about ideas personally, they will communicate their ideas more strongly than if they limit their explanations to logic and reason alone.

AN ADDING-ON PROCESS

As you can see, we're asking you to practice behaviors that are less comfortable for you than your typical behavioral preferences. But we're not asking you to change your style. We're asking you to see both your style-related assets and your style-bound problems. We want you to understand your style's limitations, what behaviors may cause tension for others, and then take some steps to control yourself. In this way, you'll take responsibility for handling your half of your relationships, because you'll be willing to use behaviors appropriate to the situation. You will become less style-bound, because you will have "added plays" to your set of defenses. People with other styles will see fewer behavioral differences between you and them, and there will be fewer conflicts in your relationships, because you will have stepped out of your corner to accommodate their preferences.

DOING SOMETHING FOR OTHERS

Once we are in control of our end of a relationship, we're ready to take the next two steps in building versatility: knowing others, and doing something for others. Knowing others means taking time to monitor the effect our behavior has on them, watching for any nonproductive tension we may be causing. Of course, if we have dealt with someone in the past, we may already have a good idea of what his or her predominant social style is. But keep in mind that although we generally display predictable habit patterns, we do vary our behavior.

Take the case of a person who typically behaves in a Driving fashion, yet occasionally wants to talk about a vacation or the family in a relaxed, slow-paced way. On those days, or even in those few minutes, this individual is showing more Amiable than Driving behavior. Here our approach should not be to force the responses we might typically use when dealing with a Driver—sticking to business in a brisk, serious fashion, and so on. Instead, we should sit back, relax, and let the Driver feel comfortable in his Amiable mood.

If we do not feel skilled enough to pinpoint another's style and adjust our responses accordingly, that's okay. In fact, the chapter on versatility did not involve style identification at all. If you simply follow some of that chapter's suggestions for reducing nonproductive tensions in your encounters with others, and incorporate some of the "control yourself" suggestions in this chapter, you'll be well on your way toward achieving successful relationships.

However, when we can pinpoint behavior themes in others—identify their social styles—the following discussion will make it easier for us to take the fourth step in the versatility process: Do something for others.

Again, remember what we mean by doing something for others. We are talking about working with another style in a way that can minimize relationship tensions, not a way that gives the other person everything they want. Normally, in a significant business or personal situation you are working with others to reach some specific objective, accomplish a task or make a decision, and each party has to take some action. So our suggestions for what you do for others are designed to improve the working relationship, not to ask you to give in or let others have their way. Our suggestions will help you maintain a productive relationship while you negotiate a mutual commitment for the actions to be taken and the performance to be achieved.

Do Something for the Amiable

Given what we know about the preferences of the Amiable individual, what course of action should we take in dealing with this person?

To deal effectively with an Amiable, we should support this individual's feelings and desire for a personal relationship. The following are some specific suggestions:

1. Take an early initiative to show personal interest in Amiables as individuals. Spend plenty of time learning about the people and things that are important—marital status, families, hobbies, and interests—and try to find a real area of common involvement, so that you can support their personal needs.

2. Establish a cooperative effort with Amiables. Amiables want to work with you on a joint basis as a means of achieving objectives. They may understate personal goals, so you need to clarify the specifics of what is to be accomplished in terms of "why," "who," "how," and "what." Avoid the temptation to overstate what you can realistically do together to achieve the

objective, or else you will create difficulties in a long-term relationship.

3. Communicate patiently, and make an effort to draw out their personal opinions. Amiables may agree with your goals too willingly, just to find a common ground or establish friendship. Thus, find out what the Amiable wants that differs from what you may want to achieve with the Amiable. Be aware of any source of doubt, fear, or insecurity the Amiable may have.

4. If you agree easily on an objective, look for possible areas of future disagreement or dissatisfaction before taking any joint action. Check, with this statement: "It's great that we agree; however, are there any areas where we might possibly disagree in the future?"

5. If you disagree with Amiables, encourage discussions about personal opinions and feelings in the area of difference to keep communications open. Give them a chance to display their priority systems, while avoiding a logical debate about facts. If you disagree too openly, expect hurt feelings.

6. Indicate all the things that you can and will do to support agreed-upon personal objectives. Clearly define what you will contribute personally to the joint effort and what the Amiable will contribute. If necessary, put this in writing, so that the Amiable will not expect too much, and so that you will remember your commitment. Once you agree on a commitment, try not to change it. If you do, it will be difficult to regain acceptance from the Amiable.

7. Be sure to define the specifics about what each person will do to achieve the agreed-upon goal. Deal specifically with any sources of insecurity or fear that may exist. Give the Amiable time to understand the separate efforts that both parties will make, and get the Amiable to agree to his or her side of the scheduled joint effort.

8. When the Amiable helps to achieve an objective, recognize the contribution with warm, personal thanks and praise.

Do Something for the Expressive

To deal most effectively with an Expressive person, we need to plan actions that will provide support for their dreams and intuitions. The following are some possible approaches:

1. Plan to ask questions concerning the opinions and ideas Expressives have about people, and about their efforts to reach future objectives. Have Expressives tell you what people should do to achieve their objectives. Then let Expressives tell you what they personally are doing to reach that objective. Thus, initially people and their future goals become the subject of these discussions, rather than results in terms of cold, factual, present realities.

2. Expressives form opinions on almost everything. Look for the opinions of Expressives and try to find some agreement in any area that you would like to be involved in with them.

   For example, an Expressive person frequently presents a very definite opinion about political candidates. One is "great," because of a stand on child welfare laws; another is "terrible," because of attitudes about capital punishment. Conversely, the Expressive may support someone without knowing anything about the candidate's platform simply because the candidate impresses him as a good human being.

   In business, one Expressive was excited when a competitor designed an imaginative new trade-show booth. It was not the purpose or the result that interested him so much as the "terrific" idea itself. He was stimulated by what appeared to be an innovative action.

3. Spend time exploring mutually stimulating ideas and possible solutions. At this point, don't rush a conversation or discussion. Instead, build ideas together. Let the Expressive take as much of the credit for the ideas developed as he or she cares to. At the same time, help Expressives get "back on track" if they begin to wander from the subject at hand in search of exciting new ideas.

4. If you disagree with an Expressive, avoid arguing, since Expressives feel a strong need to win an argument. Look for alternate solutions that you both can share with excitement. Avoid competing with the Expressive person, even when his behavior seems to encourage competition.

5. The Expressive will show little interest in *how* agreed-upon objectives are reached and usually has limited interest in details. Thus, you should offer to summarize the discussion and suggest ways to implement the actions you have both settled upon. Your willingness to take initiative in handling details will strengthen your relationship with the Expressive. Let Expressives know

that you will provide a written summary even though they may want to make some changes in the plans you have outlined. Consolidate the new information and move on.

6. Indicate all the things that you can and will do to implement the ideas you have agreed upon. Ask Expressives what you personally can do to help put their ideas into action. Be sure you agree on specifics. Avoid the temptation to proceed on the basis of a warm feeling that everything will somehow work out for the best. You should be sure there is mutual understanding about who will do what, because individuals with an Expressive style often accept more responsibility than they can really handle.

7. Reward good results quickly, in a form that gives the Expressive personal recognition. Public praise will be appreciated by the Expressive.

Do Something for the Driver

To deal most effectively with the Driver, you should try to plan your efforts to provide support for the Driver's conclusions and supply the actions needed to implement those conclusions. Initially, you shouldn't try to change this person's mind with a direct approach; instead, start by attempting to discover the Driver's objectives and find ways to support and help with these objectives.

1. In discussions with a Driver, plan to ask questions about specifics. A Driver wants to get a job done. Find out what situation or conditions would exist if the Driver had his way. It's not necessary to deal with discussions of what the Driver wants personally. Instead, you should deal with the actions and results that must take place for the Driver to reach an objective already identified as important.

2. Stick with "what" questions. Don't bog down in your discussion on "how," "who," "why," or "when" questions. Move directly and quickly to "what" specifics—what is to be achieved, what is to be done to achieve it. Don't waste time in attempts to build a personal relationship.

3. Keep the relationship businesslike. It's not necessary to build a personal relationship unless the Driver indicates that that's part of the objective. You should not anticipate friendship as a condition for a good working relationship. Listen carefully to the

Driver's statements about goals or objectives. Look for specific things you can provide to assist with the stated objective without assuming anything or trying to second guess what it is the Driver really wants.

4. If you can agree with the Driver's position, support the results the Driver wants, rather than the Driver personally. The emphasis should be on "I'm for the results you want," rather than "I'm for you." In addition, indicate all the things you can do and would like to do to achieve the objective. Then ask the Driver which of these actions he would like to have you take to contribute to the agreed-upon objective.

5. If you disagree with the Driver's specifics or objectives, take issue with the facts, not the person. Don't try to initiate a discussion of philosophies or implications. If you can't agree with any of the objectives the Driver wants to achieve, tell him "why" you can't agree and indicate "what" actions you see as alternatives. If the Driver refuses to listen to your point of view, you may need to make a head-on effort to let him know that his change of direction or independent rescheduling will hurt the results. You will have to firmly state your commitment to your existing objective or direction.

6. Reward the Driver for performance with a solid, material gain, such as a percentage of a sale or a bonus. If the Driver is the boss, reward him by getting the job done on time and by not involving him in the details.

Do Something for the Analytical

To deal effectively with the Analytical, you must demonstrate that you will support his principles and thoughtful approach. The goal should be to show understanding without being too quick with a solution or help.

1. Take the initiative to demonstrate through actions, rather than words, that you really can make a specific, organized contribution to the Analytical's efforts. Do something like preparing a written presentation of recommendations you would like the Analytical to consider.

2. The Analytical will observe your approach with the critical expectation that you will tend to oversell yourself or overstate what you can or will do. Stick with specifics, and do what you say you will do. Also, list the pros and cons of any suggestion or

plan you make. Your awareness of the disadvantages in a plan and suggestions about realistic ways for dealing with time will tend to build your credibility with the Analytical.

3. Take time to remain persistent. You can't rush an Analytical person, even when you have established a relationship. Such people move with deliberateness. However, once you have a commitment from them, they will do everything they have stated.

4. If you agree on objectives, it doesn't mean that you can expect quick implementation of action. Analyticals seek assurance that their decisions are "right" and that their actions can't backfire or clash with other activities. A scheduled approach to implementing actions with a step-by-step timetable will produce positive results.

An Analytical will frequently withhold making an early decision. For example, it may be difficult to get a firm promise to have a decision by noon next Friday. But a meeting Monday to see what additional data are required, one on Wednesday to clarify further details, and then a decision-declaration meeting on Friday may be very possible. At the final meeting, make sure that the specific "how to" and "what" remain clear, as well as the agreement on "why" and "who."

5. If you disagree, look for the possibility that you haven't really demonstrated your understanding of the Analytical's point of view. Find a way to earn credibility by making an organized, well thought out, systematic presentation of your position. A written outline can help.

6. Indicate all the things that you can and will do to support agreed-upon efforts. Be systematic about making your "can do" and "will do" contributions on the schedule that you mutually establish, and either stay with it or let the Analytical know "when" and "why" you deviated from the schedule. Don't spring surprises on the Analytical. If you pace yourself, your example will help the Analytical to stay on schedule, too. Give the Analytical time to verify the reliability of your joint actions.

7. Reward Analyticals by praising the excellence of their planning and strategies when they achieve the desired results on time, within budget, and so on. If the Analytical is the boss, reward him or her by avoiding surprises; making your presentations specific, rational, logical, and cheap; and by showing that you stayed on track.

Taking the Lead

These, then are some of the actions you can take to deal with different styles in a versatile manner. Of course, your *own* style has an influence on how easily you will be able to incorporate these suggestions. Also, how do you work with others of your own style in order to get a job done? A suggested approach, and a summary of the recommendations discussed above, are provided in Figures 5-1 through 5-4.

When you follow these recommendations, you are taking the lead in understanding others and handling tensions that can develop in relationships. As you develop this skill, you may wonder if others will resent you if it becomes obvious that you are trying to accommodate yourself to their styles. Probably not. Usually, others approve of your trying to do what they want you to do. Similarly, you may wonder—is this a kind of manipulation? No, in one sense because you aren't trying to control anyone except yourself. Yes, in another sense because you are approaching others in a way that pleases, rather than irritates them, so you can set a positive stage for effective performance from the relationship. But, if someone does try to use style strictly to manipulate, people easily detect it and the attempt won't work.

Another common question people ask is why they have difficulty using style approaches on people they know well. Our answer is that style becomes less apparent as we learn about other aspects of personality: hopes, dreams, values and so on. We get the total person in view, and don't react *just* to style differences. Style considerations are still important, but it may be more difficult to use the tips discussed in this chapter with people we know well than it is with casual acquaintances, clients, or coworkers.

In the next two chapters, we'll relate style more specifically to three areas of life: work, the community, and home.

Practice Suggestions

1. The next time you must assign someone to do a job, choose a person you know is capable, but whose behavior makes you uneasy because he or she approaches a task so differently from

Analyticals	Drivers*
Relate to your cooperative, careful, quiet, thoughtful and willing ways. Question your soft-hearted, easygoing nature, emotional responses and compliance with others.	Relate to your supportive, helpful, team-oriented, careful nature. Question your lack of initiative, need for detail, small thinking, responsive side.
To work better with Analyticals: 1. Stress the need for facts and data rather than emotion, to build a case, but let them do the workup with a time limit. 2. Provide added opportunities for classwork and study in return for meeting activity standards. 3. Build confidence in the relationship through demonstrated technical competence.	*To work better with Drivers:* 1. Be businesslike, let them tell you how to help, what they want. Don't try to build a relationship/friendship. 2. Stay on schedule, stick to the agenda, provide factual summaries. 3. Let them make decisions based on options you provide. *Working with this style will require *you* to exercise *your* versatility.
They see you as supportive, quiet, friendly, shy, retiring, team oriented, helpful, kind, thoughtful, slow to act, nonthreatening, soft-hearted, easygoing, complying, responsive, open, willing, careful, cooperative.	Relate to your supportive, friendly, responsive, helpful characteristics. Question your slowness to act, and careful, complying, noncompetitive stance.
To work better with fellow Amiables: Being hardnosed, insistent, and directive is an uncomfortable role but a necessary one in this situation. Otherwise, it is likely that no one will take the necessary initiative and the end result will be unsatisfactory.	*To work better with Expressives:* 1. Try to bring them definite opinions, backed by third-party endorsement—don't waver. 2. Publicly recognize and praise their accomplishments. 3. Stand your ground when challenged on rules and previously established procedures.

Fig. 5-1. How others respond to an Amiable.

Analyticals	Drivers
Relate to your imaginative, stimulating, thought-provoking nature.	Relate to your outgoing, imaginative, competitive and personable aspects.
Question your ability to perform as stated, follow-through, and loud, flashy, emotional side.	Question your rah-rah, demonstrative, impulsive, emotional side.
To work better with Analyticals:	*To work better with Drivers:*
1. Talk facts, not opinions, and break down component parts, preferably in writing.	1. Back up your enthusiasm with actual results; demonstrate that your ideas work.
2. Back up your facts with proof from authoritative sources.	2. Be on time, and keep within agreed-upon limits, provide materials promptly.
3. Be quietly patient while they discover for themselves what you already know.	3. Provide choices of action where possible, and let the Driver select course of action.
*Working with this style will require *you* to exercise *your* versatility.	
Relate to your warmth, enthusiasm, and your stimulating and personable nature.	They see you as outgoing, enthusiastic, warm, opinionated, talkative, intuitive, emotional, stimulating, imaginative, impulsive, excitable, loud, flashy, dramatic, personable, competitive, caring.
Question your outgoing, loud, dramatic, impulsive side.	
To work better with Amiables:	*To work better with fellow Expressives:*
1. Slow down the pace and volume, allow time to build a relationship.	Provide the discipline in this relationship, or all the fun and creativity may accomplish nothing. Keep on track and emphasize the basics, allowing carefully limited experimentation as a reward for results.
2. Work on one item at a time, in detail; avoid the confusion of too many tasks or ideas at one time.	
3. Encourage suggestions, participation on team activities, supportive roles.	

Fig. 5-2. How others respond to an Expressive.

Relate to your efficiency, logic, command of data, and task orientation. Question your haste, bossiness, decisiveness, competitiveness, risk-taking. *To work better with Analyticals:* 1. Bring them detailed facts and logic in writing. 2. Be patient while they evaluate and check the accuracy of the data. 3. Help them come to conclusions by getting them to set deadlines after you have provided time for review.	They see you as action oriented, in a hurry, bossy, commanding, efficient, stubborn, disciplined, tough, independent, secretive, logical, demanding, nonlistening, quick, decisive, unfeeling. *To work better with fellow Drivers:* Agree in advance on specific goals, and provide freedom to work within these limits. An unproductive deadlock can occur when there is too much dominance and no allowance for independence and individuality.
Relate to your efficiency and discipline. Question your lack of feeling, tough-mindedness, bottom-line orientation, impatience, secretiveness. *To work better with Amiables:* 1. Show concern for them and their families, interests, etc. 2. Slow down, and provide detail and specifics on how to accomplish objectives. 3. Support efforts and accomplishments with personal attention. *Working with this style will require *you* to exercise *your* versatility.	Relate to your accomplishments, independence, decisiveness. Question your coldness, lack of playfulness, critical nature, discipline. *To work better with Expressives:* 1. Be more open about self, feelings, gossip, opinions. 2. Relax time constraints within structure, give incentives. 3. Provide public recognition for accomplishments—let them win in front of others.

Fig. 5-3. How others respond to a Driver.

They see you as thoughtful, wanting more facts, conservative, quiet, critical, logical, cool toward others, thorough, cooperative, distant, reserved, stern, austere, dependable, accurate. *To work better with fellow Analyticals:* Recognize the need for making timetables and for reaching decisions. Reinforcing each other's desire for more information may form a self-perpetuating cycle that doesn't bring results.	Relate to your logic, command of data, accuracy, dependability. Question your overabundance of facts, lack of decisiveness, and lack of risk-taking. *To work better with Drivers:* 1. Summarize facts with various outcomes; let them decide. 2. Depend on self-discipline rather than excessive reports, precise instructions. 3. Recognize results with monetary rewards.
Relate to your cooperative, conservative nature, accuracy, patience. Question your lack of warmth and close relationships, dependence on figures. *To work better with Amiables:* 1. Show your interest in them as people, rather than as workers. 2. Use their skills as mediators to build relationships inside the organization. 3. Help them see the big picture and how they relate to it.	Relate to your cooperativeness, dependability. Question your dependence on facts, critical, stuffy nature, impersonal approach, lack of fun. *To work better with Expressives:* 1. Spend "informal" time with them. 2. Recognize their need for package sales, incentives, contests. 3. Ask for their opinions and input on a noncritical, accepting basis. *Working with this style will require *you* to exercise *your* versatility.

Fig. 5-4. How others respond to an Analytical.

the way you do. Then, don't interfere, but watch, and try to understand, how the person handles the assignment. You'll probably end up admitting that the means used weren't like yours, but the results were successful. You are becoming more tolerant of another's social style—and more versatile.

2. Each of us can practice less comfortable behaviors (growth actions) in order to expand the range of responses we can use in an interpersonal situation. The following examples are designed for a social setting where the consequences of the experiment won't jeopardize a job or a close relationship. If the experiment works well—you make others in the situation comfortable with your behavior—you can practice your new growth action in another appropriate situation. A suggested project is given for each style.

As you practice these suggestions, keep in mind that you're adding new nuances to your behavior, not trying to change your basic patterns. As you try the new kinds of behavior, you may feel so uncomfortable that you think you are failing. Keep trying; it takes continued effort before you'll reach a new level of interpersonal skill.

In addition, observe the effect your behavior has on others. For example, the Expressive is asked to tone down his "life of the party" behavior the next time he's in a social gathering. When he does, he may sense that people are disappointed when he refuses to tell his customary stories or jokes. If this happens, the Expressive should ask himself if it's possible that these same people *never* expect him to be able to carry out a serious endeavor, and do not know that he has a logical, thoughtful side to his nature. If this is the case, perhaps his rigid behavior patterns are leading to less social endorsement from others than he would like to have.

a. For Drivers: If your behavior is predominantly Driving, you may find that when you engage in a conversation, you tend to quickly see the point or draw a conclusion. Sometimes, your fast-paced, logical approach to problem solving is exactly what the other person is looking for. Other times, he or she would rather have you *listen.* To practice this less than comfortable behavior, the next time you are mingling at a party and a neighbor or casual acquaintance begins to tell you about an experience or a problem, simply listen, without trying to draw a conclusion or provide a solution.

For example, during the first few seconds of the conversation, respond by an encouraging nod of the head, direct eye contact, and a body posture (such as leaning forward) that suggests interest in what the person is saying. Then, use verbal responses that encourage the conversation to keep going in the other person's direction. Use phrases like, "oh, yes"; "that's interesting"; "tell me more." Let the other individual work out his or her own conclusion to the story or the problem, and don't offer advice unless specifically asked. Show some emotional interest in the person, but do it in a less assertive, more listening way.

b. For Analyticals: You probably have a number of firm convictions, but may hesitate to declare them to others, especially in an emotional way. To practice "declaring" behavior, choose something that interests you: a political petition, a neighborhood project, a church or club procedure you'd like changed, or a favorite charity, and set out to do something about it. If it's a petition you favor, take it personally to four or five people, sit down with them one at a time, and explain why you believe in the petition and why they should sign it. Don't state *all* the reasons, and don't just rely on factual, logical explanations for supporting the cause. Relate it to your feelings, too. Then, press for a response, a yes or no; don't settle for maybes. Declare yourself, and put some feeling into it!

c. For Amiables: If you exhibit Amiable behavior, you're generally willing to tackle a project—when asked—but you probably want to take your time and be sure everyone is satisfied with each step. So the next time a volunteer project comes along, whether it's a neighborhood get-together or a club lunch, speak up—volunteer to handle the job. But rather than taking your customary approach of checking and rechecking with people on dates, times, places, menus, and so forth, set a deadline for finishing the arrangements, check with the group *once,* and then make your decisions about the arrangements on the basis of your own judgment about the time and place best suited for the most people. Send out a memo detailing the arrangements, rather than going to each individual in person with your plan. And don't be tentative. If people complain that the time is inconvenient, don't back down. Politely, but firmly, explain that your decision is the best for the group as a whole. Initiate action, keep your emotional involvement down and the time constraints up!

d. For Expressives: If your behavior is primarily Expressive, your preference for seeking attention in a personable, competitive way may lead others to see you as the "life of the party." At the same time, you may tend to monopolize social gatherings with your jokes and antics. Or, if you're feeling irritable, you make your feelings quite obvious by completely withdrawing from the group and sulking. So the next time you're at a party, "check" your behavior—put some holds on your emotional, attention-seeking behavior. If there's a lull in the conversation, restrain yourself. Don't launch into a wild story or a joke. By the same token, don't duck out the back door or escape to a corner of the room. Instead, help others take up the conversational ball. Listen to them, and make comments that support their conversation—not yours. See if you can quietly and gently draw others into the group, rather than letting them sit on the sidelines listening to you. Restrain your impulsiveness!

3. Make a list of several acquaintances. Describe at least four of their behaviors and tentatively determine a style for them. Refer to the section in this chapter called "Do something for others," and choose a course of action for dealing with each person. Take some of these actions, and observe whether the person responds more positively to you. If these individuals are put off by your actions, you may have misjudged their styles. If so, reassess their behaviors, and adjust your approach to them accordingly. Which action project caused you the most tension? The tension may have resulted from a style conflict between yourself and the other individual, or it may be a reflection of less versatility on your part.

6

Style at Work

When we stop to think about it, our success on the job depends more on our relationships with people than we probably care to admit. It's a rare person who is able to rely solely on his own motivation and technical skills to get a job done. Instead, most of us work in environments in which we must constantly deal with people, and the more successful we are at this, the more satisfied we will be in our jobs. In fact, a study done by a New York-based management consulting firm showed that in 1979, 76 percent of the people who entered the firm's placement program had lost their previous jobs because of difficulties in interpersonal relationships, not because of technical incompetence. Thus our social style, which reflects the way we approach interpersonal situations, has numerous implications in the work world.

The vast majority of our research group's workshops have been given in business settings, and through them we have developed a great deal of information, both from personal observations and from discussions with people, about how style affects business relationships. This chapter will discuss some of the insights we have gained into style and occupation; style and type of business organizations; how people with different styles can work together; and how managers can best handle themselves and their employees to maximize style strengths and minimize style weaknesses.

OCCUPATIONS AND STYLE

Time and again, we have found that all four styles are represented in—and successful in—virtually any occupation. The behavior that seems to separate people who have succeeded in their occupations from others who are less successful is not their style, but their versatility. People who are successful seem to be better able to use adaptive interpersonal skills in order to demonstrate effective performance on the job.

For instance, if accounting work requires a very detailed, data-oriented approach, we might expect that, given a high level of technical competence, a person with predominantly Analytical behavior would fit most naturally into this occupation. Not necessarily. Although the behaviors required for accounting work might be comfortable for the Analytical, people with other styles can adapt their behaviors appropriately, if they have sufficient versatility and motivation.

An individual with Expressive behavior, for example, might be just as successful as the Analytical in the accounting profession, or more so. If Analytical behaviors, such as attending to details and logic, are crucial to the job, the Expressive can add these to his own behavior, at least while on the job. Of course, he would probably approach his work differently. We might expect that he would rely on personal contact with his data-entry support team rather than writing them memos; his office might sport a flashier calculator or a more imposing desk; and his clients might find that he looks for the "bigger and better" solution to their accounting problems, rather than using the more cautious, step-by-step approach generally taken by the Analytical. He may, indeed, attract a different type of client because of his style differences, but his success, in terms of prestige among his customers and peers, money earned, and so forth, could easily be just as great, or greater.

We have found, though, that certain styles gravitate to certain occupations in larger numbers because the job's behavior requirements match the individual's habitual style preferences. Sometimes a person is even pushed into an occupation by others because they think they see a match between the individual's behavior and the job's requirements. There are always exceptions to these generalizations, and, once again, there is no correlation between style and success, but there are some data to support the following observations.

AMIABLE: RELATIONSHIP SPECIALIST

When we look at careers such as teaching, personnel management, social work, psychology, and other helping professions, we see a large number of persons with the Amiable style entering these lines of work. We call persons who enter these career environments "relationship specialists"; to put it another way, persons with an Amiable style seem to be most comfortable working in environments where they can provide services and be supportive and helpful in their relationships with other people.

While people with every style can be found in each of these careers, if we zero in on an occupation's specialties, we often find a predictable pattern. For instance, the physician who is a general practitioner often has Amiable behavior. A doctor who teaches or does research is more likely to be Analytical. The doctor who is in charge of running a hospital often has a Driving style, and the doctor who writes books and regularly participates in talk shows is usually an Expressive.

ANALYTICAL: TECHNICAL SPECIALISTS

When we look at professions such as science, engineering, construction work, accounting, and law, we often find people with Analytical behavior. These individuals enter careers that support their style preferences to be "technical specialists."

Again, people with a variety of styles enter these professions, but they often gravitate into different specialities within the occupation. Taking the example of the law profession, lawyers who are more interested in trial law tend to have Expressive overtones to their styles; lawyers who teach the subject are likely to be Analytical; lawyers who head a law firm may have a Driving style; and lawyers who work in a storefront legal aid society often are Amiable in style.

DRIVER: COMMAND SPECIALIST

Owners of small businesses, top managers in businesses, production managers, administrative personnel, and politicians often show Driving patterns of behavior. Because of their ability to take responsibility and direct others, top management often puts these individuals into positions of control. Of course, there are many exceptions. Not all politicians or managers are "take-charge" people. But there does seem to be a cultural bias that looks for the Driving style when selecting what seems to be the best type of leader. Exceptions might include an Expressive as manager in a sales department, an Analytical as general manager for an engineering firm, or an Amiable as chief executive for a counseling center.

EXPRESSIVE: SOCIAL SPECIALIST

Persons with Expressive behavior are often found in sales, entertainment, advertising, art, music, and writing. We call these professionals "social specialists," primarily because they know how to use their social skills to gain recognition and attention and become highly visible to the public eye. Now, we certainly don't want to give the impression that all creative talent is associated with Expressive social behavior; our only observation is that people in those kinds of careers more often than not seem to be associated with the Expressive behavior pattern. As indicated earlier, you can find expressive accountants, but they approach their work with a social flair not usually associated with that occupation. The entertainer who is a political satirist may be driving, the entertainer who sings folk songs amiable, and the entertainer who provides news on TV analytical.

WHERE DOES SUCCESS LIE?

These, then, are generalizations about the relative *numbers* of individuals from any one style entering a certain line of work. Their *success* in their chosen profession, however, is another matter. As we have said earlier, people may be attracted to certain professions because of the work's compatibility with their styles; they may even be pushed into an occupation because *others* think their behavior is suitable to certain professions. Uncle John might tell his nephew, "You're so friendly to everyone. I bet you'd do great as a public relations man." Nevertheless, it's difficult to say that these individuals will be more

successful than someone with a different style in the same profession. That is why, for instance, there are successful managers
in all four styles, just as all styles are represented among successful salesmen, financial officers, or doctors.

As a case in point, we followed the study of a major Midwest-
ern insurance firm that decided to determine just what style was
most attracted to their type of selling. The results showed that
approximately 38 percent of their 3000-person sales force profiled were in the Expressive quadrant, with 27 percent in the
Driving quadrant, 24 percent in the Amiable quadrant, and 11
percent in the Analytical quadrant. Therefore, concluded the
firm, Expressives tend to be attracted to insurance selling in the
greatest numbers, with numbers about evenly split between
Driving and Amiable styles, and with the Analytical style being
the least attracted to such a career. It was interesting to note,
however, that among sales persons attending a conference to
recognize success in their careers, approximately the same number came from each of the four styles. So, though more Expressives were attracted to such a career, they did not perform any
better than the group least attracted to the career, the Analyticals, nor any better than the Driving or Amiable styles.

Thus, success is not a matter of style, but there is evidence
that success in certain jobs is related to the third dimension
of behavior—versatility.

Why? As discussed in Chapter 4, when people use versatility
in their relationships, they earn high endorsement from others.
People in certain positions, such as managers, politicians, and
salesmen, depend upon social endorsement to succeed at their
work. Thus some jobs inherently require more versatility for
success than others.

Our research group has had a great deal of experience in working with life insurance agents, and it's clear that there is a direct
relationship between higher versatility and increased success in
life insurance sales, as measured by survival in the career and the
level of commissions earned. For more detailed information on
our research in this area, see "Style and Success," in the appendix. The following story gives another example of the role that
versatility plays in job success.

Ann is a successful banker. The department she heads is one of the town's best-respected trust departments. Its solid nature is symbolized by the quiet decorum of the second floor of the First Bank & Trust Company which it occupies and by the behavior of the people who work in it. The hushed atmosphere is reminiscent of a mausoleum. The staff dresses conservatively, suggesting solid, old-world values that make customers feel that their money will be safe with the bank. The fact that the individuals who meet customers are senior staff members reveals the custodial attitude of this department toward the wealth of their customers. The younger staff members are pretty much behind the scenes in service and clerical capacities. Several quiet, bespectacled personnel remain in the background as analysts who determine the values of various securities.

Ann's behavior fits in well in this department. She is a serious, cautious individual who lives both her personal and public life in an exemplary manner. When she speaks, she expresses herself quietly and firmly, with the conviction of someone who has done her homework, and she inspires confidence almost more than anyone else who meets the bank's customers. She brings all the virtues of maturity, professionalism, and the title of a bank executive to bear on any relationship.

Almost like a librarian, she shakes her head and looks sternly in the direction of employees who enter the department with any of the hilarity that they worked up in an amusing conversation in the coffeeshop. It is significant to note that this behavior of Ann's is very similar to that of her predecessor, the elderly gentleman whose picture is now on the wall just inside the entrance to the department. The tradition of this trust function was established generations ago and has altered little over the years. Ann has fitted in well from the day she was assigned to this department, just after she finished her course as a management trainee, and she rose rapidly to the position she now holds as manager. One suspects that her success is not only the result of her hard work, willingness to study and be sure of her facts, and her ability to handle clients, but also because her demeanor brought her to the attention of the bank's officials long before she was given the assignment.

Bill is a successful banker. He has, for some years, represented the First Bank & Trust Company as a loan officer, and now he is a senior officer of the bank. His role from the beginning with the bank has been that of a marketer, functioning well in a department of other sales-oriented personnel. He now directs those who are responsible for construction loans, and his function involves meeting some of the bank's more outgoing customers, who represent a rather entrepreneurial, slam-bang approach to life, people who run speculative enterprises and develop subdivisions and shopping centers.

When Bill enters the department, it is usually in a noisy, hail-fellow-well-met manner, either with a new story about the client he has just met or a new joke that he just added to his repertoire. Bill's rise in this department has been rapid because from the moment he entered it, his behavior was appropriate to the outgoing sales atmosphere which already existed in the commercial loan department. He quickly learned the public contact and loan officer roles, and he has dealt well with business clients, showing a willingness to be helpful and making positive, constructive recommendations to his customers.

When someone enters the department whom Bill recognizes (and he always looks up from whatever he's doing to see who has come in), he is most likely to either call to them from across the room or get up and walk toward them, so that he can shake hands. Public relations is obviously uppermost in his mind.

The board at the First Bank and Trust Company is faced with a decision: They must fill the vacant post of senior vice-president. The board is considering Ann, and it is also considering Bill. Both are successful bankers. Both have also demonstrated their ability to work with other people in the bank in a flexible and adaptive manner, accommodating the special preferences of their fellow employees (subordinates and peers alike). Both are respected by the senior officers of the bank, some preferring Bill's more sociable approach and others preferring Ann's businesslike manner. Ann and Bill work well together when working with common clients, showing respect and support for each other.

Puzzled as to what should be their course of action, the directors of the bank have looked at other bank officers around the town to determine the pattern of successful senior officers, but they find no help there. Some are ex-marketing people like Bill; others are ex-stewards of the funds like Ann. The last comment to come out of the board's meeting about the imminent promotion is that it's too bad there aren't two parallel jobs available.

Our immediate reaction to this story might be, "Ann and Bill were just lucky. They happened to get into departments that suited their *styles,* and so they were successful." Often we assume that the only reason for an individual's success is because his or her behavior fits in comfortably with a certain job situation. However, if we think about this a little more, we'll realize that both Ann and Bill had to deal with a variety of people—senior bank officers, employees, peers, and customers. That they could do this well while gaining endorsement from those who came in contact with them is a truer reason for their success.

Indeed, if Bill happened to be transferred to the trust department and Ann to the loan department, we might expect that they would feel some tension in dealing with a less comfortable work environment. But the fact that both Ann and Bill have done well in a variety of interpersonal encounters in the past suggests that they have the sensitivity and ability to accommodate others no matter what the social mix of styles or the situation. Thus, it would not be surprising if they carried off the transition with a minimum of conflict. Although their styles and their original jobs happened to "fit," it is their versatility that contributed most to their job success.

Both Ann and Bill were called back for more interviews. Just as in real life, there are no obvious solutions to this dilemma. Perhaps the job went to the person with the most seniority. Perhaps internal politics dictated the decision. Possibly the board eventually brought in someone from outside the organization to fill the position. Whatever happened, though, chances are that neither Ann nor Bill would have been considered for the job in the first place if it hadn't been for their versatility.

Of course, versatility is *not* equally crucial to success in all careers. For example, if technical competence is of prime importance for a person to be effective in a given profession, then the most successful engineer might be the individual with the most knowledge and talent, and the most successful heart surgeon might be the physician with the most competence. In both of these cases, they have little need to deal skillfully with the interpersonal aspects of their jobs to be judged successful. They are successful by virtue of sheer competence and hard work.

However, the heart surgeon's patients or the engineer's co-workers would probably appreciate a show of versatility, because it would make their interactions with these professionals much more comfortable. In addition, it's unlikely that these two individuals will move into new areas of endeavor as they progress through their careers, because such opportunities almost always require people to adjust to new interpersonal situations in an adaptable way. The engineer, for example, would have a difficult time if he accepted an offer to manage a group of engineers, and the less versatile heart surgeon might become very uncomfortable if he were expected to represent other physicians in negotiations with a hospital. If the engineer's and the surgeon's definitions of success in their careers do not include moving into such situations, then their lack of versatility will not get in the way of their careers. But if these individuals want to expand their job horizons, versatility will be key to their long-term success.

ORGANIZATIONAL STYLE

Not only does style relate to certain job requirements, but it is also a factor in the business organization itself. While it is certainly true that most large organizations have enough of a mix of styles to meet the needs of various clients and situations, it is also true that large organizations tend to take on the flavor of the individuals with authority. If those at the top are Analytical in style, for example, the organization tends to be highly organized with many specific rules and procedures, and employees with other styles play off of, and seek exceptions to, that procedural orientation. We find Drivers seeking independence from, and exceptions to, all the rules and regulations; Expressives being forgetful and perhaps deliberately skipping as many of the requirements as possible; and Amiables being compulsive and conforming to the point where they may fail to participate or to influence the organization at all.

As another illustration, if Expressives are at the top of the organizational chart, they tend to be informal and other styles will play off this influence. Drivers may seek to create more of a goal orientation; Analyticals will try to institute more procedures; and the Amiables, while fitting in to a certain extent, will be somewhat uncomfortable, or even aghast, at the fast-moving pace and sometimes frightening lack of consistency seen in the freewheeling Expressive organization.

In a medium-sized organization, where there isn't such a well-distributed representation of all the various styles, we often find that an individual with a style completely opposite to that of those in leadership or management positions may find the circumstances very uncomfortable, even intolerable, so much so that he or she may leave the job. In still smaller organizations, we have observed that too much of one style can come to predominate, as the leaders tend to build around themselves a group of people with similar styles.

Of course, such an organization can succeed, but with certain limitations. For instance, an organization made up entirely of Expressives may, in the eyes of others, create a chaotic situation, or as the saying goes, "create chaos out of order." When the group succeeds, it is usually the result of individual commitment, creativity, and a high level of energy. These people grab results out of seeming disorder and move along in a course of ups and downs, rather than with a uniform effort.

Completely opposite to this kind of organization would be one made up predominantly of Analyticals. Here, we would see a rather carefully developed, deliberate plan that results in systematic progress toward a positive, and completely expected, result. Often this kind of organization seems to lack excitement, but it can continue to succeed, although in a rather mechanical way.

The more Driving small organization pushes ahead, building quickly from one step to the next and achieving results, although sometimes at great cost of wasted energy and activity. In its insistence on *some* kind of activity, the Driving organization, like the Expressive, often seems to leave behind a rather confused history of results, although it tends to move ultimately toward a definite goal.

An Amiable group can easily find strength in the firm's small size, establish very positive relationships among coworkers and clients, and provide good service. Their drawback, though, is that they may fail to take the initiative to capitalize on their corporate assets and develop much company growth.

In all of these cases, it's fairly easy to see that a balance of styles would be more productive and healthy for the organization than remaining top-heavy with one style. In many cases, adding a different style is the answer to turning a company into a more balanced, and therefore more productive, enterprise. Sometimes this move requires a change of management and leadership, to create the increased activity necessary to make a well-developed Analytical organization grow; to provide the improved system and management that will channel the creativity of an Expressive organization toward a profitable result; to build in a flexible structure and foundation of personnel to support the fast growth of a Driving organization; or to move an Amiable organization from a solid, but slow, growth rate to a more dynamic pace.

In general, organizations with a good representation of at least three or four styles have the ability to survive in times of change. On the other hand, organizations with a more homogeneous makeup tend to be unable to adapt to what can be serious problems when leadership is removed for one reason or another. For example, imagine a sales organization composed of Expressive individuals who relate to each other at an exciting, friendly level, and who encourage and support one another in a rather fun-loving, easygoing approach to business. What would happen if the top manager left the organization and his position was filled with an individual whose style was very unresponsive?

The new manager might, from the very beginning, demonstrate a less than tolerant attitude toward the (in his opinion) flippant, careless manner of the sales force. He might try to install procedures that are burdensome and unnecessary to Expressive people, and, as a result, the old salesmen might leave the company because they just plain can't get along with the new boss. This is not at all an unusual circumstance, and even though the new manager might say that he intends to keep a low profile and not make any changes, the very way in which he declares that intention can be uncomfortable for the sales force.

If many salesmen quit in a short period of time, the new manager might fill in the gaps with people whose styles are closer to his own. Again, these new people could also find themselves in conflict with the existing staff. Of course, the manager is correct to add style variety, but timing is important, and drastic style changes should only be made gradually, and when the organization is running smoothly. It's unwise to change style if the new employees are to be put into critical positions, at critical times. By knowing an organization's style patterns, top management can choose personnel whose styles complement those that are already present in the company, and avoid disrupting the organization.

TEAMING UP

Thus the strongest organization will combine various styles in a deliberately planned way, so that all the activities required for success can be provided either by individuals who have the behavior patterns to comfortably handle the assignment or by very versatile, adaptable people.

For instance, work teams or task forces can be strengthened by considering style when making assignments. An example would be a conscious effort to build a team that includes an individual who is either an Expressive or an Amiable to deal with the customer's relationship needs, backed up by a task-oriented individual—an Analytical or a Driver—who can insure precision when dealing with data and facts. In a negotiation, it would be well to plan a team composed of a fairly forceful, assertive individual, balanced by someone who is more inclined to use an asking, data-gathering approach.

In sales activities, two types of teams have been very effective. One is the door-opening individual with a Driving style who deals with the first necessities of pushing the sale to a close. This individual then works with a more Amiable-styled person who provides the necessary service and support activity that keeps the sale sold. A second team includes a door-opening Expressive who works to establish rapport with the potential client. This individual then is backed up by a technically oriented Analytical who provides specifics and helps define the best solution for the customer's needs.

In management, similar double-teaming efforts are also effective. If the assertive, fast-moving style of a manager creates too much tension for employees, it is sometimes better for an individual with a less assertive style to provide a modifying influence, rather than for the manager to shift gears himself. It's also possible for a technically oriented, less assertive manager to use a more assertive, pace-setting second-in-command to help get results. If these patterns are developed deliberately and consciously, they are much more likely to be effective than if they are formed by accident.

Using the concept of social style to determine how people behave can be invaluable for organizations as a whole. One large corporation we know of seemed to have an entirely different relationship with customers in the Northern part of the country than it did in the South. The people who represented the company in the Northern region were found to be task-oriented Analyticals and Drivers, and the firm was seen as impersonal, harsh, and overly businesslike. The representatives in the Southern region were relationship-oriented Amiables and Expressives, who created an image of a company that was friendly, supportive, and willing to "give the farm away." Once this situation became apparent, management was able to create some balance by shifting personnel.

In the past, many managers have been aware of the significance of what they have perhaps called "personality" or "managerial style." They have not, though, had a systematic style model to follow. The ability to measure social style and act on this knowledge can play a significant role in almost any type of management decision making.

WORKING TOGETHER

An organization that does employ a variety of styles should also be aware of the friction that can arise when behavioral preferences conflict, especially between individuals with nonversatile behavior. It is common for an individual who feels uncomfortable in the presence of another style not only to retreat into his or her own behavioral style, but to take countermeasures against the other person by emphasizing his or her habitual actions even more than usual.

For example, a Driving individual may see a person with an Amiable style as lacking in goal orientation. To compensate, the Driver may push for the goals, emphasize the need for results, and try to make up for what he or she sees as missing in the Amiable's behavior.

The Amiable, in turn, sees the Driver's behavior as impersonal and lacking in team effort. The Amiable may attempt to compensate for the Driver's apparent indifference by working even harder than normal at soothing ruffled feathers.

The Analytical might take countermeasures against the Amiable style by trying to superimpose systems and procedures to a machinelike degree. Again, the Amiable individual will attempt to balance the situation by injecting even more of a cooperative team spirit. And an Expressive might try to infuse excitement and stimulation into a situation in order to speed up the movement, and be countered by the Amiable, who slows down the pace in order to make sure that no one gets left behind.

Other combinations can also create conflicts. For example, if a person with Driving behavior is in charge of a small organization, this person is likely to push the team at a fast pace by prescribing goals, objectives, and the kinds of follow-up activity expected. The Expressive may counter this by questioning the directions given and expressing concern for the effect that the proposed plan might have on others. The Analytical may appear to drag his or her feet by accepting the goal, but questioning the pace and specifics of the directions. The Amiable may attempt to meet the task requirements dictated by the Driver but may nevertheless try to hold onto preexisting routines and purposes as a kind of security.

The problem with these seesaw activities is that they leave other people who must deal with the work group confused about the direction in which it is attempting to go. An exciting potential for a productive balance of styles exists, but when the organization is not able to utilize these style differences in a positive way, the clashes we have described occur.

The one person in the work group most directly responsible for helping others work together is the manager. Because this individual occupies such a key position, the following discussion will focus on managers and their use of social style.

MANAGERIAL STYLE

Just as each style can do well in any occupation, we have also found that each style has the potential to succeed in some area of management. Let's look at the positive and negative sides of each of the four styles as they apply to management.

On the positive side of Analytical behavior in a management situation is the tendency of the individual to be cautious and careful, seeking to put things in proper perspective and anticipating all of the various consequences before taking action. This is bound to be an asset in any group activity, as long as the cautiousness is not overdone. But when the careful planning approach of the Analytical begins to interfere with the preferred activities of the others, the manager's workers may begin to view him or her as indecisive, and tension may build because employees are not seeing results as quickly as they want to.

Driving behavior, which involves taking charge, making decisions, and getting things moving along, is also an appreciated asset when this kind of management task must be tackled. Of course, once again, if it is overdone it can lose its beneficial aspects. If the manager's team is not getting the results it desires, team members may begin to see the Driving behavior as counterproductive, because they perceive it as wasteful of effort and energy, precipitous, and contributing to misdirection.

The light, cheerful, move-ahead attitude taken by Expressives is also clearly a management asset, particularly in those situations where defined action is not possible and where social skills are a prime necessity. An Expressive management style can be particularly important when human relationships are tenuous and need an injection of good spirit. If overdone, however, Expressives can be seen as careless, prima-donna-like, and wasteful of time and energy, which others feel should be applied to the job in order to get results.

The positive aspects of the management style of Amiables revolve around their supportive behavior, which can be particularly beneficial where service to others and continuous relationships are required. If overdone, however, the Amiable approach can appear to lack a sense of responsibility, leaving too much in the hands of others. If the group is not achieving the desired end, the manager's behavior can be seen by others as passive, dependent, and lacking in goal-orientation.

What then is the best type of manager? Our observation is that managerial success is not associated with any one style, *if* versatility is present. Success is more a matter of what kind of performance is expected from the manager and the ability of the individual to adapt to these requirements. Of course, certain areas of management may appeal more to one style than another. Analyticals may be attracted to financial management, Expressives to sales management, Drivers to administrative management, and Amiables to personnel management. There is no reason, though, why an individual with any social style could not complete any management task if he or she has adequate versatility skills.

VERSATILITY AND MANAGERS

Versatility, which we can define here as the ability to deal with the many types of interpersonal situations which confront a manager in a resourceful and adaptable way, is required in most managerial circumstances. In fact, it's not difficult to imagine that the manager might have to use appropriate actions from all four styles in order to succeed at a job. In the planning, scheduling, and organization of activity, for example, behaviors typical of the Analytical would be employed. Giving directions and taking the responsibility to exercise control—typical Driving behaviors—are required of most managers. In almost all situations, a degree of stimulation, motivation, and cheerleading such as Expressives might demonstrate is a very strong asset. And, finally, dealing with personnel in the role of a counselor or a supportive, helpful mentor involves behavior which we have described as Amiable. The manager doesn't change his basic style as he does all this, but he should be aware that behaviors typical of styles other than his own can be very appropriate in some cases. Thus, accommodating oneself to the requirements of other people in various situations is an important skill for most managers.

Of course, there are always exceptions. For instance, Drivers with low versatility can succeed as managers, but usually in jobs that demand fewer supportive skills and instead allow them to use the authoritative, production-oriented approaches that are typical of Driving behavior. We have found that there are some job settings where it appears that workers actually prefer to have a decisive, authoritarian boss, as long as they have other strong incentives to get the job done. On the other hand, when workers are more productive in a setting that allows collaboration and provides freedom for individuals to independently achieve goals, managers probably need to exercise versatility to be successful. Thus, versatility is particularly important if, by success in management, we mean the ability to work with people in such a way that relationships don't become a vicious cycle of defensive reactions and interactions.

We are convinced that understanding social style and attempting to use versatility skills in the work setting can ultimately increase productivity in most job situations. But, organizations cannot expect short-term, immediate results, reflected on the bottom line of a profit sheet.

One reason for this, of course, is that it is impossible for industry to measure the net effect of turnover and employee dissatisfaction that results from poor communication inside the organization. There is no way to quantify the nonproductive antagonism that can develop between people such as salesmen and financial managers, or personnel and production managers, and the resulting loss of productivity.

In fact, most organizations avoid dealing with these conflicts at all, shrugging them off with the attitude that "it's all just a matter of human nature, and something we can't do anything about." We emphatically disagree. We have observed organizations that have conducted workshops in which people learn to understand and accept different styles and make efforts to improve versatility within the organization. In these situations, we have watched productivity, retention, and job performance improve. It's slow, and it takes continuing effort, particularly on the part of top management, to reap the benefits of such an approach, but it does work. Nothing strengthens an organization more than an atmosphere in which coworkers respect and support each other. Unfortunately, the pressures of meeting short-term goals, time constraints, and limitations of resources often cause organizations to seek more readily observable ways to increase productivity (see Figure A-4, Appendix).

Thus, there is still a great frontier for improving productivity by understanding social style and improving the skills for communicating in a more versatile manner. In the simplest terms, we are talking about reducing the amount of defensiveness between manager and employees, among peers, and among an organization's departments. If one just stops to think a moment about the hours spent resolving the differences that grow out of defensive cycles of interaction, or, for that matter, from attempts that people make to try to get other people to behave the way they'd like them to (usually a fruitless effort), it's easy to see that a basic understanding and acceptance of style differences could go a long way toward clearing up some of these conflicts.

For the manager, or indeed for anyone, the first step in using style at work is to consider the following fact: People need to be treated in a way that makes them feel reasonably comfortable if they are going to perform at their highest potential. When we say that an employee is not motivated, we may be saying that the employee is not doing what *we* want him to do. But if we use our styles effectively, we recognize that our job is to look at our own behavior and the tensions it may be causing for others. We must ask, "What can I do to *me* that will make it easier for other people to be productive?" rather than "What do I do to *other* people to motivate them?" We must learn how to observe our own behavior at work, as well as observing others' reactions to us. And rather than trying to change other people's behavior, we must care enough to do something about the way we act with our coworkers and employees. We've adopted a name for this effort—The Platinum Rule, or "Do for others what they would like to have done for them." This contrasts with the Golden Rule ("Do unto others as you would have others do unto you"). In other words, the Golden Rule implies that we don't steal from others because we would not like someone else to steal from us. We support the Golden Rule as an ethical principle; however, the key to effective interpersonal relations and succeeding with style is to recognize that differences between people do exist and that we should treat others the way *they'd* prefer to be treated.

STYLE AND YOUR EMPLOYEES

In this section we offer some style considerations for recruiting, selecting, training, and supervising employees. For more information on how to work with various styles, review Chapter 5. As you read this information, remember that if you offer employees what you haven't got—for example, try to recruit an Amiable by insuring him personal, thorough training when your company offers no such program—your recruit will see you as a manipulator, in the worst sense of the word. If you do deliver what you say you will, though, you are adapting yourself to the needs of your employees in a positive, productive way.

Recruiting

The Amiable: The following will appeal to the Amiable: a warm, friendly, team-building organization; opportunities to give service to others as part of the job; one-on-one supervision; and people the Amiable can feel free to call on to discuss business and personal problems.

The Expressive: People with this style will be attracted by opportunities to follow their dreams for success; a training program that gets them off to a quick start; testimony about how others have succeeded in the job; and suggestions about how they can get special recognition for their work.

The Driver: The Driver will be looking for a company that will give him or her an opportunity to earn in relation to individual effort and the chance to work fast, independently, and on complex projects. Career paths, company training, financial incentives, and specific milestones to shoot for are important to the Driver.

The Analytical: This person will want adequate training, backup experts, reasonable earnings, and the opportunity to further his or her professionalism through additional training.

Selecting

The Amiable: Don't leap to a decision to hire the Amiable because you "like" his or her warm style. Check to make sure the individual has a successful record in past jobs and can initiate action. Are you willing to provide thorough training for the Amiable and give him or her frequent attention if the individual joins your company?

The Expressive: Don't be swept along with the Expressive's enthusiasm and optimism. Check on such things as the individual's past work record and earnings, as well as the follow-through ability of the Expressive. Find out if the outside activities frequently engaged in by the Expressive will interfere with his or her work.

The Driver: If you hire this individual, be prepared for an independent, know-it-all, cool, fast-paced person. Can your organization provide the big projects and complex situations this individual may want to handle? Will you be able to integrate the Driver into your team efforts?

The Analytical: Can you adapt to this individual's questioning, probing, deliberate challenges to your training and programs? Are you willing to supply the technical expertise to train and support the Analytical's efforts throughout his career with your company?

Training

The Amiable: The Amiable will want detailed, step-by-step training; support, help, and friendly encouragement; and specific procedures to follow. Follow-up and feedback from the manager are important. Insist on completion of all training requirements and stress the importance of maintaining a high activity level. Don't let them become discouraged by failures. Stress the law of averages.

The Expressive: Keep the Expressive on track; insist on discipline, structure, and playing by the rules. Expressive people can quickly become discouraged, so make sure that their expectations remain realistic. They also like an exciting idea and may want to cut corners and overlook details in their haste to get ahead with a project that they are enthused about. Stress the importance of paying attention to details, following established procedures, and developing good work habits. Provide public recognition and rewards for achievements.

The Driver: You must sell Drivers on the business and how it can help him or her to succeed, or the individual will soon leave. This person can be vocal and critical about everything and everybody, so, during training, make sure that the Driver learns to listen to others and learns how to make positive, constructive suggestions to others. Insist on routine training and activities, but allow the Driver to waive some rules if results are forthcoming. Set high goals against which the Driver can measure performance; recognize accomplishments with financial rewards; and check to see that the individual doesn't ignore daily activities in order to concentrate solely on the big project.

The Analytical: Stress specific performance requirements to counter the Analytical's tendency to want to know all the details before beginning a project. Encourage him or her to become a little more casual and warm toward others. Go slowly during training, show evidence that your suggestions work, and insist on establishing deadlines and production goals.

Supervising

The Amiable: Continue to provide a detailed and structured environment; spell out all instructions carefully. The Amiable will feel more confident, understanding how he or she fits into the overall plan or activity. Make sure the Amiable is not neglecting individual achievement for the sake of good relationships. Make yourself available to review the Amiable's performance, and then take time to listen to success stories and personal anecdotes.

The Expressive: Keep Expressives on track and organized. Help them do what they say they will do by reviewing progress regularly. Give them competitive challenges and inspiration. They will appreciate having accomplishments publicly recognized, so try to get their names into print or congratulate them at group meetings.

The Driver: Give Drivers options, rather than shoving decisions down their throats. Do not check on them excessively or require numerous reports. Drivers want performance measured in terms of results. Make sure that they understand what is expected and that they agree with performance standards and detail requirements. Insist that they supplement the big, complex deal with the practical, everyday requirements of the job.

The Analytical: Help Analyticals find a balance between data collection and action. Allow them to use logical problem-solving approaches, and take advantage of this strength. Provide an opportunity for Analyticals to excel by offering them continued training and knowledge. Secure their commitment to a program by making sure that they agree to a plan and schedule, and by sticking to it yourself.

Practice Suggestions

1. Each of us can improve our own effectiveness on the job if we make an effort to minimize the weaknesses of our style. The following are projects for each of the four styles. Try a project yourself, and, if you are a manager, you might encourage your less versatile employees to try one. If you are doing the project yourself, discuss it with either your manager or with a coworker to get additional feedback about your progress.

a. For the Amiable: Amiables frequently hesitate to ask for things that they need because they fear they may be imposing. If this is your style, list the facts you need to know for a job situation and check off the information as it is obtained. Then get the remaining facts by simply asking for them.

A second difficulty sometimes encountered by Amiables is that people take advantage of their good nature. To let these people know that you won't be "run over" or used, you should think back to instances where you provided service or spent time making a point, but no action was taken by the other person. In these cases, go back and get a decision or set a timetable for action. Press for results; don't let people put you off. Avoid the tendency to empathize with coworkers and clients so strongly that you hesitate to ask for anything or make any demands of them.

b. For the Expressive: As one project, ask yourself if anyone has commented recently on your messy desk, incomplete information on an expense account, or a late weekly report. Following up on these details may be dull and uninteresting to you, but they are important to keep work on schedule. Make a complete list of all expenses for the week, keep weekly reports up to date, or clean your desk of all extraneous materials. Then, stand by and observe the reaction from others to this change in your behavior.

Another project involves the fact that Expressives often find it tough to build a relationship with people who are fact-oriented, cool, questioning, and unresponsive. To ease this difficulty, identify a fellow worker or client who fits this description. Look for an opportunity to discuss the style system discussed in this book, and ask that person how you can work more effectively with him by using this system.

Your reluctance to attend to details can be countered by keeping records of things important to you: how well you are doing on the job, or what activities you plan. Write these items down as a type of realistic work plan, and keep track of the results.

c. For the Driver: The first project idea concerns the observation that many people find the forceful, fact-oriented approaches of Drivers cold and distant. They miss the personal touch, and a show of concern for them as individuals, with feelings and interests outside of business. To improve in this area, make an effort to inject some personal conversation into your meeting with clients or coworkers by discussing families, sports, or the personal side of your jobs. Then, listen and respond to what you hear. This will help you to appear more human and warm.

Drivers can also create "love 'em and leave 'em" feelings in those whom they deal with—the feeling that they are interested only while results are in the offing, but hard to find when projects have been completed. To temper this tendency, develop programs that will remind other people of your interest in them periodically. This could be a regular memo, a phone call, or a short visit with others, at times when you do not have a business need to contact them.

The third project revolves around your apparent lack of empathy, impatience to move ahead, know-it-all attitude, aloofness, and lack of sharing. To moderate this appearance, choose someone in the organization whom you feel you rub the wrong way. Ask to buy the person a cup of coffee, tell him or her you are concerned with the individual's feeling about you, and ask for an explanation about what happened. Don't defend yourself, however. Instead, ask the question, "What can I do to improve this situation?" Listen, and let their answers make a difference in what you do.

d. For the Analytical: The first recommended activity revolves around the fact that other people may describe the Analytical person as someone who is overly cautious and who does not show much concern or feel much concern for others. To counter this, start with something as simple as using first names. Also, when presenting a position, try to explain your points in terms of people, by saying, for example, "This would be for Sam's benefit," and when reading information, relate the notes you jot in the margins to people.

Your peers may also feel that you are quite stiff and formal, and interpret this to mean that you look down on them. Have coffee or visit with peers occasionally and ask about—and listen to—their most interesting work projects or personal anecdotes. Try wearing brighter or more casual clothes to the office and when meeting with clients.

The last suggestion concerns the observation that although your ability to be a cooperative and willing listener has its positive side, this trait can backfire if others take advantage of it by continually putting off decisions which you need them to make. More often than not, you would probably prefer to let this happen, rather than get embroiled in conflict. So make a list of everyone who has said they would talk to you, or get something done for you, "later." Call these people and set up an appointment, or firm up a due date for a piece of work. Pin these individuals down to a definite time, even if it has to be two weeks hence.

7

Style in the Community
and at Home

When we leave work at the end of the day and return to our
private lives, we carry our social styles with us. Style can be
found at PTA meetings, church bazaars, neighborhood block
parties, tennis club matches—and in our homes.

When we interact with casual acquaintances or participate in
community activities, we behave very much the way we do at
work. For example, a person with a Driving style who volunteers
to help set up a marathon being run for charity would probably
take charge of the entire event. On the other hand, the person
with Analytical style who volunteers for the same committee
might prefer to help out by keeping track of the pledges.

In a community setting, though, there's generally less tension
than at work and, consequently, less need to use backup styles.
Although organizing a Red Cross fund drive can be demanding, it
also has a recreational aspect, and since we participate in such
activities by choice, the tension is not as great as it often is at
work. So, while there is basically no difference between the
style we use at work and that which we use in the community, in
recreational situations we tend to use our styles in a more relaxed, positive manner.

We also use our characteristic styles at home. This surprises
many people, and during our workshops participants often tell us
that they act differently at home than they do at work. In a way,
they are right; however, as we will explain below, the difference
they are talking about is not so much a difference in style as a
difference in versatility. Frequently, individuals also tell us, after
we have described their social style, "But I know this is not the

way my family sees me." Once again, they are probably right, even though style cannot be shed at the front door along with our overcoats and, in fact, was actually learned at home when we were children, as we explained in an earlier chapter.

We'd like to suggest that people close to us have difficulty defining our social styles because they do not see our behaviors objectively. Personal relationships are more complex than work-related relationships; values, beliefs, attitudes, and emotional and sexual involvement can all blur perspectives. Remember we are only discussing what others can describe about what you say and do. In a close personal relationship, shared religious beliefs may do more to hold a relationship together than concern with the superficial behavior we describe as social style. People living together accept the values that hold the relationship intact and very often are inattentive to specific behaviors or completely accepting of any behavior because a marriage relationship is more important than personal habit patterns. In Chapter 1, we quoted Dr. Willard Gaylin, "I will not be told that a young man who earns his pocket money by mugging old ladies is really a good boy." What tends to happen with close personal relationships is that we become involved with the total personality of others, like their beliefs, and establish emotional ties which change our perspectives of a person. When you observe style you don't see beliefs or values. Our discussion up to this point has looked at habit patterns, not beliefs, values and attitudes, and these have a major influence on personal relationships. The mother of the boy who went to jail for mugging little old ladies still believes he is "really a good boy." Style deals only with what the boy did and said, not emotional ties or beliefs about a good or potentially good person.

In a more everyday way, it is helpful to recognize that, after we establish a close personal relationship, we are not only poor observers of these close friends, but we sometimes do not even see obvious little changes in things as simple as personal appearance.

There's probably not a wife in the country who, at one time or another, hasn't said, "You never noticed my new dress." For that matter, a husband we know once told us that it took his wife seven days to realize he had shaved off his mustache. At home, we get so used to one another and build up such a matrix of interrelated habit patterns that we often go through an entire week, month, or even a year without taking time to observe specific actions.

Cultural stereotypes that are part of our traditional ideas about home and family also get in the way of objective observations of style. We often find that men in our workshops want to think that they have Driving styles, because they associate that type of behavior with authority, confidence, control, and with masculine behavior. Women, on the other hand, often want to be thought of as warm, supportive, and caring—characteristics of the Amiable style traditionally thought of as "feminine." Although traditional male/female family roles have started to change, these stereotypes still exist and do cloud perceptions of style at home.

But despite cultural dictates, our research has shown that these stereotypes do not hold true. There are as many males with Driving, Amiable, Analytical, and Expressive styles as there are females with Driving, Amiable, Analytical, and Expressive styles.

Taking all of these factors into consideration, then, it's not hard to understand why, when describing our social styles, those close to us "can't see the forest for the trees."

STYLE AND THE FAMILY

Even though family members usually don't consciously observe behavior, whenever people live together closely, style, even if not identified in our terms, becomes very predictable. Certain people are counted on to behave in certain ways, not just by the immediate family, but also by aunts, uncles, cousins, and in-laws.

When a good, logical solution to a problem is required, stable, thoughtful George will be asked for his opinion. When no one agrees on the way to handle a crisis, Annette, who is always so decisive, will be called on to break the impasse. When Aunt Marie is upset, Harry will be asked to intervene, because he is always sensitive to other people. And when an amusing experience occurs, Donna will be asked to recount it, because she will do it better than anyone else, using animation and gestures, and perhaps even exaggerating a bit.

It would be impossible to describe all of the interactions—both positive and negative—of different styles within the home. Among brothers and sisters, for example, most of us have seen cases where two children in a family with Expressive styles regularly engage in combat. At the same time, these children have a great deal of fun together, and others marvel at their creativity. And one can bet that years later they'll look back on the great times they had in childhood.

Similarly, we can see families where a child with an Expressive style is contrasted with a more Amiable-style offspring. Periodically, friends and relatives will remark that if it weren't for the patience and easygoing nature of one child, the more outgoing, and often more irritable, sibling wouldn't have been allowed to live.

As we've indicated earlier, most of these behavioral preferences are formed early in life, usually by the age of five, and are reinforced by parents, teachers, and peers. And because people learn to behave the way they do by imitating and satisfying those around them, they have quite an emotional investment in their styles. For this reason, it's important not to tamper with or try to change another person's style; in most cases, doing so will meet not only with resistance, but also with resentment. This is especially true with children, who will develop behavioral patterns that help them feel comfortable in the presence of their parents or other significant persons, whether or not their parents consciously try to influence the child to have a certain style.

If parents have two different styles, and don't understand each other's approaches, the child can be in for a frustrating experience. But when parents with different styles show a wide range of appropriate responses—for example, giving strict discipline when it is needed and patient understanding at other times—the child will benefit from relating to each parent in a different way. In fact, the healthiest family is the one that includes and accepts all styles without making any value judgments about them. If parents label one style good and another bad, they will certainly create discomfort, if not more serious developmental problems, for the child with the "bad" style.

The oldest child in the family is usually most influenced by the behavioral preferences of the parents, and will often follow one of their styles. The rest of the children, though, are influenced by a change in the social environment, or an older brother or sister, rather than just the parents. If a child observes that big brother behaves Expressively, and that such behavior causes tension for mother, then the child will experiment with other styles. If, though, big brother is demonstrating Amiable behavior, and is receiving approval for it, then the child will probably follow Amiable behavior, too—at least temporarily. If the child is the second child in the family, this behavior pattern will usually shift, for the second child almost always develops a style preference different from that of the oldest child, in order to get attention. Style patterns are learned by trial and error from the social setting, to achieve a comfort zone balance.

Once style patterns develop, they remain set until the teenage years, when, in the process of discovering themselves, teenagers once again begin to experiment with different behaviors. Fifteen-year-old Jed, for example, is normally quiet and reserved, but he notices that Larry is popular, makes friends easily, and is always the center of attention. So, much to the dismay of his parents, Jed learns to tell a few jokes and tries to become more outgoing. The result is often strained and strikes people as artificial. Once Jed reaches his early twenties, though, the experimenting will end, and he will probably settle back into the same style patterns he developed as a child.

The point is, of course, that style patterns are very ingrained. Even if we don't recognize it, style is present at home, and style differences do exist within the family. If we acknowledge and adjust to these differences, we can use these contrasts to broaden the value of our relationships.

Do Opposites Attract?

It's been our experience that when people are choosing a partner, opposite styles—or at least different styles—frequently *do* attract. In the past, this subject has been the source of much scientific debate, with psychiatrists and psychologists typically holding opposing points of view. Some psychiatrists have tended to advocate partnerships built on complementary needs, in which each person brings different qualities to a relationship, thus forming a mutually supportive bond. Behavioral psychologists, though, have maintained that people with similar value systems and backgrounds have fewer sources of conflict and therefore are likely to make relationship adjustments more easily. Essentially, we would agree with the latter point of view. When we say that different styles attract, we're only talking in terms of the behavioral patterns, rather than in terms of the deeper need levels.

Obviously a relationship between partners with different styles presents many opportunities for the individual partners' behavior to grate on each other. Then why does this attraction occur? It's our guess that most of us envy the qualities and characteristics of styles that differ from our own. Also, such relationships can produce complementary interactions, simply because of the natural differences. For example, a person with an Analytical style is generally reserved in social settings. This individual will often participate in a wider variety of social experiences than he would normally if he has a partner who has an Expressive style and tends to seek involvement with people.

The partner with Expressive style can also add excitement to the relationship by stimulating activity that wouldn't occur with the more conservative approach. The person with Analytical behavior might, for instance, mention that sometime it would be fun to fly to Vancouver and see the spring flowers. But unless the Expressive-style partner grabbed the idea and implemented the vacation, that "sometime" might never come—or if it did, the spring flowers would have given way to fall colors. In short, the partner with Expressive behavior will often enliven the pair's existence by jogging the conservative partner into being more spontaneous. By the same token, the conservative person's preference for facts and logic can temper the risks involved with impulsive behavior.

In another example of complementary interaction, an individual with a Driving style might possibly turn every card game into tournament play if a partner with Amiable behavior didn't point out that the game really should be played for fun and that many people don't care to play cutthroat bridge. In this way, the Amiable person's sensitivity to others has a modifying influence on the partnership, and the couple can have a more pleasant and relaxed social life. Although unlikely to admit it, the partner with the Driving style probably admires the Amiable partner's ability to bring warmth, openness, and supportiveness to social situations. In turn, because the person with Driving style appears to be in charge, confident, and able to get results without worrying about relationships, the Amiable person can rely on these qualities in some social dealings.

Still, because the seeds of eventual irritation and discomfort are so inherent in our choices of partners, it is important to recognize that the tendency to be fascinated by behavioral differences and to select partners with qualities we feel are lacking in ourselves can eventually give way to style-related conflicts unless common experience, beliefs, and values serve to support the relationship.

True, differing social styles do contribute interest and excitement to close relationships, but it is just as true that contrasting social styles can be the source of many interpersonal tensions and family problems. It's not unusual, say, for a person with an Amiable preference to go along with a "great idea" which was presented by a more Expressive-style spouse as something for "us" to do together, only to find that at the last minute the plan has been changed to include a large number of friends, neighbors, and new acquaintances. The person with the Amiable style can legitimately ask, "What happened to 'us'?" and the intimacy that was expected.

The love/hate relationships many couples have is often the result of style differences. We would prefer, though, to call these relationships fascination/discomfort relationships. Although people are often attracted to behaviors opposite from their own styles, as they become close to an individual with those behaviors, discomfort arises because the person manages interpersonal tension differently. And these differences must be dealt with if an intimate relationship is to be mutually productive and if it is to survive all the stresses that are a natural part of daily living.

There are, of course, those relationships in which two people with the same social style are attracted to each other. Such relationships seem to be rare, however, and while at first glance they might appear preferable to those that include style differences, they, too, can have drawbacks.

Although partners with the same style arrive at behavioral compatibility easily, the relationship can suffer from the lack of contrasts and can readily slip into boredom. Again, this is often offset by common experience and values. A relationship between individuals with the same social style can produce its own set of tensions. Say, for example, a misunderstanding develops between two partners who have Analytical behavioral preferences. Each partner might go for several days without speaking to the other, thus avoiding the conflict and allowing resentment to build. So, even when two partners' social styles are the same, it's important to recognize that style exists in intimate relationships, that it has both positive and negative aspects, and that it must be understood and dealt with if such a relationship is to succeed.

REACTING TO TENSION

Essentially, then, we carry our social styles with us, from the office, to the tennis club, to the home. But because of the intimate nature of the relationships in our private lives, to a certain degree we do behave differently at home than we do at work or in casual social situations.

However, this difference is not a matter of a difference in style, but in the degree of versatility we show. Most of us learn intuitively that we can't show our backup styles—nonproductive, exaggerated behavior—too quickly to our bosses, clients, or even to our coworkers and casual friends, because we would jeopardize relationships that are essential to maintaining our positions. If we attack our boss or get autocratic with him, we are likely to find ourselves either not being promoted or else out looking for another job. So while we're careful not to show our discomfort at work, the compromises we make to adjust to work relationships are, in themselves, tension producing.

If sufficient tension is built up during the day, it's not uncommon to carry it home, and when that happens, backup styles can surface rather quickly. Ironically, we tend to take out our frustrations on those people who mean the most to us, because of the "safety" implicit in an intimate relationship. There's an inclination to feel: "This person has accepted me as I am, for what I am. Therefore, I don't have to try as hard to please."

For instance, a husband with either an Analytical or an Amiable style arrives home after a stressful day at the office. His spouse is also under stress, and a conflict develops about whether or not to go out to dinner. Since the husband has been under tension all day without a chance to withdraw (his preferred behavior), rather than showing versatility and discussing the matter, he is likely to hide behind a newspaper or sit in front of the television set, thus avoiding the conflict altogether. On the other hand, individuals with either Expressive or Driving behaviors, when confronted with the same situation, might even enjoy the chance to have a good argument and let off the steam they've been suppressing all day.

This same lack of versatility shows up in many aspects of family life. As an example, let's look at what happened when a couple we know took a trip to Canada.

 Roy and Evie had looked forward to their vacation for nearly six months. With their money saved, their time commitments taken care of, and their most important business and personal affairs under control, they were totally free to just have fun traveling to and from Alberta.

Prior to the trip, Roy's disorganized life was much the same as usual. He rushed about to get everything done, which involved changing directions several times a day, working hours on end, and postponing the many unconfirmed plans he'd made with clients.

Evie, on the other hand, in between tying up loose ends at work, obtained maps with marked itineraries from the auto club, made hotel reservations, and carefully scheduled the trip to allow time to enjoy various scenic spots along the way. Evie's hope for their two-week vacation was that through her planning, their hectic, random schedule could be put aside and that their vacation would be restful, orderly, and leisurely. While Roy hadn't thought much about the details of the trip, he looked forward to getting away from the demands of clients and to having time to really relax.

After a rather late start, because of some details which Roy had forgotten to attend to until the last minute, the couple headed for

Denver, their first overnight stop. They relaxed over drinks and dinner in one of the city's finest hotels; then Evie retired to their room for her first, long-awaited quiet time. It was a chance to read the book she'd been saving for just this occasion. Roy stayed at the bar watching a football game on television. Both Roy and Evie felt that their vacation was off to a great start.

The next morning, at breakfast, Roy enthusiastically described the Millers, an interesting couple he'd met in the bar the night before. Then he announced, "We're all getting together and taking a side trip through Rocky Mountain National Park. We'll stay at their cabin. The town nearby is having a festival, and there'll be a Scotch doubles tournament and a real Western barbecue."

Roy stressed the uniqueness of this opportunity, and Evie found it impossible to disagree. She also felt that they could not disappoint the other couple. But, although she went along with the plan, she lacked enthusiasm, and it was quite apparent to everyone that she did not fully enjoy the experience. Evie's aloofness put a damper on everyone else's enjoyment.

The day they left the Millers' cabin, Evie turned to Roy and said peevishly, "Well, I'm glad that's over with. You and your wonderful ideas." She pointed out that she'd spent months putting the trip together and that now she would have to change all the reservations. Not only that—they would have to skip Yellowstone.

"So we change a few reservations—so what?" Roy replied. "It'll only take a minute." Then he joked about missing Yellowstone, saying, "With our luck, we'd probably get mauled by bears anyway!" This remark only served to irritate Evie more: "All the work I put into planning this vacation was obviously a waste of time." Roy lost his temper and accused Evie of spoiling everyone else's fun. "You never consider other people. All you ever think of are your boring maps and timetables."

During the next two weeks, this sequence of events was repeated several times. Because Roy didn't understand Evie's need for order, and for a quiet pace with time to herself, his usual approach to tension between them was to make flippant remarks about each missed schedule. On the other hand, because Evie cared for her husband, she accepted deviations from the original plan, but she was hurt when Roy didn't understand her disappointment. Rather than being relaxing, the trip began to turn out very much like their normal, pressured schedule.

Both Roy and Evie had looked forward to this vacation as a

chance to build on their relationship and reestablish some of the romance lost through the demands of everyday living. Instead, their return home was a tense, "thank God it's over," near approach to divorce. Their marriage did remain intact, primarily because their demanding daily routine created a certain separateness between them. Because this routine minimized conflict, Roy and Evie were able to keep the relationship together, but it remained far less than ideal.

Looking at Roy and Evie from the outside, it's difficult to understand why Roy couldn't see how his flippant disregard for Evie's discomfort caused tension between them. It's also hard to understand why Evie was unable to accept even a small amount of spontaneity and why she couldn't refrain from criticizing fun-loving behavior; after all, fun is what a vacation is all about.

This conflict is typical of the type that arises between two people whose preferred ways of doing things clash. And, very often, a vacation—a time when people are looking for personal pleasure and relaxation—can bring out these conflicts. Why? On vacation, people often discard their usual versatility in hopes of "doing my own thing" for a change. But, when what comes naturally to one person does not to another, tension mounts. The result is that neither Roy nor Evie succeeded with style. Nor did they succeed in creating a productive relationship, which allows people to accomplish their objectives without alienating each other. Quite obviously, Roy and Evie's return to a daily separateness was a form of alienation.

As Roy and Evie's experience shows, different styles in a partnership can lead to many tensions and frustrations. Unless these conflicts are handled with versatility, they can result in either ending the relationship, or, as in Roy and Evie's case, a situation where both partners go their own separate ways without trying to really make the relationship work.

VERSATILITY AND PERSONAL RELATIONSHIPS

Using style effectively at home, then, requires the same skills that are necessary to succeed with style at work. First we need to understand our own styles and the possible effects they have on others. If we know that a particular behavior is a source of irritation to others, we can deemphasize our own tendencies and try to be less impulsive, less pedantic, less authoritative, or less indecisive. Style-awareness helps us, because if someone expresses irritation with our behavior, we can understand why they are irritated without becoming defensive, and thus avoid turning a tense situation into a worse one.

Once we have identified the style which we use at home, we need to be able to recognize the different behaviors which make up the other person's style. Then, instead of letting these differences cause problems, we will know how to respond to the other person in a caring manner. Rather than discouraging another person's excitement, we can attempt to enhance it. Rather than criticizing someone's caution, we can attempt to satisfy it. Rather than condemning someone's stubbornness, we can try to present them with alternatives. And certainly when someone we love needs understanding and support, it isn't that hard to provide them with an extra measure of security.

In intimate relationships, we tend to avoid direct communication with our partner because of our vulnerability to his or her reactions, especially because we need their approval so much, and can be overwhelmed by our *own* emotional reactions if their response upsets us. When someone we care for has a style that's different from our own and we misinterpret this person's behavior, we can become very apprehensive. We therefore tend to evade more open or direct expressions of personal need, because it might trigger a reaction that's different from our own.

For example, we might avoid pointing out an annoying habit to someone with an Amiable style—when that would be the most honest and direct approach—because we don't want to deal with that person's hurt feelings. We might be equally evasive with someone who has Driving preferences, because we don't want to ignite this person's forceful, don't-argue-with-me response. We don't express an emotional opinion to a spouse with an Analytical style for fear this person will be critical of our illogical point of view. And we most certainly don't say anything that is likely to provoke an emotional retaliation from the person with Expressive behavior.

In close relationships, this evasive approach often cuts off genuine communication and prevents growth, even between partners with the same social style. As people hold back and dodge the need for open communication, they create more tensions within themselves. As tensions build, the point comes when they are apt to blow up unpredictably and, ultimately, create an even worse interaction, which will probably be misunderstood by both parties. As we've discussed in Chapter 4, versatility, particularly the use of feedback, is essential in breaking down a defensive cycle of communication. Practicing the skills that make for good communication and which allow us to demonstrate interpersonal understanding and strength can prevent those barriers from being built in the first place.

The following vignette is not a real-life example. Rather, it's meant to show how quickly styles can get in the way of communicating when people get tense. Watch how Terri, an Analytical person, and Dan, an Expressive one, find themselves in circumstances that could easily become destructive. Instead, they stop being defensive, start to communicate with good use of feedback—and turn the situation around. They accomplish this by expressing their feelings about the situation to one another, and neither partner insists on being right.

Terri and Dan had picked their child up at the babysitter's after a hard day at work and were driving home. Each of them had run into several conflicts on the job, and because they'd had to expend a lot of energy using versatility, tension levels were running high. Elizabeth, the baby, was screaming at the top of her lungs, which was doing nothing to soothe anyone's irritability, when Terri suddenly discovered that the baby was crying because she needed changing and now had diaper rash.

Terri lost her temper. "This is crazy! Mrs. Bauer has nothing to do all day except watch two kids, and she can't even change a diaper. I'll never leave Elizabeth with her again! But it was so hard to find a babysitter," Terri said mournfully, "and now we'll have to go through the whole routine again!" (A logical Analytical complaint.)

Dan snapped, "Well, we wouldn't have to worry about it if you didn't work. If you stayed home like a normal mother, things like this wouldn't happen!" (A personal Expressive attack.)

"And," Terri shot back, "if you made a halfway decent salary, I wouldn't have to work."

"I do make a decent salary—but with inflation, car repairs, and the baby's expenses—what do you expect? Besides, you know I was supposed to have gotten the promotion they gave to Warren." (It's not my fault—it's someone else who caused my problem.)

Pausing, both Terri and Dan realized what was happening, but neither one was ready to say, "It's okay, let's just forget it." The hostility was still there. Each one felt they were right.

Terri was the first to try to calm the situation. "It just seems that everything is too much."

Dan responded to her reflection with less intensity. "Right," he said, calming down a bit. "I don't know, sometimes it seems no matter how hard we try, we keep getting further behind."

"It's frustrating," Terri replied, looking directly at Dan.

"Yes. It sure is!"

From that point on, Terri and Dan were able to discuss the problem more calmly and reasonably. Obviously, if they had not reined in the mounting hostility when they did, this situation could have easily turned into a real knock-down, drag-out fight. Each person would have left the conflict with hurt feelings. Terri would still have thought Dan resented her for working, and Dan would have been just as sure Terri thought he was a poor provider. Instead, they were able to recognize that they were both tense from the day's events and that they were angry at circumstances, rather than at each other. By being honest with each other and by using versatile feedback skills in their conversation, they were able to understand each other's feelings and work together effectively.

BELIEF OR BEHAVIOR?

Of course style is not the only deterrent to having a successful intimate relationship. It's also essential for partners to be sexually compatible and to have common interests, beliefs, and value systems. When partners have little in common, style differences often become key sources of irritation in the relationship. And if that's the case, there's not much point in trying to simply resolve style conflicts, when deeper problems are at the root of the trouble.

It's been our observation, though, that discomfort in a relationship is often caused by differences in style—the way people manage their tension levels—rather than in beliefs and attitudes. And when partners share strong beliefs and values, there is solid motivation for learning to deal with those conflicts and for becoming more versatile.

If, as we think, it's true that many conflicts in the home result from differences in style, rather than from deeper psychological problems, how can homelife be made more fulfilling? Obviously, from our position we believe a great many of the conflicts couples experience can be resolved with counseling that focuses on understanding style and style differences, rather than in-depth therapy. Certainly there are situations that require a great deal more than learning to understand behavioral habits and deal with them objectively. But many people look for deeper reasons for their conflicts than may be necessary to resolve misunderstandings.

For example, it's important for couples to find constructive ways to release the pent-up tensions that accumulate during the day. Such outlets can prevent people from exploding at each other for no apparent reason or, equally destructive, from avoiding the relationship entirely. Outlets such as jogging, swimming, tennis, bicycling, and meditation can do a great deal to relieve tension and revitalize a relationship that's in a defensive cycle. Another method that can help reduce tension is simply setting aside a quiet, private time in which to relax and gain perspective on the day's experiences.

For those who would like to pursue this subject further, we recommend a book by Dr. William Glasser, *Positive Addiction* (New York: Harper & Row, 1976). In this book, Dr. Glasser, who has been a psychiatrist for many years, points out that physical exercise and meditation often do more to resolve conflicts in people's lives than much of the therapy he was trained to perform. In any case, we'd like to make it clear that in seriously conflicted situations it is very desirable to get outside professional counseling to assist in defining the nature of the problem, and the appropriate steps to take.

In addition to finding constructive ways to release tension, it's important to recognize the difference between belief and behavior. Of course, ways in which people behave can also be a reflection of their beliefs. But we should recognize that this is not always the case, and we should try to determine whether we are observing values in action or just behavior which is part of a style before we misinterpret another person's actions.

For example, an individual with an Analytical style might avoid attending parties. This behavior could indicate that the person doesn't *believe* in parties—possibly for religious reasons—but it might simply mean that he is shy and unable to socialize well. An individual with an Expressive style might have impulsive buying habits, but such behavior might result from the inability to resist a great bargain, rather than from a *belief* that saving for the future is pointless. Someone with an Amiable style might be openly affectionate with people other than a partner, but this behavior does not necessarily mean that the person *believes* in infidelity.

If the differences between partners are differences in style, rather than in values, they can be worked out through compromise. But, once again, because people tend to interpret and read into behaviors in terms of values, they usually don't want to change their own habit patterns and are much more apt to suggest that the other partner do the changing. For instance, at one point or another the person who exhibits Driving behavior might say to a partner, "You shouldn't be so impulsive and outgoing— it's childish." And the reply to this statement might be, "Well, you shouldn't be so cold and self-centered. You're always so busy pushing people around you never pay any attention to how they feel." Such criticisms start a vicious circle of defensiveness that must be broken so that the relationship won't end in alienation, if it survives at all.

Again, the point we teach in our workshops is that people's styles should be left alone. There's no profit in tampering with style to resolve conflict. All styles have both positive and negative aspects, and if you did succeed in changing another person's style (although this is highly unlikely), you would only be faced with a new and unfamiliar set of negative characteristics to deal with (those of the new style). Rather than trying to modify one person's behavior to match another's, we would like to suggest that successful relationships, in large part, grow out of adjustment to one another's behavioral preferences through understanding, tolerance, and mutual caring.

Thus, we would encourage couples to read this book together, as long as the partner who proposes the idea is aware that the suggestion itself could produce some defensiveness on the part of the other person. Also, we would like to emphasize again that partners might have difficulty identifying each other's styles, simply because the emotional investment in their relationships makes objective observation of style difficult. Arguing about each other's styles will only become self-defeating, so it is a good idea to get some input from outsiders—other than very close friends—to obtain an accurate picture of the way each partner behaves with people in general. We don't recommend using close friends because they are unlikely to be much more objective than the partners themselves, and are also apt to support preconceived ideas about the relationship. People you socialize with casually at church, or community groups, would be most desirable.

Any efforts made to understand each other's behavior, though, should prove worthwhile, for we've known many couples who have gained a new respect and appreciation for each other once they recognize that there are no good or bad styles, and no good or bad ways of managing tension. If these concepts are accepted, great strides can be made toward turning a relationship into the creative and rewarding experience it should be.

Yes, people are different, not just at work, but also at home. And this difference not only makes their lives together richer, it's probably what attracted them to each other in the first place. Complementary interactions are part of the strength of any close relationship. And yes, where there are differences there are difficulties, but dealing with the differences can well be worth the price.

PRACTICE SUGGESTIONS

1. Really understanding your own style will take some effort on your part, because the only way you can verify how other people perceive your behavior is to ask them. Also, because of the complexities involved in close relationships, it is often just as difficult for partners to identify each other's styles as it is for them to pinpoint their own. Since this lack of objectivity can lead to defensiveness, we again emphasize that couples should not try to determine each other's styles. Instead, we recommend using the methods suggested at the end of Chapter 3. Type four 3 × 5 cards with a description of a social style on each one. Then give these cards to people who know you—other than family or very close friends—and ask them to rank the cards in order, from the description most like you to the one that is least like you. Each partner should do this with five to seven people who are not intimate confidants.

2. Watch a movie or a television program you both enjoy, and see if you can identify the styles portrayed on the screen. Avoid situation comedies, because they tend to show exaggerated styles and often favor Expressive behavior, which can be very entertaining. Instead, it would be better to watch a variety of programs, especially ones that show people in realistic settings—some of the dramas on educational television, for example. Identify the styles portrayed on the screen and discuss them with your partner. Try to determine whether any of the characters demonstrate your own and your partner's behavioral preferences. Talking about and observing behaviors with each other will increase your ability to identify social styles, as well as to recognize what is going on with respect to style in your own lives.

3. Finally, because most of our social behavior is learned by imitation, it often helps to watch people in a social setting who are skilled at making others comfortable. Identify someone you know who has a style similar to yours and whom you believe to be versatile. How does this person behave differently than you do? Is this person more versatile than you are? Does your partner agree? Watching someone deal with a variety of social styles in resourceful and adaptive ways can help you see how accepting style differences increases versatility. And observing and discussing versatility skills together can also help you to improve your versatility at home.

8

A Perspective on Style

Throughout this book, social style has been isolated from other aspects of personality to help us better understand the ramifications of behavioral patterns in our business and personal lives. And yet we've also emphasized that no one has a pure style—each of us takes on aspects of other styles occasionally—and that style is only one facet of personality. Such things as our values, dreams, ambitions, education, and intelligence also influence our relationships. Humans *do* have complex personalities and because of this, we can easily confuse what we think is style with values or judgments, and vice versa. So, no matter how much we might like to use style as the simple solution to life's problems, we recognize that there is no single, easy-to-use answer to meet the challenge of creating productive relationships. At the same time, understanding style *can* help sort out what happens between people, and *can* lead to increased tolerance, reduced defensiveness, and less critical judgments of others.

Thus, this chapter will concentrate on placing our presentation of social style back into the complexities of everyday life. It's an important step, because none of us can hope to become social style experts, living totally objective lives that inevitably lead to mutually satisfying, perfect relationships. Instead, we respond to style as just one factor that affects the way we cope with the varying demands of a day. If we have at least some awareness and understanding of style, our relationships may not be perfect, but they will be more successful.

To look at social style more realistically, we will use a narrative. Because the narrative is intended to demonstrate behavior, it is not a complete story, but rather a series of snapshots taken from one day in the life of a working couple. We intentionally interrupt the episodes to give you the chance to study them and relate them to previous discussions of social style. In this way we hope to bridge the gap between our empirical research and descriptions of style, and the ways in which people tend to use their styles daily.

We have inserted our own notes and observations between scenes. These comments will review the principles of style discussed in earlier chapters and point out where other aspects of personality—reading into people, for example—cloud our perceptions of style.

In the following vignettes, Hadley, an Expressive person, has had instruction in social style and in building versatility skills. Nick, a Driver, has some style awareness, but he tends to rely more on his personal insights than Hadley does. Both people have high versatility, which, as you'll see, makes a notable difference in their lives.

✔ The day began normally enough. It was Friday, and Nick had a brief to prepare. Hadley, who ran her own real estate business, would be trying to close a particularly tough sale.

At 4:45 A.M. the alarm went off. Hadley groaned. She hated clocks and only reluctantly adjusted to time schedules. She was fond of saying, "When I get up, I get up," and, "It takes as long as it takes." To Hadley, clocks were evil interruptions of spontaneity. And, true to form, on this morning she ignored the alarm's ringing.

Nick, who had an internal sense of time, was already awake. He cleanly punched the alarm's off button, tugged at the lamp switch on his bedstand, and slipped on his robe.

Hadley tends to be less disciplined about time than Nick is, which is true of many people who have responsive styles. This does not mean that responsive people are always late or that they can never meet deadlines. It simply means that, generally, time is not one of their top priorities.

✔ Nick's bedstand stood in marked contrast to Hadley's. His was neatly organized: a pencil holder filled with sharpened pencils, a note pad, a small pocket dictaphone, a book on succeeding in business, and yesterday's *Wall Street Journal*. He admired its orderliness, but smiled as he remembered the time Hadley had crept over in the night and purposely put it all in disarray to "teach you frustration tolerance in the morning."

Nick and Hadley are having fun with differences in each other's habitual ways of doing things. We can all recognize other people's patterns of behavior, and, when there are differences, we can either accept the differences or argue about the right way to do things. Every person has a preferred way of acting, which is right for that individual but could upset someone else. A versatile person, though, can be understanding and playful about style differences.

✔ Nick tucked the *Journal* under his arm, headed down to the kitchen, and put the paper on the roll-top desk. The night before, he had circled certain articles "for my files." He had worked out a deal with Hadley: she would cut out special articles for him if he would toss the rest of the paper away. Before this compromise, he'd been in the habit of keeping every *Journal,* and Hadley had joked that she feared for their lives if the boxes of newspapers in the hall closet ever fell on them.

Nick has a preference for keeping data and ideas that might be useful to him at a later date. Even though Hadley was only joking about his habit, he arranged a way to meet both their needs— evidence that he is a command specialist, a Driver, and a versatile person.

✔ Next, Nick ate his breakfast, showered, and dressed in a crisp three-piece suit. He was back at the breakfast table for a second cup of coffee, briefcase in hand, before Hadley poked her head into the kitchen.

"Mornin', Nick," she said. "How are things in the White House?" She couldn't resist one playful jab at his professional appearance.

Nick was prepared. It was part of their intimacy. "Good morning to you, Ms. Fitzpatrick," he said in his best professional, on-top-of-everything voice.

"Is that how you greet the young lovelies at the office?"

"Precisely," he said.

"Precisely," she repeated in the same tone, then kissed him on the cheek and walked over to the coffee pot.

"I sure wish we didn't have to live by clocks and coffee timers."
She returned to the table and reached for the morning papers.

"It seems too efficient," Nick observed.

"Exactly."

"I found a couple of items in the *Journal* on the commodities market. They're on the desk."

"Okay." She was still waking up. "I'll cut them out before I leave this morning."

"Thanks. See you tonight."

Nick and Hadley clearly acknowledge their different approaches to organizing themselves for the day, and their joking exchanges suggest they accept these differences, instead of debating about the "right way to act." Such behavior is evidence of versatility. They make no judgments about one another, but instead, they understand and appreciate the differences that do exist. Whether we think about it consciously or not, we all organize ourselves in habitual ways to maintain our daily comfort levels, and these habits contribute to our effectiveness.

After Nick left, Hadley turned the radio to her favorite station and listened to Willie Nelson as she read the real estate ads in the newspaper. ". . . Mama, don't let your babies grow up to be cowboys. . . ." Fired by Willie's admonition to "let 'em be doctors, and lawyers, and such," and thinking of Nick, the lawyer, and her own efforts to close the sale on the Harrison estate, she raced upstairs to get ready for work. "Today's going to be a good day!" she affirmed. Hadley was known by all as a person inclined to make sudden emotional declarations.

As usual, Hadley dressed quickly. She put on a light-weight blue suit, pulled her hair back behind her ears, and tied it with a silk scarf. She felt that the outfit made her look quite dignified.

"I've got an idea for selling that estate that's surefire—the sale's in the bag!" she thought to herself.

Hadley grabbed her briefcase and checked to make sure she had turned off the coffeemaker. She hadn't. "Whew, that was close," she said. Then she went out the door, leaving Nick's *Journal* with the circled articles untouched on the desk.

Hadley's thoughts and self-perceptions are an aspect of her personality, rather than of style. Style is what you do and say that others can agree upon and report about you. While what you think about yourself may often reflect what others can see, you can also have many thoughts that are never public information.

✔ Just as Hadley was leaving the house, Nick pulled into his firm's underground parking lot.

"Looks like another hot one," the attendant at the entrance commented as Nick got out of the car.

"Looks like," Nick answered, his mind on business.

"She sure is a beauty." The man ran his hand down the clean, sweeping roof of Nick's Porsche.

"Uh, huh." The reply sounded mechanical and unresponsive. Nick handed the attendant the keys and quickly headed for the elevator.

George, the parking attendant, slipped behind the wheel and pulled the Porsche into a vacant spot. He took the keys to the office and tagged them with the license plate number.

"Some guys just don't appreciate what they've got," he said to the girl behind the desk.

George's reaction to Nick is typical of the types of judgments we all tend to make when observing others. Rather than accepting Nick's behavior, George concludes that Nick doesn't appreciate what he has; that he is distant and unfriendly. In everyday life we often "read into" people's behavior to make ourselves more comfortable with the way a person is treating us. "Reading in" explains away our uncomfortable feelings about an individual's style and becomes a value judgment that condemns the other person's natural way of acting.

✔ A few minutes after Nick left the garage, George smiled and said to the office girl, "Here comes my buddy."

George greeted Bernard Sadler, the senior partner of Nick's firm, with, "Morning! Looks like another hot one."

"Sure does, George. Here. You take good care of this old gal." He got out of his Cadillac and gave the keys to George. Sadler was a portly man who preferred to be called Bernie by everyone and nearly always had a cigar in his mouth. As he ambled to the elevator, he waved to George and called out, "Don't work too hard."

"That man's never too busy to say hello. What a great guy." Then George pulled out a cigar of his own and lit up.

George is still reading into the relationship. Mr. Sadler is a "buddy" because he treats George the way George wants to be treated. George appreciates a style that is agreeable, friendly, and supportive. Mr. Sadler acts this way naturally, with everyone he comes in contact with, because his style is Amiable. Because of their styles, George likes Amiable Mr. Sadler and puts down Driving Nick. Neither man may be any more or less George's buddy, but one style makes George feel comfortable, and the other not so comfortable.

We all make similar assumptions every day, to one degree or another. What we need to do is realize that people tend to use their styles in the same way with almost everyone, and their natural actions very often don't carry any special meanings— except in the eye of the beholder.

➤ By now, Nick was in his office talking to his secretary. "Claire," he said over the intercom, "I'll have the Thompson brief to you by noon so you can type it up." His voice was even with resolve.

"Yes, sir," came the reply, but Nick had already turned off the machine and didn't hear her. He was now picking up pace, putting on his best professional demeanor, purely out of habit.

Nick heard Bernie Sadler entering the reception area. You couldn't *not* hear him. He was chatting casually with Claire, and when Bob Weiskopf arrived, Nick could imagine Bernie's big hand slapping Bob on the back as the two went into Bernie's office.

"Come on in, Robert. I want to talk with you before you and Nick get all wound up."

Nick respected Bernie Sadler, even admired him as a lawyer, but he never really felt comfortable with Bernie's affable animation. Nick turned his thoughts away from Bernie and began working on the Thompson brief.

Nick's thoughts about Bernie Sadler are not observable actions, and therefore we would describe them as part of personality, not style. However, there is a style difference between the two men (Driver versus Amiable), and although Nick is not comfortable with Bernie's habitual way of handling relationships, he does respect his competence as an attorney. When we're uncomfortable with the social habits of another person and there is a reason to maintain the relationship, we look beyond style to factors such as professional competence. Since, more often than not, we don't discuss the style discomfort, it can set the stage for conflict and disagreement, if things don't run smoothly when we are performing daily tasks.

▶ In the meantime, Hadley was the first person to arrive at her office. She always met time schedules when the situation required them. The recently hired secretary was late once again.

"Suzanne is good with clients, but," Hadley thought as she made the coffee, "there are a couple of things we're going to have to work on. Like getting here on time to answer the phone and taking better messages."

Hadley went to her desk and, after sorting through a pile of the papers, found a clean pad and sat down to organize her day.

"Let's see. Number one is to talk with Suzanne about her job performance. She's fairly undisciplined about time like me, yet when she gets rolling she sure can do a lot, and quickly, too. Her rapport with clients is excellent, so I just need to confront her on the time thing. I'll wait to work on the phone messages later.

"Number two is to talk with Fred about his sales record. He's pretty cautious about closings and wants to give every client so much time and so many facts that I think he loses some sales. So we need to talk about better closing techniques.

"Number three is for me to get ready to talk with the Johnsons about buying the Harrison estate."

Part of versatility is recognizing style similarities and differences and planning ahead to treat people the way they need to be treated so they can perform more effectively. Versatility is a conscious process that permits you to think about how you can keep a relationship productive, whether your style is similar to or different from someone else's. Since Hadley's thinking process is not observable behavior, it is not a part of what we call style.

To confront Suzanne, Hadley plans to use the skills she has learned in a versatility workshop, and she recognizes that she can expect a series of defensive responses. Her objective is to specifically point out the actions that trouble her, indicate her feelings about them, and state clearly why she is upset. Then she intends to listen to the predictable defensive responses, without getting hostile or defensive herself, and repeat her concern until Suzanne accepts responsibility for improving her performance. If you are not familiar with confrontation skills you may find the following conversation a little stilted, and it is. But reflective listening and confrontation skill has a great deal to do with developing improved versatility. Versatility skills don't come naturally to most of us; we have to plan to use them, and we have to practice them.

Just as Hadley was underlining number four on her list—"Call Nick"—Suzanne walked in. As the door opened, the sleigh bells which were tacked to it jingled; Hadley felt they added atmosphere, no matter what the time of year.

"Hello, Suzanne."

"Hi, Hadley. Boy, is it going to be hot today. It's so hot we'll be able to use our refrigerator as a microwave oven!"

"That's hot," Hadley agreed. Then she added, "Suzanne, once you get your things put away . . ."—she didn't want to go too far without letting Suzanne know that something was coming—"I'd like to talk with you about how we work around here."

"Sure," replied Suzanne, tempering her response and sensing that Hadley was displeased about something.

As Suzanne went to her desk, Hadley asked, "When will Fred be in?"

"Oh, let's see," she checked some phone message slips but couldn't seem to find the one she wanted.

"I think he said when he called yesterday afternoon that he wouldn't be in until just before lunch. I can't seem to find the exact message."

Hadley let the answer go by, even though she was tempted to comment on that part of Suzanne's performance. Instead, she stuck to her original plan.

"Suzanne, since we seem to have a few minutes, there's something I need to talk to you about."

"Yes?" Suzanne could feel it coming, and Hadley could see her getting red.

"Suzanne, it's about your coming in late. You see the office opens at 9:00, and when you get in later than that, I get upset, because that means that we may miss some client calls or important messages." Hadley stopped speaking and focused her complete attention on Suzanne, letting the carefully constructed message sink in.

Trying to shrug it off, Suzanne said, "Come on, now. I know sometimes I get in a little late, but if anyone calls and it's important, they'll call back."

Hadley soaked this up, not giving in to an impulse to reply angrily. Instead she repeated, "So because you believe clients will call back, you think it's unnecessary to be here at 9:00." It wasn't a question, but rather a reflection of Suzanne's statement.

"Well, not exactly, now that I hear what I just said. But what's with you anyway, Hadley? We're friends. What's gotten into you, being so tough?"

Hadley was prepared for Suzanne's defensive attempt to seek acceptance, and she controlled herself enough to say, "This seems unusual to you, my being persistent on this time thing." Again, it was not a question.

"You're darn right. What gives?" Suzanne's discomfort was subsiding.

Hadley came back with her original message. "What gives, Suzanne, is that when you're not here to answer the phone when our business hours start at 9:00, I get upset and irritated because it means we could lose potential clients or miss important messages." Again, Hadley controlled her emotions but kept her full attention on Suzanne.

"Well sure, Hadley, I know it's important not to miss calls from clients, but I'm not late that often, and anyway, you say yourself that time isn't everything."

"You're right, Suzanne, I do feel that time isn't everything." Hadley had to acknowledge this; still there were certain procedures she felt must be followed. "But it's company policy. Besides, when you don't arrive on time in the mornings, I really get concerned, because we could lose potential sales."

Hadley's insistence was beginning to dispel Suzanne's defensive reactions. "Okay, I see what you mean. It's not me you're mad at. It's just this thing about not getting here on time?"

"Exactly." Hadley kept her response short, so that Suzanne would go on.

"Tell you what, Hadley, since it is important to be here on time, I'll try to work something out. Okay?"

Hadley sensed that Suzanne was still trying to evade the issue.

"Suzanne, I hear you saying that you recognize being here on time is important, but I don't hear a firm commitment to do something.''

"My gosh, Hadley, you really are serious about this. I never knew you were like this.''

"My persistence is unusual. It's puzzling you.''

"Right.'' Suzanne paused, and Hadley kept quiet, letting her accept the problem and come up with a solution.

"Tell you what. I'll buy a second alarm clock and set it each day so I make sure I'll be here at 9:00 A.M. sharp. Deal?''

"That's a deal, Suzanne, and let's check on how you're doing in a couple of weeks. How about going to lunch two weeks from today?''

"I've got to hand it to you. You're really serious. Two weeks from today is a date.''

Hadley is demonstrating versatile use of feedback skills in this confrontation. She uses a model that she learned in the versatility workshop which helps others to accept your message and motivates them to modify their performance in an effective way. Of course, this is an ideal example of what can happen when correctly using confrontation skills, and more often than not, Hadley will fall short of the ideal, even after her training. However, she has learned that attempting to be a versatile manager is always better than not trying at all. By communicating clearly and specifically, making her feelings known without being judgmental, and indicating the effects of Suzanne's actions on the business, Hadley starts to solve a problem that could have gotten out of hand.

It was 9:30 A.M., and Nick was really getting into gear on the Thompson brief. "At this pace,'' he thought to himself, "I'll be finished by 11:00.''

There was a short knock at his door, and Nick knew who was there before he looked up. The odor of cigar smoke had preceded Bernie Sadler.

"Good morning, Nicholas,'' Bernie said in his most affable, jovial voice.

"Hello, Bernie. What's on your mind? I'm kind of busy this morning.''

Nick was as cool and uninviting as he'd been in the garage with

George. Much as he liked and admired Bernie, he'd more than once lost a morning's work by starting to listen to one of Bernie's stories, and he wasn't about to let it happen today. Nick was aware that he came across to others as demanding and slightly aloof. Sometimes he even used this knowledge to his advantage, although he recognized the tradeoffs—on occasion, personal relationships suffered. Still, when he was organizing his work life, the task came first. Nick glanced at his wrist watch: 9:35 A.M.

Bernie watched Nick, saw his growing impatience, and felt compelled to ask, "Nick, how long has it been?"

"Since what?" Nick returned.

Bernie chuckled. "Since you walked away from your briefs and forgot about this ratrace." He pulled up a chair, and the leather groaned with his presence.

Bernie was very impressive, in an understated sort of way. As a young criminal lawyer, before he become a corporate lawyer with this firm, he had earned quite a reputation for charming his juries. His deliberateness connoted a patient, momentum-gathering power. And his style and competence had paid off: In four years as a criminal lawyer, he had never lost a case.

"Nick?" Bernie quietly pressed for an answer.

Recognizing that he was going to have to reply, Nick ran through the options in his mind. "Do I just tell Bernie I'm too busy? He's the one who gave me this brief. After all, I'm in charge on this one. Or, do I go along with him, at least for a while? See if he's got anything on his mind or just wants to talk. Old Bernie Sadler. Old B.S."

"Nick," this time Bernie's voice insisted.

"Yes, sorry, Bernie, I was just concentrating on this brief. You had a question?"

That Nick had been this inattentive bothered Bernie. "Nick, you're one of the best young corporate lawyers I know. Maybe the best. That's why I hired you, and I pay you what you're worth. But listen to me," Bernie could see Nick getting uncomfortable. It was the praise before the criticism that Nick knew was Bernie's habit, and it made him edgy.

"Nick, you've got the best wife in the world. Why don't you take off a little time and the two of you get away for a while?"

"What's Hadley got to do with this?" He felt himself bristling at the advice.

"Nick," Bernie's voice grew softly insistent, powerful, "what

I'm getting at is that the last brief you prepared wasn't up to your normal ability. It had flaws. You need a break."

"Listen, Bernie, don't start telling me how to write briefs. I'm the best there is. Remember? You just said it yourself."

Nick could feel himself tensing. He really wished he hadn't taken the extreme position that he was the best, but Bernie had pushed, so he pushed back.

Bernie took a long draw on his cigar and let the smoke settle, rolling the Havana between his thumb and forefinger, looking not quite directly at Nick. He remained quiet. Nick grew equally silent. A full minute passed. It was a mental tug-of-war.

Bernie was the first to break the silence. "Nick," he said paternally, "I can't remember the last time you went home without a briefcase full of papers. You're a workaholic. On top of that, you're very talented. These two things have resulted in tremendous productivity. But, son, I can see that you're burned out. It's showing in your work. Please, think about taking some time off, for the good of the firm, if not for you and Hadley."

"Bernie, there you go again, thinking you know me better than I do." The diagnosis, delivered father-to-son, had made Nick reject it, even though he knew there was some truth in the statement. "I'll run my own life. I'll straighten things out."

Bernie could see that Nick was irritated, so he tried to recover by softening his advice. "Nicholas, being a workaholic is dangerous. You should think more of Hadley and yourself than to let something like this slowly ruin your life."

"Listen, Bernie," Nick came back, "you're treating me like a kid. Stop it with the 'shoulds.' "

Bernie stood slowly, coming up out of the chair balding head first, then belly, then arms, hands, and finally thick legs. He drew deeply on his cigar and with a pained expression replacing the earlier charm, he ran his free hand over his forehead and sighed. "Nick, I want you to seriously consider taking next week off. Do you understand what I'm saying?"

Nick stood. "Yes, Fine," he said, his voice carrying just the opposite meaning. "I'll consider it."

"Good." Bernie left the room.

In this example, Bernie's intentions are good, but because of the way he presents them, the message is not received appropriately, and Nick is still defensive and uncomfortable. You can predict that productivity and effectiveness will decrease until Nick resolves what's happened. Neither Bernie nor Nick demonstrate much versatility in this conversation and both display signs of reverting to backup styles. By acting as if he were telling a son what he ought to do, because father knows best, Bernie appeared judgmental and patronizing. Nick predictably became defensive, since he is independent and likes to make his own decisions. He autocratically says, "I run my own life. I'll straighten things out." Bernie uses his position of authority but leaves his message open to interpretation. This response is not versatile. Neither is it likely to motivate Nick toward effective performance.

On the other side of town, at Hadley's office, Fred came walking in, the sleigh bells jingling on the door.

"Morning, Suzanne," he said laconically.

"Hello, Fred. How'd it go?"

"Oh, the usual. They seemed interested, but they kept getting concerned about things like how this room or that room 'felt,' or what kind of people lived in the neighborhood. I tried to keep bringing them back to the facts, but it was no-go."

Uncomfortable having said as much as this, Fred smiled good morning to Hadley through her open door and went to his desk. Fred's desk was so clean and well organized that a visitor to the office might conclude that no one was using it.

Hadley went over to the coffee machine and on the way said to Fred, "I heard you tell Suzanne that it was kind of tough this morning. If you have ten minutes or so before lunch, stop in, and maybe we can figure out a new strategy."

Hadley planned her words carefully. She didn't want to make Fred feel rushed or accused, but to appeal to his thought processes by offering a new, mutually devised plan.

"I've got ten or fifteen minutes now."

"Great, come on into my office.

"Well, Fred, tell me about this morning." She turned her attention to the salesman in a nonthreatening manner.

Somewhat reluctantly, Fred slowly replied, "Oh, Hadley, you know how it is. Same old thing."

"Kind of discouraging for you."

"Yeah, sure is." Fred grew silent.

Hadley stayed with him. She tried to draw Fred out again. "Come on, Fred, tell me what's troubling you."

This remark opened Fred up. "We've gone over it before. It's just that it's so hard for me to relate to people who have no appreciation for the real features of a house. All they care about is who's living next to them or the 'feeling' a room creates. Can you imagine that, a room having a feeling?" Hadley was silent, not wanting to get trapped into answering Fred's question and stopping his flow of communication. "I don't know, maybe I need a new approach. Something that would help me move those people closer to a decision."

Hadley recognized that Fred was looking for solutions. She wanted, however, for him to come up with his own. That way he'd be more inclined to act on it and follow through. "So maybe a new strategy is the answer," she suggested.

"Right." Fred was thinking. Hadley gave him plenty of time, but her tendency to want to move along quickly made it hard for her to hold back. She could feel herself wanting to just plain tell him what to do.

Fred was still thinking. Hadley looked at the clock, 10:50. She couldn't help thinking about her upcoming sales call with the Johnsons. Finally, Fred offered, "Well, Hadley, I don't have any answers. I think it's too difficult to solve right off the bat like this."

Hadley was unable to be versatile anymore. "Maybe you just haven't tried hard enough, Fred."

It was an unusual statement from Hadley, this form of judgmental put-down, and Fred, beginning to feel her haste, grew more reticent.

"Come on, Fred. Got any ideas?" Hadley was giving in to irritation. She knew if she forced Fred into admitting that he didn't have a solution, she could push hers on him. He'd have to take it. It would be done with, and she could get on with her plans for selling the Harrison estate.

Fred backed off. "No, Hadley, I guess I don't have any ideas. How about you?" The balance had shifted.

Hadley sensed that the focus of the conversation was different now, that she was telling him what to do, rather than letting him arrive at his own answer. She had the sinking feeling in her stomach that she had pushed a little too far, but she went on.

"Sure, Fred, I've given it a little thought."

"Thought you had," he noted cryptically.

Hadley ignored his remark. "Fred, your toughest problem comes when you have prospects who are more emotional than you."

"Right." He was listening, but more out of necessity than because he really accepted what Hadley was saying.

"You tend to get bogged down with them."

"Uh, huh."

"So what I'm suggesting is that you take a course in how to deal with people who rub you the wrong way."

Fred was suspicious. "Is that anything like this sensitivity, let-it-all-hang-out garbage you read about? I won't do that."

Hadley knew that even though she felt her solution was a good one, she was forcing it on Fred without his agreement. She also recognized that Fred wasn't buying it, and so she tried to recover a little of the relationship.

"You really dislike that sort of thing."

It was a good reflection and helped Fred. "Precisely."

"Fred, what I have in mind isn't anything like that at all. I took a course last year on how people communicate, and it was very helpful. I think you should take it."

"Have you got any literature on it?"

"Sure. Let me find it. You can read the brochures and then we'll discuss the idea again. Deal?"

"Well, I'm not sure. Let me look over the information first."

"Fred," Hadley pressed, "I really want you to go to this workshop." She tried to hold any emotionally charged words out of her sentence, but, as was often the case, her real feelings were expressed indirectly.

"Sure, Hadley." He paused, looking at her. "Well, I'd better get back to work."

"Thank you, Fred." She made a last stab at setting things straight. "Oh, Fred, you know me, when I get onto something, I really can push. I don't mean anything personal by it."

"Right. I never thought you did."

"Oh," said Hadley, slightly surprised, and a little self-conscious about her defensiveness.

Fred left Hadley's office. She felt let down. She knew she had the right solution for Fred, but she somehow wasn't satisfied with how the conversation had gone.

In this situation, Hadley is dealing with a person whose style is exactly the opposite of her own (he is Analytical and she is Expressive). Practicing versatility skills is naturally difficult when extreme style differences are involved in an interaction. The easy answer is to assume that it's impossible to work with people who are this different. In addition, Hadley was concerned about her own personal sales call, and she couldn't find the extra energy to use her versatility skill training as effectively as she had with Suzanne. In this situation, you see her backup style surface in the form of a judgmental attack: "Maybe you just haven't tried hard enough." When Fred gets defensive, his back-up behavior is to avoid the issue, so he has difficulty coming up with ideas to solve his own problem. This makes the situation worse, and although Hadley recognizes what's happening and tries to recover, Fred does not make a commitment, and we watch the encounter end unproductively. It's important to recognize that no one is versatile at all times and that it does take energy and discipline to exercise feedback skills. However, when it comes to long-term effectiveness, the versatile manager can make a big difference in an employee's performance.

Nick left the office for lunch at 12:15. It was too late to get into any of the better restaurants, so he decided to walk down the street to the park and buy a hot dog from the sidewalk vendor. He left his coat in the office, and without rearranging his tie or rolling down his sleeves he wandered toward a fountain and sat nearby, feeling a mist of water against his face and forearms. A mime was dancing around the plaza, entertaining the crowd.

Occasionally the mime would mimic one of the onlookers, imitating the person's walk, carrying imaginary packages, tugging at invisible children. People tossed quarters into a hat that a helper was passing through the crowd. Then the mime noticed Nick, sitting on his haunches, eating his hot dog with a deadpan look on his face. He danced over to the fountain opposite Nick, sat down, put a most serious contemplative look upon his white, painted face, and ate a nonexistent hot dog. The crowd looked about, searching for the model.

They soon discovered him, and Nick, who had lost interest in the mime's earlier antics, slowly began to realize that people were looking at him, laughing. At first, he was angry, and the mime mimicked his stern, severe look. The crowd roared. Nick thought of Hadley's frequent suggestion that he loosen up and show his emotions, but the irony of being faced with himself caused him to flush with embarrassment. Nick had to give in. He stood. The mime stood. The crowd chuckled in anticipation. Then Nick, with his best medieval flourish, saluted the crowd and the mime, who returned the gesture. The obvious good fellowship Nick exhibited drew huge applause from the swelling crowd. The mime shook hands with Nick and made off with the hat full of quarters.

A mime capitalizes on social style by reflecting what others can see—only those actions that are available to the public—rather than what Nick is thinking or feeling. Nick's response is ultimately versatile, because he acknowledges the mime in a nondefensive way. People readily recognize and endorse nondefensive responses, just as the crowd applauded Nick.

After lunch Nick returned to the office. He'd been working for about thirty minutes when Claire announced, "Nick, sorry to bother you, but Bob needs to talk to you."

Bob Weiskopf was a lot like Nick: hard-driving, tight-lipped, with a disciplined approach to work. Nick had only seen Bob take his suit jacket off once and that had been two years ago at an impromptu New Year's Eve party. Nick remembered how surprised he'd been at Bob's muscularity. When he asked Bob about it, he discovered that Bob had played varsity hockey while at Harvard. "Strange," he'd thought to himself, "how you can work with some guys for years and never know much of anything about their personal or past life."

"Sure, send him on in." Nick knew that whatever was on Bob's mind was important, or Bob wouldn't bother him. He liked Bob, respected him.

"Afternoon, Nick."

"Bob." Nick stood motioning for Bob to take a chair. "What's up?"

Bob was silent for a minute. "Nick, Bernie asked me to talk to you." There was no hint of what was to come on Bob's face.

"Yes?" Nick felt his tension mounting.

Bob readjusted his posture in the chair and leaned forward toward Nick. "Bernie wants me to finish the Thompson brief."

Bob's words reverberated through Nick's mind. "What do you mean? That's my project. I've done all the work all the way along.

He has no right. You have no right." Nick stood. "Bob, get out of my office."

Bob sat unmoving.

"Bob, I said get out."

"Nick," there was still no trace of emotion on Bob's face, "settle down. It's nothing personal. It's work. Bernie wants you to take a rest. Now."

"Come on, you're kidding. He's kidding." Nick sat down. "You're not kidding."

"No. Sorry."

"Sure." Nick couldn't believe it. "What do you need?"

"Just what you have there on your desk. Claire's already given me the rest of the files."

"You mean she's in on this, too?"

"Nick, come on. Bernie just wants, as he puts it," the slightest smile crossed Bob's face, " 'to rest his best horse.' He said he talked to you about it this morning."

"Yes, but not about the brief. Why didn't he tell me himself?"

"He just came to the decision this afternoon, right after lunch. He was with clients, and they saw your little performance with the mime."

"And that's the reason?"

"Part of it."

"Well?" Nick was insistent.

"Bernie thinks you're burned out."

"So he sent you in to do his dirty work?"

"Nick, get off it. You know how he hates confrontations. Besides, he had to catch a plane. He'll be in Dallas all weekend with clients."

"Yeah, that's right." Nick knew this was true, but still, he thought, what an evasive way to handle things.

"I'd have done it a little differently," Bob offered.

"Yes. I know that. Well, let me get out of your way."

Nick threw his coat over his shoulder and walked out of his office. Claire avoided his stare. Nick didn't look back, went straight out the door to the elevator, and walked to the parking lot office to pick up his keys.

Nick and Bob confront each other in the typical driver-to-driver mode. Both become autocratic, and although they may respect and even like one another, Bob has a job to do, an assignment from Bernie, and Bernie has the power. Bernie clearly handled this tough situation by acquiescing during the face to face encounter and finding someone else to do his job. Not very versatile, and certainly not effective, communication. Everyone loses, even though the job of sending Nick home gets done.

Nick arrived home and pulled into his drive. He left his coat in the car and walked into the kitchen. Hadley was busy over a wok, preparing Nick's favorite steamed vegetable dish, while a bottle of Rhine wine cooled in a bucket.

"Hi, Nick. I came home early. Thought we'd have a special dinner. Take a shower, and it'll be ready when you are."

Nick was trying to hold his tension in, control himself, but, because he was feeling safer with Hadley than with the people at work, he lost it. "So now *you're* telling me what to do!"

Hadley turned around, sensing Nick's unusual response to a rather simple statement. "No, Nick. Sorry." She looked at him sympathetically, encouraging him to tell her what was bothering him.

Nick wanted to put his arms around her, but couldn't bring himself to do it just yet. He realized the situation could go either way; his emotions were ready to explode. On the one hand, he could make the first move toward easing the tension he'd created, while on the other hand, he could let loose and watch the situation deteriorate. He didn't know what to say, but didn't want a fight. "And now you're feeling sorry for me. You and Claire Stephenson."

Hadley knew Claire was one of the women at the office, and though she'd teased Nick, she still felt occasional jealousy. Despite all the day's difficulties, Hadley had controlled her tension, but now she too was beginning to lose her grip.

She knew what was happening, but she couldn't stop it; she was too exhausted from coping with Suzanne and Fred and hadn't closed the sale as expected. "And I suppose sweet little Claire gives you lots of sympathy." She emphasized "lots" haughtily.

"Get off it, Had."

"Don't you call me Had." Hadley was becoming emotional.

"Fine," Nick said, as he strode past the old roll-top on his way to take a shower. "I won't. With pleasure, Ms. Fitzpatrick." Nick controlled his voice, knowing that would get to Hadley.

"And don't use that pompous tone on me."

Nick turned around to answer her, and as he did his eyes fell upon the desk. There was yesterday's *Wall Street Journal* with the circled items untouched.

"You've been home all afternoon, and look at this." He held up the *Journal*.

"Listen, Nicholas, I'm not your little secretary." She felt pushed into a corner, even though she realized that she'd volunteered to cut out the articles.

"You can say that again." Nick's tone was purposely ambiguous.

Hadley sensed the double meaning. She turned her back on Nick and slowly stirred the vegetables in the wok. "Maybe you better go call Claire. You always said she's there when you need her." A few tears slid down her cheeks, despite her efforts to hold them back.

Nick could see her shoulders shaking, and caught himself. Then the ridiculousness of the argument struck him, and he smiled at himself.

"Hadley, Hadley," he finally managed to say. "I'm sorry." He threw the *Journal* in the trash, walked over to her and gave her a hug.

We all tend to store up uncomfortable feelings when we are in situations that demand some social conformity, and we often unload this tension on those close to us. In this scene, you can clearly see Nick's autocratic, and Hadley's attacking, backup styles. Because you saw glimpses of both their days, you can understand what happened: the harsh words were a way of releasing pent-up feelings. If Nick hadn't caught himself in time and put things in perspective, if he had let Hadley have another blast, this situation would have continued to get worse. What Nick did was not easy, but it was versatile; he stopped the cycle of defensive communication. Nick, of course, had many reasons beyond style for loving and accepting his wife. Even so, just as with any relationship, being aware of style and style differences can add another dimension to personal relationships and help make them more effective, too.

As you can see, Hadley and Nick went through a day dealing with style differences, work pressures, and common irritations.

Their ability to understand and use style to advantage was not, of course, the whole reason their day ended on a happy note, but it certainly helped matters.

We hope that you, too, have developed an awareness of social style and will be able to use that understanding to cope with life's demands. It makes little sense to try to change your style, because it has served you well in the past. But it does make a great deal of sense to develop insights and skills that can help you create productive relationships—whether at work or at home. If you can accept your own style and the styles of others, and if you use versatility to adapt to style differences, you will find that your potential success will increase. You will improve not only your own effectiveness, but also that of others.

Appendix
The Social Style Profile

FACTOR ANALYSIS AND RELIABILITY MEASUREMENTS

The Social Style Profile, an adjective checklist that shows how people consistently describe others, was developed by using factor analysis. We found that if a respondent to the checklist felt a certain adjective described someone's behavior, then that same respondent would answer yes or no to certain other adjectives. In other words, there was a clustering of adjectives. This factor analysis process was done by computer. If there was a correlation of 0.35 or greater between two adjectives, these items were included in a scale. These clusters—scales—were then analyzed to see if an overall word could be attached to them. Originally, our factor analysis had shown us five clusters or scales: 1) assertiveness; 2) versatility; 3) responsiveness; 4) aloofness; and 5) easygoing.

In the field of statistics, reliability is a measure of how consistently people respond to the same test items or scale. Reliability can be measured either over time or over items. In the case of the adjectives on our checklist used for each scale on the Social Style Profile,[1] the reliability scale was done over items (for a copy of the checklist, see Fig. A-1).

In each of the five scales, the adjectives included in the scale were numbered *1, 2, 3,* etc. The adjectives were then divided into odd- and even-numbered categories. Then responses from the odd category were correlated with responses in the even category for each scale. For example, one-half of the responses to

1. The Social Style Profile is a tool of Personnel Predictions and Research (PPR), a division of The TRACOM Corp., 200 Fillmore St., Suite 200, Denver, CO 80206. (Telephone: 303-388-5451)

adjectives in the dimension called assertiveness were scored to see if they compared reliably with the adjectives in the other half, the odd-numbered ones against the even-numbered ones. Perfect reliability would be shown as 1.0. For the assertiveness scale, a very high odd-even reliability of 0.93 was found. The versatility scale had a reliability of 0.91. In testing the responsiveness and aloofness scales, we found some overlap of adjectives; thus, we combined these two scales, with a resulting reliability of 0.70. The easygoing scale did not have a high enough reliability to be statistically meaningful, and it was dropped. Thus, we were left with three scales by which people consistently describe others: 1) assertiveness; 2) responsiveness; and 3) versatility.

As another type of reliability index, our research group investigated the question of whether one rater's evaluation of a subject correlates with that of two other raters describing the same subject. In other words, we wanted to see whether the three raters agreed with each other about the individual. In a 1967 study, 23 sales trainees were profiled by three individuals. The raters were: 1) a supervisor, 2) a training coordinator, and 3) a manager familiar with the subject's job behavior. Each rater's score was correlated with the average results from the other two raters for the same subject. The results were that assertiveness and responsiveness showed a significant positive correlation among raters; versatility was also positively correlated among raters, but the correlation was not as strong as for the other two scales (+ 0.44 for assertiveness; + 0.49 for responsiveness; + 0.30 for versatility). This study supports our contention that the assertiveness and responsiveness dimensions of style are seen most consistently among raters. Depending on an individual's choice of raters, versatility can vary more than the other two scales.

COMPARATIVE NORMS

At that point, we had defined three sets of measurements by which people described others. However, for the scales to have practical application for an individual, these scales needed to have some comparative value. In other words, if a person can be

Fig. A-1. The structured adjective checklist.

DESCRIPTIVE CHECKLIST

NAME

STREET ADDRESS

CITY, STATE

SOCIAL SECURITY OR SOCIAL INSURANCE NO.

Listed below are adjectives that people frequently use in describing themselves and others. If you feel that the word applies to the individual requesting this information, blacken the **Y** (yes). If you feel the word does not apply, or that it would be incorrect to use the word in describing this person, blacken the **N** (no). Please do not use a dictionary — when in doubt about a word, use the **?** question mark. There are no right or wrong answers on this list. Please respond to every adjective.

Before Mailing - Check each column for responses.

PLEASE USE NO. 2 PENCIL. BE SURE TO ERASE COMPLETELY ANY ANSWERS YOU WISH TO CHANGE.

	Y	?	N
ABRUPT			
ADVENTUROUS			
AFFLUENT			
AGGRESSIVE			
ALTRUISTIC			
ANXIOUS			
APOLOGETIC			
APPREHENSIVE			
ARGUMENTATIVE			

	Y	?	N
CRITICAL			
CULTURED			
CYNICAL			
DEFENSIVE			
DEFIANT			
DELIBERATE			
DEMANDING			
DEPENDENT			
DISCERNING			

	Y	?	N
FUSSY			
GIFTED			
GUARDED			
HAPPY-GO-LUCKY			
HARDHEADED			
HARMLESS			
HEADSTRONG			
HUMBLE			
HUMOROUS			

	Y	?	N
METHODICAL			
METICULOUS			
MILD			
MODEST			
MORALISTIC			
NON-CONFORMING			
OPINIONATED			
OPPORTUNISTIC			
ORDINARY			

	Y	?	N
PROSPEROUS			
PROVOCATIVE			
PRUDENT			
RATIONAL			
REACTIONARY			
RELIGIOUS			
REMARKABLE			
RESERVED			
RESTLESS			

	Y	?	N
STIMULATING			
STRICT			
STUBBORN			
STUDIOUS			
SUBORDINATE			
SUBTLE			
SUGGESTIBLE			
SUSPICIOUS			
TALKATIVE			

Each word below is followed by the response options [N] [?] [Y].

BLUNT [Y] [?] [N]	DISTINGUISHED [N] [?] [Y]	HURRIED [N] [?] [Y]
BOISTEROUS [Y] [?] [N]	DOMINEERING [N] [?] [Y]	IDEALISTIC [N] [?] [Y]
BOLD [Y] [?] [N]	DOUBTING [N] [?] [Y]	IMPATIENT [N] [?] [Y]
CALM [Y] [?] [N]	DRAMATIC [N] [?] [Y]	IMPERSONAL [N] [?] [Y]
CAREFREE [Y] [?] [N]	DYNAMIC [N] [?] [Y]	IMPULSIVE [N] [?] [Y]
CAUTIOUS [Y] [?] [N]	EGOTISTICAL [N] [?] [Y]	INDIVIDUALISTIC [N] [?] [Y]
CHANGEABLE [Y] [?] [N]	EMOTIONAL [N] [?] [Y]	INFLUENTIAL [N] [?] [Y]
CLEAR-THINKING [Y] [?] [N]	EXCEPTIONAL [N] [?] [Y]	INOFFENSIVE [N] [?] [Y]
CLEVER [Y] [?] [N]	EXCITABLE [N] [?] [Y]	INTELLECTUAL [N] [?] [Y]
COMPLACENT [Y] [?] [N]	EXTRAVAGANT [N] [?] [Y]	INVENTIVE [N] [?] [Y]
COMPLIANT [Y] [?] [N]	EXTROVERTED [N] [?] [Y]	JUDICIOUS [N] [?] [Y]
COMPROMISING [Y] [?] [N]	FEARLESS [N] [?] [Y]	LIGHTHEARTED [N] [?] [Y]
CONFORMING [Y] [?] [N]	FLUENT [N] [?] [Y]	LIMITED [N] [?] [Y]
CONSTRAINED [Y] [?] [N]	FORCEFUL [N] [?] [Y]	LUCKY [N] [?] [Y]
CONTEMPLATIVE [Y] [?] [N]	FORWARD [N] [?] [Y]	MASTERFUL [N] [?] [Y]
CONVENTIONAL [Y] [?] [N]	FUNNY [N] [?] [Y]	MELLOW [N] [?] [Y]

ORTHODOX [N] [?] [Y]	REVERENT [N] [?] [Y]	TEMPERAMENTAL [N] [?] [Y]
OUTSPOKEN [N] [?] [Y]	RIGHTEOUS [N] [?] [Y]	TENDERHEARTED [N] [?] [Y]
OUTSTANDING [N] [?] [Y]	SCHOLARLY [N] [?] [Y]	THRIFTY [N] [?] [Y]
OVERCRITICAL [N] [?] [Y]	SCRAPPY [N] [?] [Y]	TOUGH [N] [?] [Y]
OVEREAGER [N] [?] [Y]	SECRETIVE [N] [?] [Y]	UNASSUMING [N] [?] [Y]
PAINSTAKING [N] [?] [Y]	SELF-CONSCIOUS [N] [?] [Y]	UNBIASED [N] [?] [Y]
PERFECTIONIST [N] [?] [Y]	SELF-EDUCATED [N] [?] [Y]	UNCOMPLAINING [N] [?] [Y]
PERMISSIVE [N] [?] [Y]	SELF-SACRIFICING [N] [?] [Y]	UNPREJUDICED [N] [?] [Y]
PESSIMISTIC [N] [?] [Y]	SELF-SUFFICIENT [N] [?] [Y]	UNPRETENTIOUS [N] [?] [Y]
PHILOSOPHICAL [N] [?] [Y]	SENSITIVE [N] [?] [Y]	UNSELFISH [N] [?] [Y]
POLISHED [N] [?] [Y]	SHREWD [N] [?] [Y]	VAIN [N] [?] [Y]
POSSESSIVE [N] [?] [Y]	SHY [N] [?] [Y]	VIRTUOUS [N] [?] [Y]
PREOCCUPIED [N] [?] [Y]	SKEPTICAL [N] [?] [Y]	WELL-READ [N] [?] [Y]
PRESUMPTUOUS [N] [?] [Y]	SOPHISTICATED [N] [?] [Y]	WISE [N] [?] [Y]
PROFOUND [N] [?] [Y]	STALWART [N] [?] [Y]	WITTY [N] [?] [Y]
PROMINENT [N] [?] [Y]	STERN [N] [?] [Y]	WORLDLY [N] [?] [Y]

DISTRIBUTED AND SCORED BY
PERSONNEL PREDICTIONS & RESEARCH
A DIVISION OF THE TRACOM CORPORATION
200 FILLMORE STREET DENVER, COLORADO 80206

described with adjectives representing the assertiveness, responsiveness, or responsiveness, or versatility scales, he needs to know if he is more assertive than others or less, more responsive or less, more versatile or less. So the next step in the development of the profile was to set up a population norm against which other individuals could be measured.

The subjects that we selected to represent the norm were people who had achieved a certain level of success in their careers. Included were life insurance salesmen, employee relations managers, public school principals, advertising-space salesmen, small-loan finance managers, and others with similar occupations.

The initial population totaled 997. Each of these people was evaluated by others, using the adjective checklist. The individuals had the freedom to select their scorers and were encouraged to mix both social and business acquaintances, but to exclude family and relatives.

The raw scores (as computed from the adjectives checked) were then tallied for the 997 people for each of the three scales. Here it should be noted that 50 adjectives describe assertiveness, 83 describe responsiveness, and 50 describe versatility. Some adjectives can describe more than one scale, depending on whether they are checked "yes" or "no." This explains why the total is 183, not 150. An example of this is the adjective *cultured*. If a respondent checks "yes" to cultured, it is computed as a versatility adjective. If "no" is checked, it is computed as an assertiveness adjective.

After the raw scores had been tallied, the scales were divided into fourths, so that 25 percent of the population was in each quartile. The raw scores at each breakpoint between the quartiles were noted, so that future profiles could be measured against this norm. Thus, for example, on the assertiveness scale there are four ranges, labeled *A, B, C,* and *D*. Those in the *A* quartile are seen as more assertive than 75 percent of the population; those in the *D* quartile are seen as less assertive than 75 percent of the population. Responsiveness (using labels *1–4*) and versatility (labeled *W–Z*) are likewise divided. (A copy of the checklist and of the Social Style Profile form are shown as Figs. A-1 and A-2.)

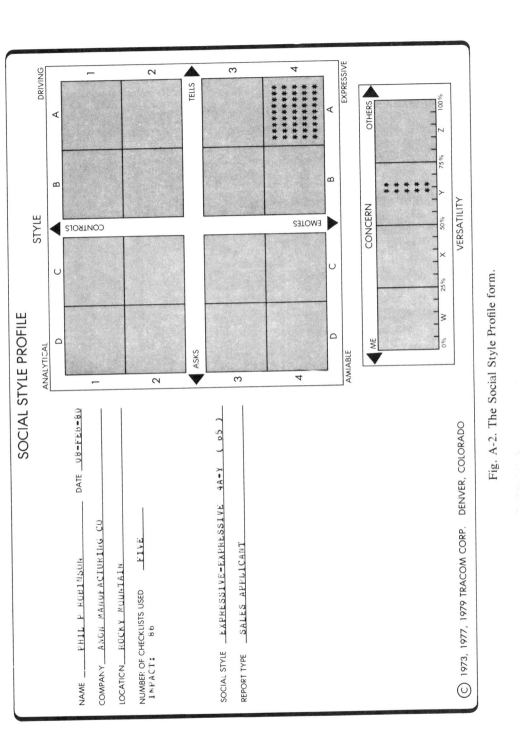

Fig. A-2. The Social Style Profile form.

Now that norms had been established, an individual could have five people fill out a checklist on him and the resulting tabulation would tell him how he measured against the specific norm of 997 individuals in sales or management positions. As the profile was put into use, these norms have been periodically updated to represent everyone participating in the program. It is important to note that the norms come primarily from a business and professional setting and that therefore participants are not measured against a population of, for instance, housewives, hourly workers, artists, or unemployed persons. However, the norms have proven to be very stable over time and for varying groups of people. Therefore we believe that the way people perceive social style is a function of how we observe behavior, not of a person's role or position in life (see Research Study No. 1, Fig. A-7, at the back of this appendix).

Social Style Quadrants

During the early part of our research, persons profiled were given their scores on three horizontal, independent scales: assertiveness, responsiveness, and versatility. However, by the very act of doing factor analysis on the adjectives, the scales form a cube: they become three-dimensional. Thus, a natural crossing of the scales occurs. However, because it appears that the versatility score, unlike the other two, has some positive and negative connotations to it—more endorsement versus less endorsement—we chose to keep it separate from the other two scales. Versatility is shown as a separate, horizontal scale, but can be thought of as a third dimension at right angles to the social style quadrant, forming a cube. Numerous studies have proved our contention that assertiveness and responsiveness are not a measure of success or endorsement, but that versatility is.

Validity Measurements

Validity, in the scientific sense, is more difficult to measure than reliability. However, it is of clearer practical importance for users of the profile than reliability. Validity studies answer the question: Am I measuring what I say I am measuring?

Regarding the Social Style Profile, a number of validity studies have been completed to back up our statements about the profile. We have made the following statements about it: The tool measures how a consensus of people "see" another person's behavior. No one style is more successful than another. However, versatility is a factor in success. (Success, in this context, means either career position or whether or not others perceive you as successful.) We also state that the profile measures behavior—not other aspects of personality, such as intelligence. Finally, we state that the profile can be used as a predictor of success in life insurance selling, as measured by retention ratios.

Validation of the Assertiveness Scale

If the profile says that an individual is seen as more assertive than X percent of the population, does another, separate measurement say the same thing?

Yes. In a study conducted by General Electric Company staff psychologists in 1968, it was found that the assertiveness scale in the Social Style Profile correlates to an independent measurement of a study group's aggressiveness. The study was conducted by Walter D. Storey, Ph.D., who was manager of GE's Talent Review Program, and Dr. Herbert H. Meyer, a behavioral research psychologist with GE.

The study was carried out with 87 men who had participated in GE's Talent Review Program, a week-long assessment program used by the company to analyze managers' performance in a series of exercises, tests, and group discussions. For our study, each individual asked his immediate superior on the job and two persons of his choice familiar with his job performance to complete the adjective checklist. These descriptions were mailed directly to our research group in Denver. There they were computer analyzed, and the profile picture was developed, which reported how these individuals were seen by their three raters.

The ratings were then compared with evaluations of the individuals based on their performance in the Talent Review Program. The Talent Review Program provided peer ratings of aggressiveness, leadership, and overall social effectiveness.

In his draft report on the study, Dr. Meyer wrote: "There was very clear evidence that the Social Style Profile scores on assertiveness, based on descriptions made by superiors and two others in the job setting, correlated very well with the peer ratings of 'Aggressiveness' obtained during TRP [the Talent Review Program]'' (+0.64). His conclusions:

1. Dr. Merrill's tool, the Social Style Profile, seems to have definite potential for identifying individuals who display assertiveness on the job in terms of social aggressiveness.

2. Superiors and others familiar with an individual's job performance can provide a consensus description of social behavior in the area of assertiveness which appear to be related to behavior shown in other social situations beyond the immediate job setting (in this case, TRP).

3. To the extent that social assertiveness or aggressiveness is important to job performance, such as in sales work or to some degree in a leadership role, the descriptive rating from others about an individual, as collected in the Social Style Profile, can be helpful in assessing one aspect of a man's present performance and help to predict performance in a related situation.

Validation of the Versatility Scale

In the late 1960s, we conducted a validity study of the versatility scale. In this study, home office employees for three companies—a casualty insurance company, an investment company, and a life insurance company—were used. The study separated males and females. Four hundred thirty-seven females were in one group; their jobs included secretary, file clerk, keypunch operator, and programmer. Their managers were asked to rank them from best to worst for: 1) competence on the job and 2) attitude on the job. The rankings were then correlated to the group's versatility rankings, as measured by the Social Style Profile. For the group of females, a positive correlation of +0.52 was found between the employees' competency ranking and versatility. A +0.46 correlation was computed between attitude on the job and versatility. (Psychological statisticians see 0.35 or above as a practically significant correlation figure for samples of this size.)

The same comparison was carried out using 150 males from

the three companies. Their jobs included salesman, credit manager, accountant, and adjustor. A correlation of 0.48 was found between competence on the job and versatility, and a +0.44 correlation with rankings of attitude on the job and versatility.

Style and Success

Because one objective of our research has been to determine if the profile can be used to predict success, a number of studies have been conducted to determine whether successful individuals are found on certain points on the three scales. (Once again, success is defined either by career position or by whether others perceive the individual as being successful.)

In 1967, for example, we studied 34 middle managers in a manufacturing plant. Taking the personnel records, the managers were ranked from best to worst in performance on the job. Then, the 34 men were rated by three others, using our checklist. The results showed that the worst group's and the best group's positions on the scales of assertiveness and responsiveness were not significantly different, as determined by a statistical computation known as the T-test. The T-test was considered significant if it showed a level of confidence greater than 0.05. However, the versatility scores were significantly different: The best group had a higher versatility rating than the worst group. Similar findings were also found in studies with a group of life insurance salesmen and a group of sales trainees in a consumer products manufacturing plant (see Research Studies Nos. 2–5, Figs. A-8 through A-11, at the back of this appendix). One study in a bank setting suggested that less responsive and more versatile persons were judged to be more successful, but again assertiveness was not associated with success.

When our research was completed, we concluded that we had evidence to challenge the notion that the most successful persons in business are more assertive. In addition, responsiveness or lack of it did not appear to be consistently related to success. Successful, well-regarded career persons were found along all ranges of the assertiveness and responsiveness scales—just as were less successful individuals. What consistently separated the two groups, however, was the scale of versatility. In other words, more successful individuals received higher endorsement ratings from others.

WHAT THE PROFILE MEASURES

A common source of confusion about the profile is that people often associate their social style with some other aspect of their personality, such as intelligence. We emphasize that only behavior is being measured, and that no other inferences about the Profile should be made. Two studies conducted in 1967 bear that statement out. In one study, 70 operating middle managers and potential managers in a manufacturing plant were rated with the adjective checklist by an immediate superior and two other staff members familiar with the subjects. Verbal ability (a form of intelligence test) was being assessed using the Employee Aptitude Survey Test No. 1, Verbal Comprehension. The verbal comprehension ratings were then correlated with each of the three profile scales. The results showed no consistent correlation (Assertiveness with Verbal Comprehension: -0.06; Responsiveness with Verbal Comprehension: -0.36; Versatility with Verbal Comprehension: $+0.24$).

In a second study, 46 of the best and poorest sales trainees for a manufacturer of consumer products were rated with the Social Style Profile. They were then given the Guilford Verbal Comprehension Test, Short Form. The correlation between social style and verbal comprehension again showed no useful pattern (Assertiveness with Verbal Comprehension: $+0.007$; Responsiveness with Verbal Comprehension: -0.19; Versatility with Verbal Comprehension: -0.36). The two studies did suggest a slightly negative correlation between responsiveness and verbal comprehension which has since been verified. This suggests that people with better verbal comprehension may have a slight tendency to be less responsive, but the correlation is much too low to have practical use.

At this point, the Social Style Profile's use as a predictor has been described in general terms. For example, the Profile can predict that a person with a higher versatility score is more likely to be rated as successful than another. And, research shows that the versatility scale can vary more among raters, but that there is greater agreement among raters about the individual's assertiveness and responsiveness.

SOCIAL STYLE IN LIFE INSURANCE SALES SELECTION

In pursuing our interest in prediction, we have done extensive work in predicting success among life insurance salesmen using the Social Style Profile. Since 1963, Roger H. Reid, M.A., has been assisting us in this work.

The life insurance industry has a notoriously poor retention rate for salesmen: typically it loses two of every three new employees each year. Was there a way to predict success (in terms of staying on the job) that would improve this retention ratio? To research this question, life insurance applicants were studied from 1969 to 1975. Approximately 4000 salesmen were involved in the studies, representing Mutual Benefit, Travelers, Metropolitan Life, and New York Life. The first study was done with Mutual Benefit applicants who were hired "blind"—that is, hired without providing profile results to the person making the hiring decision. Twelve months later, the group was checked for retention, and the "yes" or "no" answer to whether the individual was still on the job was correlated to his raw scores on the three scales of the Social Style Profile. From this, a statistical combination of scores was computed which resulted in new scores, called Impact Scores. They were numbered 53, 56, 63, 66, 73, 76, 83, 86, 93, and 96. The higher the score, the better the chances of retention.

The next year, 1970, we tested the Impact Scores we had developed in 1969 on another insurance company, the New York Life Insurance Company. At that time, New York Life had decided to make a major effort to raise its retention-ratio figures above the industry standard of one out of three. It put its emphasis on improving selection by beginning a series of steps that successively tightened selection standards. One step involved better use of the Aptitude Index Battery (AIB) of tests, which is widely used by the life insurance industry to screen applicants. The AIB is a self-reporting tool: the applicant provides information about himself that gives clues about past experiences and success. From this, some predictions can be made about the applicant's potential for future success in life insurance sales. The opinion and attitude portion of the AIB had been originally developed by one of the authors, David W. Merrill, before he began his research with the Social Style Profile. The opinion and attitude survey had proved to be an effective tool for predicting success in life insurance selling, and in 1965 it was adopted as part of the AIB by the Life Insurance Marketing and Research Association (LIMRA), a national professional association of life insurance companies. Since then, more than 500 life insurance companies have used the test for agent selection.

Another step involved testing the use of the Social Style Profile as a supplementary screen for certain applicant categories. The question: Would the tool, which provides consensus information about how other people describe an applicant's behavior, help the companies to retain more people? To answer this question, a "blind" research experiment was set up that involved testing a sample of 203 newly hired insurance agents. The Social Style Profile test was given prior to contracting with the individual, and the results were given to New York Life's headquarters, but not to the hiring manager. The criterion of successful performance was a simple one: survival. Was the agent still with the company 13 months after the contracting date? Those who did survive were analyzed to determine if they had higher AIB and Impact Scores (as computed from the Social Style Profile) than those who were terminated. New York Life found that the Impact Score was a significant predictor of retention. From this study, we determined that if we advised New York Life to hire only those applicants with an Impact Score of 83 or above, retention rates would be improved (see Figs. A-3 and A-4).

It was found in the New York Life Insurance Company research that, when the AIB and the Impact Scores were both low, there was a retention rate of 10 percent. When there was a low AIB and a high Impact Score, the retention rate was 31 percent. When the AIB was high and the Impact Score was low, the rate was 20 percent, and with a high AIB and a high Impact Score, there was 39 percent retention. In short, the Social Style Profile measurement could make a significant predictive contribution to agent retention.

**Percent Retained
into 13th Month**

	Low Impact Score	High Impact Score
High AIB	20%	39%
Low AIB	10%	31%

Fig. A-3. Research results, New York
Life Insurance Co.

The systematic improvements in retention shown in Fig. A-4 were achieved by refining the selection strategy as additional experience was gained. Obviously, better selection is not the only answer to improved retention, and top management has continued to develop comprehensive selection, training, and management techniques to improve human resource development and decrease operating costs.

Since those early studies, we have continued to enter data from applicants' raw scores into the computer and to further refine the computation of Impact Scores. In addition to Mutual

Percent Retained Figures
are Moving Averages

Time Periods Selected as They Represent
Changes in Selection Strategies

A	July 70–May 71	27.5%
B	June 71–January 73	29.3%
C	February 73–January 74	32.2%
D	February 74–June 74	31.2%
E	July 74–December 74	31.5%
F	January 75–December 75	37.6%
G	January 76–May 77	43.5%

Fig. A-4. New York Life Insurance Co. improved retention rates. (The figures are shown over time as the selection strategy was modified.)

Benefit and New York Life, Travelers and Metropolitan Life have also been included in the data. In about 1975, Impact Scores based on a population of 4171 applicants from these four companies were analyzed. The relationship between position on the three scales and whether or not the individuals were on the job 6 months after contracting is shown (in percentages) in Fig. A-5. The results show that the responsiveness and assertiveness ranking had less relationship to retention than did versatility, and that the middle ranges in versatility indicated better retention than either extreme.

As a result of these studies, a number of life insurance companies are using the tool as a standard part of their selection procedures. For example, New York Life found that one of the

Versatility   **% Retained**

Retention ratio to: Z (highest versatility) = 0.414

Y = 0.632

X = 0.538

W (lowest versatility) = 0.417

Assertiveness   **% Retained**

Retention ratio to: A (most assertive) = 0.513

B = 0.563

C = 0.530

D (least assertive) = 0.520

Responsiveness   **% Retained**

Retention ratio to: 4 (most responsive) = 0.500

3 = 0.547

2 = 0.562

1 (least responsive) = 0.566

Fig. A-5. Retention in four life insurance companies. (The retention rate is shown in relation to versatility, assertiveness, and responsiveness.)

tool's best uses was to screen "gray-area" applicants and select the "potential performers" from this group. That is, in the past, if the company was considering 100 applicants, typically it would reject 50 applicants for such combined reasons as low AIB scores, "single," "no previous related work experience," "under age 25," or "no college." However, it knew that there were candidates in this group who would emerge with a fairly good retention rate. The company decided that if it could salvage half of these potential "selection rejects," it would save considerable costs; typically, it costs an insurance company a minimum of $5,000 to recruit, select, and train each new salesman.

Historically, before the advent of the use of the social style tool, the category with below-average AIB scores (below 9) always had inferior retention. Use of the supplementary Social Style Profile screen now salvages many good appointments with mid-range AIB scores (7–12), contributing to overall cost effectiveness.

To compile these retention percentages, life insurance companies send contracted and retained information for salesmen selected to us on a monthly basis, using the Impact Score and the AIB tool. All life insurance companies start by using a general industry Impact Score; with time and sufficient results, adjustments have been made in assigning a special Impact Score to each company in order to reflect an individual organization's management style. (For example, one company might be more supportive of a sales force that is essentially unassertive than would another company, thus making the quality of high assertiveness less important in determining whether an individual would stay with the company.)

The tool is being continually refined by our behavioral researchers, under the guidance of Dr. Wesley Du Charme. For example, using the data which we have stored concerning retention ratios, Dr. Du Charme has assigned weights to each combination of raw scores, so that statistically, persons with a score of 96 will be retained in greatest numbers, those with 93 will be second, and so on down the scores. This ordering of Impact Scores had not been done with such precision in the earlier years; rather, all those with 83 or above were given a better chance of staying with the job for 12 months, but the differences between 83 and 96 scores were not clearly significant. Today, 96 scores are significantly better than 83 scores for predicting first-year retention.

In our continuing research, versatility remains the major contributor to predictions of success. Assertiveness and responsiveness only influence the predictions of success when there is an organizational management style consideration or when very extreme scores occur on these scales for a particular individual.

EEO REQUIREMENTS

Does the selection tool meet Equal Employment Opportunity (EEO) requirements? If we are to answer yes to this question, the profile and resulting Impact Score must provide data for the answers to two questions. First, does the selection procedure have an adverse impact on members of minority groups or sex groups? To put it another way, can it be demonstrated that all persons have an equal opportunity to score well or receive a passing mark with our selection procedure?

Second, does our selection procedure show evidence of validity? Can evidence be provided that shows that this selection process is significantly related to performance on the job? (These questions are interpreted from "Proposed Uniform Guidelines on Employee Selection Procedures," published in the *Federal Register,* January 1978, as part of Equal Employment Opportunity Commission's (EEOC) enforcement of Title VII of the Civil Rights Act of 1964.)

We have already answered the second of these two questions affirmatively above.

In response to the first question, we have collected data on the mean scores and standard deviations of the social style dimensions for various ethnic and sexual groups. The results of these computations show that the mean and standard deviations are virtually the same for all groups, as collected from life insurance sales applicants. Thus, there is no discrimination, when our selection procedure is used.

The way the three social style dimensions are used for selection has been discussed; those with Impact Scores of 83 or better are recommended for hire. EEOC guidelines require records to show whether minority or sex groups have a significantly more difficult time receiving "passing" scores. The EEOC rule of thumb is that no discrimination is shown if the passing rate of a subject group is at least 80% of the passing rate for the group with the highest pass rate. In our sample of 35,532 applicants, black females had the highest statistically significant percentage of all applicants recommended for hire, at 70%. The breakdown of the other groups studied in 1980 is shown in Figure A-6.

As the figure shows, all groups of significant size recorded through April 1980 readily meet the 80% rule of thumb. The numbers are small for some categories (such as American Indian females and Hispanic females), but we have no reason to believe that any group will ultimately have a significantly lower pass rate than the highest category of black females. Thus Social Style Profile selection scores have no adverse impact on any applicant group for life insurance selling.

EEO Group	No. of Applicants	No. of Applicants with Impact Score of 83 or Greater	% of Applicants with Impact Score of 83 or Greater
White male	24,413	14,440	59
White female	6,801	4,518	66
Black male	2,233	1,437	64
Black female	830	578	70
American Indian male	118	66	56
American Indian female	41	21	51
Asian male	431	276	64
Asian female	123	80	65
Hispanic male	468	277	59
Hispanic female	74	50	68
Totals	35,532	21,743	61

Fig. A-6. Applicants with passing scores compared for ethnic background.

Although these data are specific to the life insurance industry and to life insurance underwriters as salesmen, we believe that similar results can be demonstrated in the selection of other salesmen in other industries. We base this position upon extensive data collected from life insurance sales applicants, which represent a very diversified population of people exploring sales opportunities. It is reasonable to contend that the Social Style Profile will not adversely discriminate against minorities or sex groups in any sales applicant population. Continuing research is under way to support this contention.

CURRENT RESEARCH

Currently our research continues toward the development of new behavioral measurement techniques. Since the "versatility" scale measures the most significant variable in social style, that quality is receiving considerable in-depth examination.

We are making two significant efforts toward developing better means for social style identification. A major effort is addressing the "versatility" variables, and, second, a more routine program is reevaluating the present-day semantic connotations of each individual adjective.

During 1980, a new approach to measuring a major aspect of versatility was completed and field tested. The new measure is called an Interpersonal Feedback Rating (it correlates with the original versatility score $+0.65$). This measurement also comes from what others say about a person's actions in statements such as "Evidences strong personal convictions" and "Says the right thing at the right time." Our effort is to measure only the feedback skills associated with versatility—not appearance, oral presentation, or competence. A program has been designed to specifically teach feedback skills, in order to improve versatility and assist people with their interpersonal success.

We continue to focus upon predictors of human behavior as a basis for improving individuals' potential for discovering personal success and satisfaction in all aspects of their careers.

		Original Norms (N-997)			Norms Oct. 1978 Life Insurance Applicant (N-200)	
		Mean	S.D.		Mean	S.D.
Assertiveness	(A)	20.52	7.78		19.50	6.29
Responsiveness	(R)	41.37	5.03		43.14*	4.35
Versatility	(V)	33.58	5.63		34.53	4.81
		(R)	(V)		(R)	(V)
Scale	(A)	−0.14	+0.16		+0.17	−0.17
Intercorrelations	(R)		−0.34			−0.27

*Note: Life insurance norms have consistently had a systematic bias toward more responsiveness.

Fig. A-7. Research Study No. 1, October 1978. (Original norms compared to life insurance applicant norms; random sample.)

Company   Manufacturing: Petroleum Products

Description   Managers and two staff personnel completed the Profile on middle managers in operating positions. Best and poorest middle managers were identified from personnel records, independent of the Profile results.

Results

	Best Mean	Group (N=12) S.D.	Poorest Mean	Group (N=22) S.D.	T=test
Assertiveness	20.42	5.28	19.91	7.78	0.195 N.S.
Responsiveness	44.08	3.45	44.23	3.73	0.107 N.S.
Versatility	30.25	6.34	22.86	6.06	3.34 Sign. 0.01

Fig. A-8. Research Study No. 2, May 1967.

Company   Life Insurance

Description   Managers and two staff personnel com-
                     pleted the Profile on salesmen. Best
                     and poorest sales performance was
                     identified from sales records indepen-
                     dent of the Profile results.

Results

	Best Mean	Group (N=27) S.D.	Poor- est Mean	Group (N=25) S.D.	T=test	
Assertiveness	22.22	11.36	19.60	9.35	0.885	N.S.
Responsiveness	46.15	8.55	43.96	4.56	1.12	N.S.
Versatility	29.52	8.15	21.76	7.29	3.54	Sign. 0.001

Fig. A-9. Research Study No. 3, May 1967.

Company   Manufacturing: Consumer Products
                     Sales Trainees

Description   Managers and two staff personnel com-
                     pleted the Profile on sales trainees.
                     Best to poorest potential for sales work
                     was ranked by the local sales mana-
                     gers. Rankings were collected from
                     twenty-two different branch locations.
                     Ranks were independent of Profile
                     results.

Results

	Best Mean	Group (N=24) S.D.	Poor- est Mean	Group (N=22) S.D.	T=test	
Assertiveness	18.08	7.01	16.91	8.46	0.50	N.S.
Responsiveness	44.38	5.09	43.55	4.93	0.55	N.S.
Versatility	33.00	6.58	23.14	6.47	5.01	Sign. 0.001

Fig. A-10. Research Study No. 4, May 1967.

Company   Commercial Bank: Officers

Description   Managers and two peers completed the
                   Profile on each officer. Best and
                   poorest officers were identified by per-
                   sonnel records, independent of the
                   Profile results.

Results

	Best Mean	Group (N=10) S.D.	Poor-est Mean	Group (N=23) S.D.	T=test	
Assertiveness	18.00	6.36	18.91	10.66	0.244	N.S.
Responsiveness	35.00	5.35	41.87	5.92	2.78	Sign. 0.01
Versatility	33.00	6.37	25.13	8.31	2.57	Sign. 0.02

Fig. A-11. Research Study No. 5, May 1967.

Recommended Reading

About Style

R. C. Carson, *Interaction Concepts of Personality*. Aldine, 1969.

A. Mehrabian, *Silent Messages*. Wadsworth, 1971.

About Feedback Skills

Gerard Egan, *You and Me*. Brooks/Cole, 1977.

Robert Bolton, *People Skills*. Prentice-Hall, 1979.

Index